During his sixteen-year police career, Lachlan McCulloch was a wide-eyed uniformed constable, a tearaway detective, an undercover operative and finally a corruption whistleblower. After he resigned from the Victoria Police Force in November, 1999, he was awarded a Chief Commissioner's Certificate for exposing corruption.

He has written two best-selling books – *The Street* and *The Street 2* – and was the subject of the award-winning television documentary *The Brotherhood*. He is married, remains a committed angler and works as an investigator for the Victorian Ombudsman.

PACKING DEATH

by LACHLAN McCULLOCH

Published in Australia by
Floradale Productions Pty Ltd and Sly Ink Pty Ltd
October 2005
Reprinted Nov 2005

Distributed wholesale by
Gary Allen Pty Ltd,
9 Cooper Street,
Smithfield, NSW
Telephone 02 9725 2933

Packing Death
Lachlan McCulloch

ISBN – 0 9752318 6 3

Cover photograph by James Braund
jamesbraund@bigpond.com

It's a mystery to me
The game commences
For the usual fee
Plus expenses
Confidential information
It's in a diary
This is my investigation
It's not a public inquiry

I go checking out the report
Digging up the dirt
You get to meet all sorts
in this line of work
Treachery and treason
There's always an excuse for it
And when I find no reason
I still can't get used to it

And what have you got at the end of the day?
What have you got to take away?
A bottle of whisky and a new set of lies
Blinds on the window and a pain behind the eyes

– *Private Investigations,* Dire Straits

DEDICATION

To Fran, who taught me
leopards can change
their spots, and to Peter
'Beatle' Bailey, a trusted
investigator who taught
me you can lock up
crooks without losing
your sense of humour.

CONTENTS

CHAPTER 1

The start

'Alcohol is the downfall
of more coppers than
women and property put
together. I'll see you this
afternoon at happy hour.'

I PARKED my car in the famous McKenzie Street car park and looked up at the brick building towering overhead – the Russell Street police station that housed, among other units, the Victoria Police crime squads. Up there, on the second and third floors, was my new home – the drug squad. The next floor up was where the armed robbery squad conspired against its many enemies. In fact, I was standing on a battleground. And the battle had waged for years.

The crime squads, as they were called, simultaneously fought serious crime throughout Victoria, but the greatest enemies of all were Melbourne City Council parking inspectors. These inspectors loved to book police members' private vehicles. These inspectors knew how to really hurt police. They knew that for a police officer, receiving a parking ticket was like being stabbed in the heart, like losing their first born. Police, particularly detectives, were the givers of pain and punishment. They weren't trained to receive it. You could say they could dish it out but didn't take it very well.

Parking inspectors had complained to police internal investigations that they had been shot several times with air rifles as they booked vehicles belonging to armed robbery squad and drug squad members. I thought it must have been all lies because there's no way the 'Robbers', as we call them, would use air rifles, as such pussy weapons would be a reflection on their manhood. The resulting inquiry never found any air rifles or any other evidence that police were responsible. The internal inquiries always resulted in a file that read, 'This complaint has been fully investigated. Due to a lack of corroborative evidence the allegations have been unsubstantiated'. In other words, the internal investigators had a pretty shrewd idea that it had happened, but they had no chance of proving it.

On another occasion, a parking inspector was in the process of writing out a ticket and placing it on the windscreen of a vehicle owned by an armed robbery squad detective. For some unknown reason the parking officer suddenly, without provocation, attacked the owner of the vehicle as he approached. The parking officer was subdued after a short scuffle and handcuffed. He was then taken to the armed robbery squad offices for interrogation and identification. He was charged with assaulting police, resisting arrest and anything else that seemed applicable. He was bailed on the condition that he not go within 100 metres of the McKenzie Street car park area.

I know this parking officer must have assaulted the owner of the vehicle because there were many witnesses to the apparently unprovoked attack. The witnesses were not all from the crime squads. There were witnesses from the uniform section as well. It seemed everybody who worked at Russell Street police station that day had witnessed the incident. Parking officers never worked alone after that, at least in the McKenzie Street car park.

Over the years, whole forests were cut down to make the paper for police to type reports to get out of paying parking tickets. Police would fudge their diary entries in support of the fact that they had all the intentions in the world to move their vehicle but on the way they witnessed mythical armed robberies, gave vital evidence at the County Court or had to assist the homicide squad in urgent enquiries.

Most of these excuses did not work of course, but cops always had to try. The bottom line was always the basic fact that cops just don't like paying for anything. Crime doesn't pay and neither do detectives.

The uniform section joined in by booking some of the parking inspectors as they drove around near the police car park. Parking officers were booked for speeding, changing lanes without indicating and so on. So the parking officers started to work in packs. They employed guerrilla tactics. They would zoom in and book as many as they could and leave.

This dirty little war seemed rather amusing at the time, but the fact was that most parking officers were just trying to do their jobs without fear or favour. When they fined a cop who expected to get away with manipulating the system, they were actually doing the right thing. It wasn't until later that I realised there was a lesson in it for me – about the way cops stick together, right or wrong.

I left the Police Academy on a Friday in June 1984 and started at Richmond police station on the Monday. This was my training station. I recall working in the watch house area when several internal investigation department officers walked in.

Apparently the town hall clock had copped a dose of lead poisoning at precisely 2.17 that morning. I walked out the front door of the station and looked up. Yep, the clock was shot right in the face. Forensic science officers estimated that the shots came from the area around the police station barbecue.

The theory going around at the time, well decades of theory actually, was that there was a tendency for the town hall clock to get shot in the early hours of Monday. Monday mornings, coincidentally, had traditionally attracted end-of-night-shift compulsory drinkathon sessions. For some unknown reason, when you mix an armed, trained-to-shoot, frustrated copper, with 27 or so green cans (Victoria Bitter), you end up with a shot clock. When I arrived in 1984, it was an entrenched tradition. The other entrenched tradition was for the internal police to not catch, charge or even identify the police responsible.

During the latter stages of my five-month training session at Richmond, I was standing next to the barbecue holding a green can glancing up at the bullet holes in the clock's face. The clock was just at that challenging distance, not an easy shot but not a hard one either. Even a sober clock shooter would be entitled to a few misses at 50 metres in the dark. While I was standing there, I made some mental calculations: Smith and Wesson .38 calibre revolver with a four-inch barrel at 45 degrees ... I guessed it would be unwise to live around Burwood Road, Hawthorn.

There was always a lot of talk but never any admissions. Some time after midnight an old senior constable asked when I was going home. I took this to mean, 'Piss off, we want to shoot the clock'. I left the imminent crime scene. It was blatantly clear that the shooting of the clock was not something that was going to happen in the presence of a snotty-nosed trainee. I must agree, as I have never been accused of being a silent witness.

In 1995, Richmond council covered up the shooting incidents with putty and paint, quietly repairing the clock face – during daylight hours of course. It's always good to get on well with your neighbours, especially when they all carry guns 24/7 and spasmodically get on the piss and shoot your clock. A complaint might cause them to shoot other things.

Then in 1997 someone blew the whistle by sending the Chief Commissioner a bill for the clock being used as target practice. On receipt of the $1500 repair bill, police command had the ethical standards department start another investigation. After an exhaustive seven-month search, they failed to identify who was responsible. They did find the 22 bullet holes were caused by .38 calibre standard police issue rounds. Police then asked for legal advice to ascertain who should pay the bill. Legal advice suggested that although it was possible that criminals could have scaled the high-security station fence and shot the clock from the barbecue area 22 times with police-issue bullets, without alerting the 24-hour police station attached to the barbecue, it was most unlikely. So they coughed up.

The tradition of shooting the Richmond town hall clock flourished throughout my career. No-one was ever charged, let alone convicted. At first I thought police shot the clock for the same reason Sir Edmund Hillary climbed Mount Everest. I was wrong. Now, looking back, I think some cops shot the clock to make a sort of 'Cops rule' statement.

Early one Sunday in June 2005, I grabbed my camera and drove to the Richmond police station and looked up at the clock. The clock was clean, no bullet holes. This was making a new statement: 'Cops don't rule'. The change of culture within the force has removed the code of silence. The now constant, professional and effective fight against corrupt and inappropriate behaviour by our police is making a difference. Then again, maybe someone just shifted the barbecue.

Seven years after walking into Richmond as the new boy, I got the same feeling when I moved to the drug squad.

I CAREFULLY carried three boxes of correspondence and associated useless junk past the 'The Club' – that is, The Victoria Police Club – around the corner from the main entrance of Russell Street, as everybody called the old police station. The front of the Russell Street building bore deep scars from a massive car bomb that killed Constable Angela Taylor. She had lost a coin toss to see who was to buy lunch. She walked outside just as the bomb went off. Angela was a sensational young woman and will never be forgotten. This was not a terrorist act, but a criminal one. The crooks who did it wanted to destroy the Victoria Police communications centre so they could conduct a series of armed robberies around Melbourne.

Acts like these really did make me believe we were in a war – a sort of clandestine war that never ends. At the time, I thought the battle line was drawn at the front door of Russell Street, with us on one side and them on the other. Events in the drug squad were soon to show me there was no line. The war was all around … and within, although I didn't know that then.

As I walked up the bluestone steps, I pushed the massive doors open. The air was thick with history. Pure police history. I imagined what the Russell Street foyer must have seen and heard in the previous century. Back when the station was built, the crooks were not poisoned by drugs. Back then, armed robbers wore overalls and balaclavas and robbed banks carrying sawn-off shotguns and old army revolvers. And burglars cased their targets for weeks before doing a top job, leaving no evidence. Times change.

Now the building was as cold as it was old. The powers that be must have decided it could slowly die. Cracks in the walls were left to grow into the ceiling. The labyrinth of hallways and distant ceilings were covered in tired beige paint. Not that I noticed much of the decor on my first day. I was too keen to get started.

I stuck my badge in my shirt pocket and walked on, past fresh-faced uniformed men and women. Past interview rooms containing crying mothers consoling their shop-stealing young. Past cops whispering about what they should do next. Past laughter and the smell of lunches coming from the mess room. Russell Street had a police flavour. I had never felt more like a cop in my life.

I felt like it was my first day in secondary school. Even though I had been a cop for seven years, I felt like I was starting all over again. The new kid on the block and all that. I was a nobody in the detective business. Policing drugs was always my best bit. I wanted to become the best drug squad investigator and undercover operative the Victoria Police had ever seen.

I knew I had the energy and drive to do it. I would just have to work on my punctuality, correspondence, spelling, my occasional lack of professionalism and overall work ethic. If I could fix up those things, I thought, I'm there. While I'm at it, I'd better become a bit more serious. Policing is a serious business, or so I've been told. Just ask Melbourne's parking officers.

I walked through one building across a hallway into another, up stairs and up to a push-button security pad. I pushed a small button marked 'Reception'. Moments later, I was taken to the boss's office. He welcomed me into the drug squad. I got the standard reception speech: 'Bring the drug squad into disrepute, you're out. Keep your nose clean and do your job properly or you're out. Whatever you do, don't get drunk and come back to the office and want to fight me, or you're out. Any questions?'

I said, 'Is this a bad time? Should I come back later?'

He said, 'Alcohol is the downfall of more coppers than women and property put together. I'll see you this afternoon at happy hour.'

I left. There were 86 members in the squad. I found out that one of them had just gone out for a long lunch, drunk too much Dutch courage, then decided to go back to the office and tell the boss what he thought of him. Bad move. If you drink, don't work – and if you work, don't drink. If you do drink, don't talk to the boss because you just might tell the truth. Another example of the truth hurting the truth teller. The truth is often better to be known silently than said aloud. If marriage doesn't teach us this, bosses do.

Anyway, I soon found out that 'happy hour' was drug squad drinks. At 4pm every Friday all members were expected to attend at the mess room for drinks. Each week a different crew from the squad was responsible for the mandatory cheese, salami, cabana and biscuits. In typical police force style we were allowed to serve only light beer – yet all spirits, wine and mixed drinks were available. Work that out. As if the mere fact that there was no full-strength beer meant none of us were ever going to drink and drive. None of us could ever work out the rationale behind this rule. But a lot of us got a taste for wine and spirits we hadn't had before.

When I first got to the squad, it was made up of three sections. Section one was the task force investigation section. It mainly targeted large organised drug suppliers. Throughout most of the

1990s it targeted Italian crime groups trafficking huge amounts of cannabis and cocaine. It also targeted some large Asian heroin traffickers. The longest and most successful investigation was codenamed *Afghan*.

Section two's charter was to locate and shut down clandestine laboratories manufacturing amphetamines. In other words, we hunted speed labs. Section three's charter was to locate and destroy large-scale cannabis crops. The charters for the three sections were written down in the overall drug squad charter. In practice, what actually happened was that everyone in the squad could work on any sort of job. For instance, if we were chasing a particular crook who we knew was making speed and received information that Fred Nerk was selling heroin, we could bust Fred, no worries.

The squad was really good like that. We were always able to catch drug dealers and suppliers should they suddenly need catching.

Most of the time it was great to catch crooks instead of following them around and listening to their shit all the time. It used to drive me up the wall working on the same targets month after month without arresting them.

One day I was sitting in court waiting for my case to come up. A prison officer approached me and said, 'Hey mate, do you mind if George comes over and sits with you for a while?'

I said, 'No that's fine.' George Papp was a good crook. George was in custody and we were waiting for the magistrate to arrive. I had charged him with stealing $2.4million in cash. He came over and sat next to me. I said, 'What's your go, George?'

He said, 'The worst thing about prison is that it's full of fuckwits. Total imbeciles that think I want to listen to their shit. Prison's full of stupid drug-addicted fuckwits. I've listened to their shit for months now. Please can you just talk to me?'

gations. They are far more likely to use a piece of phone cable and a large amount of gaffer tape.

The problems don't end there. In my seven years at the drug squad, there were on average about two or three labs a year found by the fire brigade. This is because the crooks who make speed do not often follow health and safety guidelines. They actually boil highly explosive chemicals like ether over a naked flame. They should, of course, use a heating mantle like any sensible criminal scientist, but they are not scientists nor are they sensible. Proper heating mantles are very expensive and hard to get hold of. They work like a very large and extremely hot electric frying pan. But the stupid crooks often go to the nearest Ray's Tent City store and buy a large gas flame burner. It works well until fumes build up and then – POW! Or maybe that should be KABOOM! Then we get a call from the fire brigade. To this day there are some well-known amphetamine cooks carrying large fire and chemical burns.

Why do they risk being incinerated? Because this crime pays big time. It's hot and dangerous but it pays millions of dollars in cold hard cash for those who survive.

CHAPTER 2

Bananas in Pyjamas

The only thing bigger
than her tits were her
tatts – and the port wine
birthmark on her neck.
She was without doubt
the happiest, most jovial
informer I had ever met.

MY first big job turned to shit in a few months. Known as *Operation Cane*, it had looked promising but it was sold out from within my own squad. It would take years to find out who turned traitor, but in the end it destroyed him and almost me as well. That was in the future. For now, I was happy to go fishing. I flew to Tasmania and stepped onto a 54-foot boat named the *Seafarer*. I happily fished and scuba dived for two weeks. I had such a good time it almost took my mind away from the work events of the previous few months. Almost.

When I got home, I was a little more relaxed. I got a call from my best mate, Darren O'Loughlin, for a social chat. We spoke about our wives, family, all the private off-duty stuff for the usual 3.5 seconds before the conversation turned to cops and robbers. Darren was a detective senior constable stationed at

Frankston criminal investigation branch. He started to tell me about a really good informer he had. Her name was Fran Zeal. He went on and on about how good she was. Darren's not the sort of bloke who talks for the sake of it. 'The Job' and everything in it is serious for him. He comes from a long line of police, from constables to Deputy Commissioners. His father, mother, sister, brother, cousins, uncles, are or were all coppers. He was bred for it. I joined because it sounded like fun.

Darren met Fran after he raided her house searching for her husband, Butch. Butch was a mad, bad-arse armed robber. Darren charged him and locked him up in the cells at Frankston police station.

For Butch, this was the end of a series of being arrested, charged and then being bailed. Now it was no more bail for bad-arse Butch.

Fran and the kids wanted to say goodbye. Darren organised it so they could say their final goodbyes in private. He showed Fran some common courtesy. Fran respected Darren for that. Months later, in the County Court, Butch got ten years jail with a minimum of eight.

Fran started to telephone Darren almost daily. She liked Darren. They shared a common hatred of drug dealers. Fran kept in contact with all her associates. Darren went on to explain that Fran smoked cannabis several times a day. Even so, she hated with a passion anyone who sold powders. She blamed powders for all of her husband's problems. Fran hated powders so much she went out of her way to find out who sold them and made sure they were arrested forthwith.

Then Darren got down to the point of this particular phone call. He went on to explain that he was flat out keeping up with his own investigations and that his boss wouldn't allow him time to run major drug inquiries. I agreed that for major drug inquiries I was the man. Darren said he had spoken to Fran about 'Lenny' (me) and she wanted to have a meeting. I could tell by the way Darren spoke of her, the tone in his voice, that she was special, not your average informer.

On February 2, 1993, at 9.25pm in the rear car park of the Frankston Lawn Bowls club I met with Fran. The only thing bigger than her tits were her tatts – and the port wine birthmark on her neck. She was without doubt the happiest, most jovial informer I had ever met. Darren introduced me to Fran as Lenny. It was obvious from the outset that she loved Darren. Not that sort of love, she just loved to be around Darren. She was quite large and had a loud booming voice. Most of all she appeared to be having fun. She seemed to enjoy all this cloak and dagger stuff.

She called Darren 'Legs'. Her voice was an absolute classic. Another thing I noticed was that she had her own language. She was great at swearing and slang. She attached sexual connotations to just about everything she said. Darren had to race back to work for some reason and left Fran with me. As Darren left, he suggested I take her out to lunch. With that she called out, 'I might have Lenny's lunch'. With a big cheesy grin she added, 'You got a big lunch, Lenny?' She looked down toward my crotch. Laughing, I called out to Darren's car as it drove off, 'Don't leave me, you bastard'. Fran laughed and said, 'Come on Lenny, let's get to know each other better.' She even made my name sound crude. Darren, your day will come.

She was covered in perfume. I couldn't help but say, 'What type of perfume is that?' I really did want to know, just so I could make sure I never ever bought it for anyone I loved. She said, 'It's some sort of cheap shit. They put the good stuff behind the counter so I can't pinch it.' Ask a silly question, as they say. Darren hadn't told me the full truth. She was full-on in your face. She had a way about her that made me feel comfortable. She had an infectious smile backed up by a real laugh.

Informers can be extremely dangerous. Female informers can be deadly, especially ones who use sex as a tool. At detective training school we were taught: 'Informers are like manure. Pick it up with a shovel and use it properly and you can grow beautiful roses in no time. Use it incorrectly and you can end up smelling like shit'.

Fran got into my car and I drove her to the nearest hotel for a counter lunch. All along the way I visualised the robot from the TV series *Lost in Space* with his arms flailing about screaming, 'Danger, Danger, Danger Will Robinson'. One part of me decided she was way too dangerous to deal with. That was up until we sat down and had lunch.

Fran settled down and became quite serious. I think she sensed I was summing her up and putting her in the wrong basket. I said, 'Fran, what's the go? Why do you want to talk to me?' She looked puzzled, as though I must be some kind of idiot.

She said, 'You hate drug dealers, don't you?' She hung on the word 'drrrrrrrug' – she sort of slipped it out the corner of her mouth and spat it on the floor.

I said, 'Yeah.'

She continued, 'I do. They kill kids, they fuck people's lives and I fuckin' well hate 'em.' The way she spoke made me feel glad I wasn't a drug dealer.

She went on to explain that her man Butch was doing eight years for armed robberies. She blamed speed. She was dead against all drugs except 'choof'. When she was putting shit on drugs, she'd always stop and clarify that choof was okay. 'There's nothin' like a good smoke'. At one point she clarified the fact that she didn't want to talk to me about any choof dealers. I thought that was fine. I was busy enough without wasting time and effort arresting cannabis dealers as they were just as hard to catch as dealers in powder and they got stuff-all jail time.

A very good childhood friend of mine smoked a lot of cannabis. He eventually developed schizophrenia. After extensive treatment, he committed suicide. I believe that cannabis use contributed to the early onset of this disease. He was a great mate. He was at his best sitting around a campfire singing *Stairway to Heaven*. But that was a lifetime ago.

That first meeting was what is called a 'meet and greet'. I didn't sit there taking down all the specifics of who was dealing what. That was to come later. At the conclusion of our long lunch, I was most impressed. She was certainly unlike any informer I had ever met. She was mutton dressed as mutton. She didn't put on false airs or graces. Fran was Fran. I began to realise what it was that made me feel comfortable. Even though she was obviously a small-time crook, she exuded a sort of honesty. I know that sounds strange, but it's like truth to her was more natural and easier than lying.

I made one mistake during that first meeting. I was just informing Fran what we could and couldn't do in the future. I said, 'As an informer, we cannot, of course, pay you. We can pay for some of your expenses though.'

Her face changed, I suddenly thought I was going to be punched off my chair. She said, 'Puttin' me on the informer are ya? Didn't Legs tell ya I ain't no informer? I'm a witness, I witness things. Fuck, you're a rude bastard.'

'Sorry, Fran'.

She said, 'Witness sounds better.'

I said, 'Much better, the more you witness the better.'

With a sly smile she added, 'Do you pay witnesses?' That broke the tension. That didn't need an answer; we just smiled.

I said, 'If you happen to be in the right place at the right time, like any good witness, you can page me on this number.' I handed her a piece of paper with the name Lenny and the pager number on it.

She said, 'Will ya come runnin', will ya?'

I said, 'Second thoughts you better give it back.' I held out my hand. She smiled and stuffed it down her cavernous cleavage. There was no way I was going there, not without at least a block and tackle.

At the end of that first meeting I knew that if I liked Fran, the crooks must love her. I dropped her off at home and raced back to the office. I started filling out forms. I walked down the other end of my office and had her registered at the drug squad intelligence section as an informer. I was handed her official title. Fran had now become B2 of 1993. I now had one of the Bananas in Pyjamas as an informer. All my official reports from now on would refer to her as simply B2/93. No-one need know her true identity. Not then anyway.

Darren rang me right after the meeting to see what I thought. He couldn't stop laughing. I told him how I had referred to her as an informer. He explained that one time he was in talking with Fran and he had to answer his mobile phone. During the call Darren had said, 'I've got to go, I'm talking to a 'gig'. (Short for the police term for informer – 'fizz-gig'.)

Fran had grabbed the phone off him and said to Darren's boss, 'I'm not a fuckin' gig.' Then she said, 'What's a fuckin' gig, anyway?' Daz had me in fits. We both laughed at what a classic she was.

I said, 'Don't tell her, but I just made her into a Banana in Pyjamas, as an informer she's now known as B2 of '93.'

Darren said, 'She's not going to like you, "putting her on" the Banana in Pyjamas.'

I said, 'What's this way she says 'Put her on things'? Put her on this and that.'

Darren replied, 'It's her language.'

B2 had several prior convictions. She had a couple for shop stealing and one much more serious one. I managed to track down the copper who arrested her for the serious charge. This is what she did.

Several years before, when Fran's son was quite young, Fran heard that a paedophile lived a couple of streets away. He had apparently interfered with one of the local children. So being the community-spirited person she is, and the fact that she doesn't like paedophiles, she took it upon herself to ask him to relocate.

Her armed robber husband was away doing time, but he kindly left Fran a sawn-off shotgun hidden inside the bathroom door.

One evening Fran grabbed the shotgun and walked around the corner to the front of Mr Rock Spider's house. She politely screamed, 'Hey cunt, fuck off out of here or I'll blow your fuckin' balls off you paedophile cunt' or similar. She then fired both barrels into the front of his house. Being a sawn-off shotgun, the shot spread quickly and peppered through his front windows and door. She then walked back home.

The following evening, Fran saw that Spider's car was in his driveway. He had obviously not taken her advice. So she went home, re-loaded her shotgun, filled a large glass jar with petrol and stuffed a cloth in a small hole in the jar's lid. She rushed back to Mr Spider's.

To get his attention she fired the shots and then lit the petrol bomb and smashed it onto the front door. Then she screamed out her message again.

The following day she couldn't believe her eyes when she

observed his car parked in the driveway. The front of the house was a bit worse for wear, but he hadn't moved. That evening she loaded the shotty, made another bomb and hurried back to pay another visit.

The ever-vigilant, highly-trained local police had worked out there was a pattern. So on the third night in succession, Fran arrived carrying her large handbag.

A car full of cops was parked down the street. They observed a large-breasted woman start to walk past the house. They hardly paid her any attention, until she stopped and began to reach into her bag. The funny part was that Fran managed to fire the shots and blow up Spider's car before the cops even got out of their vehicle.

Fran was off, bouncing up the road when she was tackled to the ground. Fran went into shock when she found out it was against the law to evict paedophiles in such a manner. During the police interview she was asked, 'You are now going to be charged with the offence of conduct endangering life. Do you have anything to say in answer to the charge?'

She smiled and said, 'I was just helpin' me local community.'

Fran was convicted and sentenced to four years' imprisonment with a minimum of eighteen months. She served a total of about twelve months at Fairlea Women's Prison. I later spoke to her about that crime and she assured me that it worked out well because he did get the message and moved house after the third attack.

It proved Fran could be a force to be reckoned with. I treated her with extreme caution. I had of course taped that first meeting. In fact I taped every word of the first three meetings I had with Fran. I had enough information from her to start several operations. They were a mixture of both speed and heroin dealers.

I named them *Operations Marlin*, *Swordfish*, *Tuna* and *Flathead*. As you can tell, I'm into fishing. Over the next two months I started purchasing small amounts of heroin and speed from numerous targets.

It was during these meetings that I started to really get to know Fran. I was beginning to discover that she really did have a heart of gold, even if she was a bit rough around the edges. Getting to know Fran ultimately involved getting to know her children. Young Charlie was only eight. He was a great young kid. He thought Lenny was a new friend of his Mum's. Fran also had two daughters. For security reasons, I couldn't risk the kids finding out I was a cop. Fran and the kids went to visit Daddy in Barwon Prison every Saturday. I felt sure he would be less than pleased with, 'Hey Dad, have a guess what Mummy brought home? ... an undercover cop'.

By this time I had supplied Fran with her own full-time tape recorder. Crooks were always ringing her up or calling over to her house. I'll pause at this moment to tell you about a couple of funny things that can happen when you have your own $12,000 high definition secret tape recorder handy. One day Fran had a visit from woman named Sandra who lived down the road.

Sandra asked Fran if she could help her out with a problem she had. Sandra wanted to torch her house but had no-one to help her out with an alibi. Fran, always on the lookout for an earn, happily agreed.

Fran rang me, all excited, saying, 'You're not going to believe this, I'm onto a really good earn.'

I said, 'Legal, of course.'

She said, 'Stop your bitchin', it's legal for me.'

'Fran, do I need to know?'

She said, 'Not yet. You're going to laugh.'

I said, 'Only ever tell me what I really need to know, okay.'
'Chill out, Lenny.'

Fran was always ringing me for a chat. She was always happy and up to something that I didn't need to know about. I had no idea what she was up to until the following day, when she rang again. She said, 'They fuckin' well did it.' She went on to tell me the whole story about Sandra and the fact that her house just burnt down.

Fran was all excited because she had just had Sandra over for a cup of tea and an alibi. Sandra explained in detail how she burnt her house down for the insurance. Here I was thinking that Fran wanted her own special tape recorder to tape our targets. Fran was streets ahead of me and had her own targets in mind.

I said, 'You really are a bitch. You probably came up with the idea in the first place.' I'm sure she did. I could just see Fran egging them on hoping for 'an earn'.

Fran just laughed. She said, 'Sandra was laughing with me on the tape, laughing about burning her house down. What a classic. I've been hangin' and hopin' she'd do it.' I helped Fran report the crime to the local police. Long story short – Fran negotiated a tidy sum from the insurance company. Her tape was more than enough to knock back the claim and have Sandra and her husband convicted of arson.

As it happened, Sandra and her husband didn't see the funny side to Fran's alibi. They felt a little bit burnt, so to speak. They had burnt their house down for no reason at all and were about to go to jail for it. They thought the least they could do was to kill Fran. It wasn't going to get their house back, but they would feel better. Death threats came thick and fast.

Fran's problem became my problem. A dead gig was worse than no gig at all. I contacted the priority shifting department of the Victorian Housing Commission. I sent them some paperwork explaining Fran's death threat situation.

What happened next became a large issue at future court proceedings. I maintained that I didn't know who lived in Fran's new street. The defence maintained that I had set the whole thing up. I'll let you work out the truth.

My story is that Fran was given several addresses she could shift into. They were all around Melbourne. One address was in Wedge Crescent, Rowville. Rowville is a nice quiet suburb about 25 kilometres east of Melbourne.

Fran drove out to check this address. It was a large three-bedroom house in a quiet little street. Fran rang me that evening to say that the house looked really nice. She added, 'Lenny, Victor Peirce used to live in it.'

I said, 'Well, you wouldn't want to live there would you?'

Fran said, 'That would be cool.'

EDITOR'S NOTE

VICTOR Peirce was one of Australia's worst criminals and the son of the notorious underworld matriach, Granny Evil – Kath Pettingill.

If Kath Pettingill had been barren, one of Australia's most prolific and notorious crime dynasties would never have been established. Kath, as she is universally known, had six sons and a daughter. All had criminal records and three of her sons were to die young – though not necessarily prematurely.

The eldest was Dennis Bruce Allen, known as Mr Death, who was a suspect in eleven murders, and managed to keep out of jail by becoming a police informer ... and a valuable one. It was suspected that, as added insurance, he also paid a corrupt cell of detectives for protection.

Not content with her own six sons, Kath virtually adopted another young man. It was a bad move for Gregory Vivian Pasche. He was stabbed to death and his body was dumped in Olinda, in the Dandenong Ranges east of Melbourne, in 1983. Police believe he was murdered in a drug dispute involving Dennis. Sibling rivalry gone mad.

But Kath did not need to live off the reflected 'glory' of her family.

One of her eyes was shot out by a woman in October, 1978. Police with knowledge of ancient mythology and a black sense of humour later named an investigation into Kath's criminal empire Operation Cyclops.

She had worked as a madam, a drug dealer and had provided aid and comfort to many of Australia's heaviest gunmen.

Dennis and another of Kath's sons, Jamie Pettingill, who was then just a teenager, committed an armed robbery at the United Kingdom Hotel in Clifton Hill. During the raid a barman was shot and later died from a blood clot. Police threatened Pettingill with a murder charge unless he talked. Jamie told them he knew they were bluffing because he had read a story in the paper that the evidence would not sustain a homicide prosecution.

In May 1985, he bombed the Coroner's Court as a warning to prospective witnesses in an inquest that could have implicated Dennis in the murder of a prostitute called Helga Wagnegg. A few days later, Jamie died of a drug overdose.

Two other sons, Victor George Peirce and Trevor Pettingill, were charged and acquitted with two other men of murdering two police, Steven Tynan and Damian Eyre, in Walsh Street, South Yarra, on October 12, 1988. Investigators maintain the four suspects killed the police as a random revenge attack after Victor Peirce's best friend, Graeme Jensen, was shot by armed robbery squad detectives in Narre Warren just thirteen hours earlier.

The detectives said a group of criminals had formed a pact to murder two police in an ambush attack if police killed one of them. Any two would do; they would die because of the uniform they wore. The star witness against the four suspects was Jason Ryan – Kath's grandson. Kath would turn up at court often wearing a T-shirt that read, 'Life's A Bitch. Then You Die.'

In the 1980s Dennis Bruce Allen was making a fortune through the drug trade. He had a substantial property portfolio and was depositing $7000 a week in his bank accounts. He once bragged that he paid $15,000 to two top police to leak him information on a police investigation into his operations. With inside mail he was able to launch a counter-attack. He fired ten shots into supposedly secret police surveillance posts that had been set up to monitor his activities near his home in the back streets of Richmond. Shots were also fired at a policeman sitting in the Prahran police station. Investigators had no doubt who fired the shots – the policeman was involved in the investigation into Allen.

When Allen feared he would be killed because he was a police informant, two detectives gave him a bullet-proof flak jacket. He used a small local hotel as his business headquarters, once chaining an enemy from a rafter in the ladies' lounge. He drank in the bar and every time he walked past he would beat the man hanging from the beam.

Allen was charged with the murder of one Wayne Patrick Stanhope, although a body was never recovered. In August 1984, Stanhope and Allen were drinking in his home when Allen produced a silver pistol and emptied it into his guest's head. The reason for the murder was never clear, although Dennis often didn't need a reason. One suggestion was that Stanhope *changed a record without asking. Another was that Allen had earlier seen a photo of Stanhope wearing a policeman's hat. Believing Stanhope was a police informer, he shot him.*

Allen made between $70,000 and $100,000 a week from drugs and was on bail for 60 different offences in the early 1980s. The sureties alone were $225,000 – then the price of several inner suburban houses, which were another of Allen's hobbies. He had more houses in Richmond than he had coppers on the take.

It was in one of these houses that Mr Death killed a Hells Angels associate, Anton Kenny, on November 8, 1985. He took the body into the garage and used a chainsaw to amputate the legs before stuffing the remains in a 44-gallon drum. He stopped in the middle of the job to have a beer because, he would later claim, dismembering bodies was surprisingly hot work. The drum was dumped in the nearby Yarra River. Allen was later to tell homicide squad detectives where the body was, but blamed others for the murder.

A police task force believed he was the prime suspect in a fatal shooting, three suspicious drug overdoses, two missing persons cases and five confirmed homicides. He was connected with the mistaken identity murder of Lindsay Simpson, who was killed on September 18, 1984, in Lower Plenty. Allen and Roy 'Red Rat' Pollitt, were supposed to kill a drug dealer called Alan Williams but shot Williams' innocent brother-in-law instead.

Williams was to be killed because he was involved in the attempt to murder NSW undercover policeman Mick Drury and was seen as a potential prosecution witness against two other men said to be involved – hitman Christopher Dale Flannery and notorious Sydney detective Roger Rogerson.

Many in the underworld claimed that Allen was a specialist at 'hot-shots' – giving drug addicts pure heroin so they would overdose.

At one stage his heroin ring supplied nearly 100 people a day though an inner-city massage parlour.

He died in April 1987 from a rare heart disease at the age of 35, proving that not only the good die young.

When Victor Peirce, Trevor Pettingill, Anthony Farrell and Peter McEvoy were acquitted of the Walsh Street murders, they became the most hated men in Victoria by police. Emotions were running so high that straight after the verdict a D24 message was sent: Announcement all units. The verdict in the Walsh Street trial was all four not guilty, repeat not guilty. All units are warned, keep yourself in control.

Victor Peirce may have been found not guilty of the Walsh Street murders, but there was only one way he was going to leave the underworld. He was shot dead sitting in his Commodore in Bay Street Port Melbourne, on May 1, 2002.

Following the Walsh Street acquittal, police had to be particularly careful in any investigations into the Pettingill/Peirce clan. Police saw them as cop killers, so any undercover investigations were potentially life-threatening and any investigation that did not result in uncovering rock-solid evidence would be seen as part of a vendetta to jail the 'Walsh Street Killers'.

This was the environment that McCulloch had to deal with when he took on the family run by Granny Evil.

AT THE time I knew Victor Peirce was serving an eight-year sentence for heroin trafficking and his wife Wendy alias 'Slut Guts' Peirce was serving eighteen months' jail for perjury. In the middle of Victor's Walsh Street murder trial, Wendy changed her evidence and said he didn't commit the murders. He got off and she was convicted of perjury. Testimony to our great legal system. To put the whole thing in perspective it must be understood that it was 1993 and there was an ugly, still raw, wound that affected every copper in Victoria. On March 26, 1991 Victor and Trevor and the other two had been acquitted of the Walsh Street murders. The feeling within the Victoria Police Force was absolute outrage and disgust.

Revenge and retribution were high on the agenda of all police. Straight after the jury verdict McEvoy baited police, turning to a group saying: 'What do you think about that? … "I'll fix you, I'll fix you". Is that what you said? I'll be waiting. I'm not afraid to die.' Police outrage was exacerbated by the fact that a national television current affairs program picked up Victor and Trevor from the Supreme Court in a chauffeur-driven limousine. They were filmed drinking champagne, toasting their victory with Granny Evil, Kathleen Pettingill.

Anyway, Fran loved the idea of living in Victor's old house. Each to their own – it was hardly Graceland. Her heart was set on it, so who was I to interfere? Two days later, on April 21, 1993, Fran had me driving out to Frankston, helping her shift house. Wouldn't it have to be the worst job in the world? I dragged along another undercover cop and fellow crew member, Baldrick. He is bald and his name is Rick. Baldrick and I helped Fran pack everything into boxes. As I was packing, I noticed it was funny how all her pictures looked the same as those found in hotel and motel rooms. Her cutlery had that Sizzler and The Keg restaurant look about it. I made a comment about the similarities. With a cheeky grin Fran said, 'Coincidence. What are you? You a cop, are ya?'

Good point, Fran, I thought.

We filled a giant removal van and off we went in convoy. I had an almost new white Holden Berlina at the rear, the removal van was in the middle and Fran led the convoy in her chocolate brown 1973 Ford Cortina. It was my job to make sure we weren't being followed.

Quiet little Wedge Crescent was about to wake up. Fran arrived like an earthquake. Within seconds of her car door opening, the whole crescent knew she was there. She stood on her front door step and screamed, 'Lenny, welcome to the neighbourhood'.

I tried to hide as all the neighbours peered through curtains or peeped out front doors. I thought how happy they must have been to get rid of Victor Peirce. After a few days of Fran they might want him back.

While I was slaving away helping Fran, I noticed a little grey-haired old lady standing on the footpath looking in at us. She stood there for a while and moved on. We would have looked a sight: Big Baldrick looking like a bikie, me with long hair dressed in all black, big buxom fake blonde Fran showing off her tatts and young Charlie dressed as a cowboy.

I couldn't stop laughing at the poor bloody removal van driver. He was huge and fat and had a bad back. He couldn't lift anything at all. He just told us off for slacking and ordered us around. After a quick bottle of Spumante to celebrate, I left with Rick.

Later that evening, at 7.18, I was at home relaxing when my pager went off. The message was 'Ring Fran Urgent'. Fran had only one phone – on her kitchen wall. I rang. Fran answered in a whisper, 'Have a fuckin' guess who is in my lounge room?'

'Who?'

She said, 'Kath'.

Now, there is only one Kath in Australia, but I couldn't help clarifying, 'Kath Pettingill, with a glass eye, is in your lounge room?'

She said, 'Yep, she put it in my drink when we were in jail.'

She meant the glass eye – I hope. It was obviously one of Kath's cleaner party tricks. The others don't bear thinking about.

I said, 'What is she doing in your lounge room?'

She said, 'She's having a cup of tea and a bong.'

As you do when you're a lovely old grandmother.

I thought, 'Fuck'. In fact, I said it out loud. Then I asked why Kath was there. I was a trained investigator, after all.

Fran said, 'She lives across the road. I was wrong. Victor lived over the road, not here, and now Kath lives there lookin' after his kids – you know, her grandchildren.' Fran whispered, 'Kath wants to sell me some drugs. Do you want any drugs?'

I said, 'Of course I want drugs, fuck, of course.'

Fran said, 'Lenny, what do you want? Fuckin' tell me.'

I had a lot going through my mind. I had just shifted my number one gig across the road from Kath Pettingill. Fran was having a cup of tea and a bong with Kath 'Fucking' Pettingill. I knew Kath could get any drug that's possible to get. So I said, 'Crack. Crack cocaine.'

Fran said, 'Sweet. Bye.'

The phone went dead.

I can't recall ever being so excited in my life. I did the perfect impression of a gobsmacked stunned mullet standing up with a phone in his hand. I rang Baldrick. With a few, 'You're not going to believe this' thrown in, I explained what Fran was up to. Baldrick couldn't believe it either.

Later that night, Fran paged me again. I rang her back. Kath had just left. By this stage of the evening several bottles of red wine had lost their corks. Fran wasn't much better after bonging on with Kath. Fran had supplied the tea, and Kath brought over a few large heads of hooch to welcome Fran to the neighbourhood. It turned out that Kath knew of Fran's husband and Fran had been in prison with Kath when she was doing time for blowing up the paedophile. Fran knew quite a few of Kath's friends. They had a good old chat.

I sat down with my crew. I briefed them. Then I had to brief my inspector, Dave Reid, and the officer in charge of the squad, Chief Inspector Tom McGrath. Bob, our sergeant, had left the squad on a six-month secondment. So our crew was without an immediate boss.

The overnight developments astounded Mr McGrath. Everyone saw that this was an opportunity to strike back, to lock up the smiling assassins, so to speak. The first thing Mr McGrath was concerned about was security. He said, 'From this moment on, the only people to know what you are doing are people who have to know.' We all knew the Pettingills had been surrounded by death for many years. And that Kath had been associating with corrupt cops for over 30 years.

It was common knowledge that just after the Walsh Street murders a telephone intercept was placed in Kath's phone. Investigators found she was having regular sex with an old detective sergeant from an inner suburban criminal investigation branch. This was even after Walsh Street. He resigned and quietly disappeared.

My crew and I left the briefing. The bosses stayed and closed the door. An hour later Inspector Reid appeared and asked me to organise a meeting between himself, Fran and me. We met in the food court of Brandon Park Shopping Centre. I had about half an hour with Fran before the boss arrived.

I explained to Fran that it was time to stop laughing. This is serious shit. On the phone, Fran had said that she was willing to buy drugs from Kath on our behalf. Here I was, sitting at a tiny little vinyl-topped table with Fran, about to ask her to go one step further. I wanted to ask her if she was willing to purchase drugs, make statements and give evidence in court. The bottom line was that I was about to ask her to put her life and that of her whole family in jeopardy forever. Risk your life forever and can you please do it for nothing? Her only payment would be that she did the right thing. Big ask. I didn't want to ask myself if I'd do it, mainly because I knew the answer. I eventually said, 'Have you thought about collecting evidence, making statements and actually getting in the witness box against Kath?'

Fran looked right into my eyes and said, 'Lenny, I can do it. You can help me.'

I said, 'Witness protection, are you willing to go there?'

She said, 'I'd have to, wouldn't I?'

I nodded.

I said, 'You organise drugs for me, we arrest Kath, you're gone anyway. You do one thing with us against Kath and you're gone. Your life will end then and there – life as you know it. Think about it.'

Fran cried. Just then Reid arrived. I introduced her to him. I said that Mr Reid was coming to speak to her, to ask her some questions. Fran knew exactly why he had come. She wiped tears from her eyes and said, 'You must be the guy in charge of all the money.'

Reid laughed and said, 'Spot on.' He had been around for a long time, the old school. He cut straight to the guts and said, 'Why?'

Fran appeared taken aback by his honesty. She thought about it. In the most professional voice I'd never heard her use she said, 'Kath and her sons destroy people. I reckon they did do the wrong thing. I reckon they shot those two young uniform coppers because they were too scared to shoot coppers from the armed robbery squad.' Fran went on about how that was no way to act. 'Their friend Jensen had been shot dead by the robbery squad so they killed two young uniform cops, shot 'em in the back. Gutless.'

Reid said, 'Why do you want to risk your life, your family's lives?'

She said, 'I can do this. I can get 'em all. Can you promise me that in the end we can go and tell my husband what's happened? I want him to find out from me before he is killed. Victor Peirce and his mates are out there, in Barwon.'

Reid said, 'Certainly, then you'll be taken away by witness protection.'

She said, 'Where would they take me?'

'Anywhere that's safe. You get a new name, they'll help you start a new life somewhere.'

'What about Butch?'

Reid replied, 'The authorities will make sure he's protected.' Then he said, 'Fran, it all depends on how this job goes. We will just take this slowly. It could take weeks or months.'

I said, wanting my boss to back me up, 'Fran, as I have said, the most important part of all this is that you do not commit any crime. You can only deal drugs on authority from me, from us.'

Reidy nodded, saying, 'Exactly, or you will jeopardise the whole operation. Back at the office, I am going to authorise you to breach sections of the Drug Act. Only for this operation. You step outside that and you face prosecution.'

Fran said, 'I know I've been drug dealing with Lenny for a couple of months.'

Reid shook his head, 'No Fran, you were not going to give evidence in those, *Operation Marlin*, those bloody fish operations.' We all laughed at me and my fish. In his most serious manner Reid said, 'Fran, this is serious shit. I'm here to evaluate you, to satisfy myself you can do this. I believe you can.'

Fran looked down at the table, 'I hope you guys have lots of money.' She smiled, putting a tissue to her nose.

Reid said, 'You obviously know what you're getting yourself into.'

Fran said, 'I've only ever spoken to Legs and Lenny.'

I said, 'Boss, Legs is Darren O'Loughlin.'

Reid smiled. He was in charge when we were at St Kilda police station and had recommended us both to become detectives.

Fran said, 'If it's okay with you, can you be the only other cop I meet because I don't want to deal with anyone else?'

I said, 'Boss, Fran believes there are a few corrupt cops about.'

Fran laughed and said, 'I fuckin' well know there is.'

Reid said, 'Around our office, at the drug squad you are referred to as B2 of 1993. No-one uses your real name.' Fran sat back in her chair and said, 'I'm B2, I'm a fucking Banana, a Banana in Pyjamas.'

Reid gave me a dirty look and I said, 'I didn't tell her. I was keeping that a secret, boss.'

Fran said, 'You wait, I'm going to tell Legs that you've named me after a fucking dancing banana. You could have called me 007 or something. I'm risking my life and you're puttin' me on the banana.' But she was smiling as she said it. She was going to find out her new codename when we start taking statements from her anyway, so it was good to get it over with.

Now that the boss had stirred her up, he was ready to go. He stood and held out his hand to Fran. Fran stood and said, 'See ya in the soup.'

Reid shook her hand firmly, 'Lenny is going to keep me up to date. I have no doubt you're going to do well. All the best.'

I noticed the boss didn't say, 'Good luck'. Maybe because luck's got nothing to do with it. In this game, if you need luck in the equation, you wouldn't do it.

I stayed and had a chat to Fran. After the boss left, she said, 'He's a serious bastard, doesn't smile much.'

I said, 'He didn't come here for fun.'

Fran snapped, 'I did.'

I said, 'I've got to go now and do a couple of trees worth of paperwork.' I shook her hand and said, 'Once you start, there's no coming back.'

Fran, 'What would Maxwell Smart say? "And loving it".'

I said, 'You are a fucking nut.'

I looked at her and realised we both felt the same way. We were about to do something special. We were about to embark on an escapade jam-packed with death-defying action. Only Fran was going to play at the start. I wanted Lenny to join her as soon as possible. I said, 'Slowly, slowly catch the monkey. We've got plenty of time. Let Kath come to you. Don't forget to mention your boyfriend Lenny.'

Fran laughed, 'Get it right, Lenny, you're not my boyfriend. You just come over to fuck me now and then.'

'Aw, Christ,' I said, and thought to myself, 'death-defying action is right.'

We left each other and returned to our opposite worlds.

NOW is a good time to explain a few things. Fran often spoke about sex. All the time, in fact. Not about having sex, but sexual comments. Lenny and I are a bit more coy about such matters. Like the comment earlier, about lunch. Fran would refer to penises as 'lunch'. She was only joking of course, but I could see such comments might cause problems down the track. Especially in court. And sure enough, I was right..

I got back to the office. Reid said he was impressed enough with Fran to let an operation go ahead. He asked me what the name of it was. I said, '*Operation Earthquake*, sir.' In those days police were able to pick their own codenames but that changed after an armed robbery job called *Short Time* ended with a dead bandit and a lot of paper work. Cynics tried to suggest the name related to the life expectancy of the suspect rather than the length of the job. Then there was the previous investigation into Kath codenamed *Cyclops* in honour of her one good eye. Now the names are spat out of a computer. Not as much fun, but a lot safer.

Reid handed me a mobile phone and said, 'That's for *Earthquake*. As of now, all your other jobs are on hold. You are in charge of handling B2. You are to report to Steve Cody. He is now your new sergeant and controller.' There would be an *Earthquake* meeting in the conference room in fifteen minutes, he added.

I returned to my desk just as my pager went off. It was Fran. I went into one of the interview rooms and closed the door. Fran sounded upset. She whispered excitedly, 'As soon as I got home Kath come over. She wants to know if I can move some gear.'

I said, 'What gear? What is it?'

'I don't fucking know, I just said yes.'

I said, 'Fran, did you fucking well ask? Do you just sell anything? Fran, if you're going to be a drug trafficker, you've got to know what you're selling for fuck's sake.'

Fran responded, 'Do you care what she sells me?'

I said, 'Well no, we want to buy anything, as long as it's illegal.'

'Well it won't be fucking Panadol.'

I said, 'What, you're going to walk up to Kath and say, "I'll have $200 worth of mixed drugs, thanks"?'

Fran was getting annoyed. 'I'm doing a good job, so go and get fucked.'

'Fran, have you ever sold gear before?'

'No.'

I said, 'I'm serious. Now have you or not?'

'No, Lenny, I haven't. I've bought a shit-load but never sold it.'

I suddenly realised that Fran had no idea.

I said, 'Don't for fuck sake pretend that you have. Kath will see through you in a second. Don't try and bullshit Kath. Just tell her that you want to get into it. She'll teach you, no worries. Always say that your man, that's me, Lenny, does it all.'

Fran said, 'What do you sell, Mr Big-time fucking drug dealer?'

I said, 'Everything, whatever she wants to sell.'

I knew it, bloody Fran had me.

Fran said, 'You have a go at me for keeping my options open and your fucking options are opener that mine.'

I said, 'Okay, okay. Ummm. Go for heroin but take anything else she wants to sell.'

Fran said, 'You are red-hot, aren't ya?'

I said, 'Don't commit yourself to anything. Get some samples and we'll work it out.'

I gave Fran my new mobile phone number. I told her to only ring me when she really had to. She really had to every ten minutes.

She reduced that to about every five minutes when I told her the drug squad was going to pay for all her phone bills.

At 7.15 that night Fran rang me again. Kath had come over to her house with her granddaughter Katie. Victor and Wendy had named her Kath after her lovely grandmother. Kath again had the mandatory cup of tea and a bong. Kath wanted to know how much cannabis she could sell for $400 an ounce. Kath also offered Fran as much morphine and Serapax as she could move. Fran told her that she would only want the choof and that she would have to speak to her man Lenny to see how much we'd want. I told Fran that we were in no hurry and to just take things slowly. Fran went back to Kath and ordered an ounce.

Back at the drug squad, we were flat out starting off the operation. We had several warrants to complete to get telephone intercepts and listening devices.

As Fran was ringing me on the mobile the whole time I soon discovered how difficult it was to talk around the office. This was a highly covert operation. Lives were at stake and as far as we were concerned we were dealing with killers. I had no doubt that Kath would kill Fran in a minute if she knew what she was up to.

At our desks the mere mention of the name Kath would have given the game away. There is only one Kath. For security reasons I started to call Kath, Mary. The whole crew followed. Fran and I spoke of Mary the whole time. It was around this first couple of days that I started to drive over to Fran's house at around six in the mornings. I would sometimes park in her driveway, or park in a back street and walk in to her house. I wanted Kath and the nosy neighbours to think I lived with Fran most of the time.

We found there was much more than we expected going on in little quiet Wedge Crescent. There was Frank, an old crook with cancer up the road who sold cannabis and speed for Kath, and another friend of Kath's who was a very proficient shoplifter who could steal anything, it would seem, except underwear.

I was looking out the front window at Fran's, munching on a bowl of cornflakes when I spotted the shoplifter heading for the letterbox to check her mail. She was wearing a white T-shirt and, when she bent over, I suspected a black, fluffy G-string. A second look indicated I was wrong. I lost interest in breakfast.

I said, 'Fran, ever thought about getting a job?'

She replied, 'I used to work. Now I have kids I don't. They keep me flat out.'

'What did you do?'

'I was a receptionist,' she said.

'What sort of company, who did you work for?'

'It was a brothel called 'The Pink Bits' in Frankston.'

I said, 'You were the receptionist? Why is it that every woman I meet who works in a brothel is always the receptionist?'

Fran laughed, 'I dunno. That's what I was.'

I said, 'Well, I don't know who does all the work in these brothels then?'

Fran walked back into the kitchen smiling. She called out, 'Hey Lenny, don't you put me on the prostitute.'

I called, 'I wouldn't do that. You were just a highly paid receptionist.'

I HAD been having huge problems with wiring up Fran for sound. It turned out to be totally impractical for Fran to wear a tape recorder all day every day. So I came up with the old tape recorder in the handbag trick. I borrowed her handbag for a few days and made it suddenly worth over $12,000. I informed her that she had to guard it with her life, or more accurately, my life. As I had to sign property such as recorders in and out, I had an incredibly hard time convincing my bosses Fran could be trusted with such an item all day every day.

As it turned out, this handbag became a permanent attachment to Fran. In the beginning Fran felt awkward. She said she felt nervous about always having her handbag and she thought someone might get suspicious. As time went by, Fran understood that the only reason we were going through all this bullshit was to get evidence. After a while, Fran became confident and totally professional – well that's an exaggeration but I would have not swapped her for anyone.

On May 8, 1993, Kath knocked on Fran's front door. Kath

knew that Fran visited her husband Butch in Barwon Jail every Saturday morning. Kath asked Fran if she could take an ounce of speed into prison and give it to her husband, who would then in turn give it to a close friend of her son Victor Peirce. At this time Victor was in Pentridge Prison. Fran told Kath that she couldn't. In truth this petrified Fran. Kath went on to explain that Victor could sell the drugs and the money would be put into a TAB betting account. Fran politely refused again, saying that she didn't want to get her husband into trouble. Fran was afraid that Butch might pinch some of the drugs, as he would, and then there could be big trouble for everyone.

The reason money is put in to a TAB betting account is so no money has to change hands in jail. It can all be done via the phone. The buyer doesn't get any drugs until the dealer checks and finds the money has been put into his account. Kath wasn't happy with Fran but what could she do?

The following day, Kath again knocked on Fran's door. She said, 'Righto Fran, it's not going to involve your husband. I want you to pretend to be Victor's girlfriend and you can take an ounce of "gowie" (speed) into Pentridge for him, okay love?'

Fran couldn't believe it. She said she couldn't as she's always searched. In the end, Fran stopped giving reasons and just refused. When Fran rang me, she was filthy. She said, 'Lenny, I'm fucking filthy with that bitch. Now she wants me to stick an ounce of gowie up me fanny and give it to her son Victor.'

I wanted to stay well away from anything to do with the prison system. If I thought the drug squad was a leaky boat when it came to security, the prison system was a sunken shipwreck in comparison. I would have loved to do a controlled drug delivery into Victor, but it would be blown out of the water before it got in the water.

I remember once when I was a detective at Carlton CIB. I was having a coffee in the watch-house of the uniform section. A prison van arrived. The city watch-house was full or something, so this prison van delivered a crook from Pentridge to Carlton instead. Two prison officers walked the prisoner into the watch-house.

As his details were being entered in the watch-house book, one of the uniformed members stepped forward to search the prisoner.

Right in front of me, one of the prison officers stepped forward and stopped the copper from searching him. The guard said, 'It's all right, we have already searched him. He's fine.'

The copper couldn't believe the guard's action. Neither could I. The copper ignored the guard and went to search the prisoner again. Again the guard stopped him. By this stage the prisoner was giving us one of those smart-arse smiles. I pushed the guard back, grabbed the prisoner and pushed him up against the wall. Then it was on. I was backed up by more uniform coppers, who had to hold the guards back. The prisoner was jacking up and it was on for young and old, all abusing each other.

I have two very good friends who are prison guards. They're top blokes and I would go to war with them tomorrow. But obviously this crook was a 'somebody' within the walls of prison. Here he was, actually receiving protection from his guards. The guards must have formed some type of admiration to the point of having to show him respect. This crook had reversed the roles.

Fortunately, coppers don't have to live inside prison walls our entire working lives. Attitudes displayed by these guards are alien to us. To us a crook is a crook. The guards feel they have to actually guard the crooks from us. I find their mindset disturbing.

The guards were forced to back down. I explained that they were not in a position to protect their mate any more. Their mate was in a whole new world, a world free from prison politics and hard-earned loyalties. The guards reluctantly left. It took five of us to hold the prisoner down and search him thoroughly.

During the next week Fran met with and bonged on with most of her lovely neighbours. Daily, they would take turns to go to each other's houses to smoke choof and gossip. Fran also met another of Kath's friends, Fred. As I was leaving Fran's one morning, Fred walked past me. He was about 70 years old, with a face that looked like it had been through a blender and then stuck back on. His tatts were so faded, they were barely visible. He was short and thickset. Just a classic old-time crook.

So, near Fran's house were the knickerless shoplifter, Frank the cancerous speed dealer and then faded-tatts Fred.

These were only the neighbours we knew of. What about the rest?

On Saturday, May 15, 1993 Frank rang Fran at her home. He wanted to meet Fran at the milk bar around the corner. She walked there and met him and Kath. They both asked Fran to hop in Frank's car and drive off. Fran with her special handbag taped the meeting:

Kath asked Fran: *Right love, how much speed do youse want?*

Fran: *I just want a quarter* (quarter ounce or seven grams). *Lenny and me just want to check it out.*

Kath then handed her six small plastic bags, each of them containing about one gram of speed. Kath went on to explain on tape that two of the bags contained much stronger speed than the others. Frank added that the price was $300 for the six bags.

Later that evening I drove out to Fran's home. As Lenny, I parked my Berlina in her driveway, Fran appeared at the front door. All smiles. In a whispered shout she said, 'Lenny, it's not much, but I did it.' We walked inside and she handed me the six small bags of white powder. This moment was huge. This drug squad seizure wasn't quite going to cause thousands of Melbourne's speed addicts to go without, but I wouldn't have swapped those small bags for twenty kilos of pure speed from anyone else.

These came from Kath Pettingill, no less. I've spilt more speed than that during a drug deal, but this operation was never about how much. It was all about **who.**

This case had to be rock solid. Any mistakes and it would have looked as though it was an attempted payback to get the Walsh Street gang. Plus they were known killers – and cop killers as well. They had shown they would do anything to avoid apprehension.

Make no mistake, Fran and I knew her life was in danger every minute. I was just a tourist in comparison. Apart from me, she was very much alone.

A few days later Kath turned up at Fran's front door with an ounce bag of hooch. Kath said she could have it for $350. Fran took it and promptly sat down with Kath and had their usual cup of tea and a bong. Fran rang me when Kath had left. I could tell Fran had been smoking because she always became totally paranoid about everything.

She thought people were hiding under her house or listening to her phone calls. I quickly put the phone down and drove over to pick up what was left of our exhibit before it all went up in smoke. The following day Fran gave Kath her $350. *Earthquake* had started with a rumble, but it was slowly getting louder. Like Fran, Kath was always looking for an 'earn'. On May 19, 1993 Kath turned up unannounced at Fran's front door. By now Fran had the whole thing down pat. Kath would come in, Fran would say, 'I'll just grab me smokes.' Fran would come back rummaging through her handbag. Grabbing her smokes and turning her bag on, she would place it nearby. The smoke would calm her nerves as the tape rolled on.

Kath said, 'Come on Fran, you can come with me now. We hafta go and see a bloke, Indian John. He's got three ounces of speed for us. We can get it on credit. It's all organised.'

Fran grabbed her handbag. Kath wanted to go in Fran's car. Just as Kath was getting to Fran's car she stopped and said, 'No, fuck that, you just go love, see this friend of mine Noel. He'll take you to see Indian John.' Fran was not too happy with this. Kath gave Fran a piece of paper with an address written on it. Fran drove off and picked up Noel. Noel then directed Fran to the Narre Warren caravan park. Indian John lived in an on-site caravan.

Fran told John she was there to pick up the three ounces of speed for Kath. John said he never gave anyone credit, and that he had not organised any credit with Kath. Fran was smart enough to still buy a small sample of speed from him. John laughed at the fact that anyone would give credit to Kath. He added that she would never pay after getting credit, why would she?

John knew that shooting himself in the head would be safer that putting pressure on Kath to pay up. Fran gave John her phone number. She told John that her man Lenny was in the market for a few ounces. John said that his speed supplier was a bloke named 'HJ'. We identified Indian John to be John Humphrey. He was a low-level crook with prior convictions for thefts and drug-related offences. We were unable to identify any 'HJ'.

I found this job was different in many ways to the average drug squad jobs. Normally someone like Indian John would never speak his speed supplier's name, but then you have to remember that Fran came to him on Kath's behalf. To John, this made Fran 100 per cent safe to deal with.

Another interesting fact was that none of the crooks showed any signs of wealth. Living in caravans and housing commission houses, they weren't your Mr Bigs. But they were serious, not to be fucked around with, low-lifes. In my experience, the lower the crook is, the cheaper life becomes. This was a worry. If I was to go in undercover with these guys, I was going to have to come down to their level. By listening to tapes and speaking with Fran day-in, day-out, I slowly started to come down. And come down I did.

Back in the drug squad we would all lock ourselves in the conference room, put a tape recorder on the middle of the table and push 'play'. Kath's nasally old, unmistakable voice would pierce the air.

It was nothing for Kath to say two or three 'fucks' and a couple of 'cunts' in the one sentence. Fran tried to outdo her, but didn't come close. Kath's total vocabulary consists of about ten words. And I reckon about four of them contain 'fuck'. She thought a split infinitive should be treated with Dettol and a Bandaid.

You know when she gets to a topic that she's passionate about because the 'fucks' increase. Like, 'What about that fuckin' fat fuckin' security sheila at fuckin' Coles, the fuckin' slut keeps fuckin' eyeballin' me.' One time Kath was telling Fran how she had stolen a soft toy dinosaur to give young Katie. She had hidden it under her jumper. As she was paying for some other items at the checkout, she got the fright of her life when the toy started growling. Quick as lightning, she pretended it was her stomach rumbling and got away with it.

We would play most of the tapes to our crew. This way everyone got a feeling for the job. Baldrick was elected brief coordinator. Right from the start, we made sure that all the evidence was collected, collated, logged and its continuity maintained. We all knew every aspect of this operation was going to be thoroughly tested at court.

Each time I collected drugs from Fran, they would be logged in my diary, placed in an exhibit log, photographed and analysed. The same would happen with all of Fran's tapes. Not only was Fran taping her conversations with 'Mary' and her mates but every time I spoke to Fran I recorded the conversation. I would tape every time we spoke, in cars, at her home and all telephone conversations. At the end of business-talk I would often turn the tape off.

Fran knew when we spoke I would be taping the call. It was legal to tape my calls as I would hold a small tape recorder up to my telephone earpiece and record both what came out of my phone and what I was saying. It only becomes illegal if you attach a device to the phone.

This enabled me to take instant exact notes of everythings as it happened. Before and after each conversation I would state the date and time. One of the biggest problems I had was the transcription of the tapes. I eventually solved this by giving my tapes to a group of stenographers employed by Victoria Police.

Several of them were blind, which meant they were much better at listening than most. They did in hours what would have taken me years.

I HAD one problem that I could not ever fix – Fran. I would ring her straight after she had a meeting with the crooks. A typical conversation would go something like this:

'G'day Fran, what happened? Did you meet Mary?'

'G'day Lenny, how's it hangin'?'

'Fine, what's happened?'

'Lenny, is it on the left or the right?'

By this stage I'm pissed off. Fran knows I'm pissed off but does not care. She knows I'm taping the conversation and wants me to squirm. 'Fran, I am being serious, don't do this.'

Fran would say, 'You're just interested in the business, I'm not tellin' you nothing till you answer.'

'All right Fran, it's hanging on the left today.'

Fran would be rapt. She won.

You put yourself in my position. I am trying to be a highly trained professional detective conducting a professional, totally impartial, drug squad operation. Here I am, on tape telling the main witness which side my penis is hanging on today. I couldn't just turn the tape on and off, whenever I wanted, because that would be editing my notes. They would lose all credibility at any trial. So I had to play along with Fran, unsafe in the knowledge that I am going to cop it big time in the witness box. More on this subject latter.

On May 25, 1993, Fran rang me. She had an old girlfriend of hers turn up on her doorstep. Fran told me that she was going to let her stay with her for a while. This was the last thing I wanted to hear. It got better. Fran wanted me to help her out with her problem. Fran said that she was wanted by the police for car theft and house burglaries. Great.

I said, 'So she's a junkie?'

'Yes, she's on 'smack' (heroin) but I'm going to help her get off it. She's got no-one else in the world and we're mates.'

Who was I to deny Fran a friend? I sensed the real reason was that Fran loved the idea of company. She not only wanted a friend, she wanted a friend in need.Fran promised to never tell Sally Lenny's secret. This was another danger that Lenny did not need. I asked my boss where we stood, with me knowing Sally was wanted on arrest warrants, and me doing nothing.

Several hours later I was authorised to ignore the warrants and continue with our covert investigation. A quick check of the computer revealed that Sally was no Florence Nightingale. She had heaps of convictions for armed robbery, possessing firearms, assault and robbery, prostitution, thefts and burglaries. She had spent several years in jail and was one hardcore scumbag.

Sally was a real problem for us. Fran was the only one that loved her being around. Sally was a real hard case. One afternoon I started to research her past. She hated police with a passion. That was obvious from the way she spoke. I had met her several times as Lenny Rogers and she was fine. She was smiley and happy. But I found she had a dark side.

She had been the de facto wife of a serious old robber ten years before. She had assisted him in executing several large bank robberies. I thought at first she must have been the getaway driver. No, she had entered the banks with her de facto carrying a loaded sawn-off shotgun. She ended up with eight years with a four-year minimum. She got off light as she claimed she was forced to assist. She was also a chronic heroin addict.

When Sally got out of jail, she met up with an old friend, Jimmy Reimers. Jimmy was a well-known mad gunman, junkie and armed robber. Jimmy, his brother Billy and Sally then went on a disgusting drug-driven rampage. They hit their criminal career lowlight when one day, while driving along a back road in an outer eastern suburb of Melbourne, they decided to rob a 78-year-old man walking down the street. To speed up the process they bashed him first. After taking a small amount of cash and a cheap watch, they sped off.

The soft targets seemed easy. So over the next two months they struck fear into the elderly from Frankston to Ferntree Gully. They were eventually charged and convicted of fifteen assault and robberies. Sally received another eight-year sentence. Now she was free again after serving only four. Just what I needed to make undercover life interesting.

On May 27, 1993, at 8.25pm I received a phone call from Fran. She was upset. She cried as she told me that she had just told Sally I was an undercover cop. Fran said, 'I've told her about my handbag, and the sticky tape.' I thought Christ, the job is blown, big time. Urgent damage control was needed. I asked Fran to take Sally to the Mountain View Hotel. I could hear Sally crying in the background. We had gone through so much and now it could all be lost.

Deep down I knew there was no way Fran could ever have kept our secret. I phoned Steve. I told him I would be all right to go and talk to Sally. We had no choice. Either Sally joined us or the job was over. It would become too dangerous for Fran or myself to go undercover on Kath. I also knew that if Sally joined us it could really boost our credibility. In the world of cops and robbers, credibility is everything. You're only as good as the person who introduces you.

I walked into the dimly lit lounge of the Mountain View Hotel. In a small cubicle, right down the back were Fran and Sally. They both had drinks. I nodded to them and walked to the bar. While I waited for a beer, I took a few big breaths. Sally had to join us or the whole operation would fold. If she walked out now, we could not trust her not to say anything. With a beer I walked over. Fran was saying something to Sally to try to make her laugh. Sally reacted with a fake giggle. Fran said, 'G'day Lenny.' Fran half stood and we did the half kiss on the cheek thing. Sally was shrinking inside her chair, on the verge of tears. She still hadn't looked at me. I'd met Sally several times; we'd cracked a few jokes together. Now, for several seconds – nothing. In that pause she started to sob.

How do you ask someone to ruin their life forever? To finish their life as they know it. Big ask.

For Sally to join us meant her becoming a dog forever. Becoming something she was not. Fran sat silent. She was sitting too far away from Sally to comfort her. She leant forward and squeezed Sally's arm.

I said, 'Sally, I'm Detective Senior Constable Lachlan McCulloch.'

With a whispered cry she said, 'I've never, I've never spoken to a jack before.' Interviewed heaps of times but never really spoken a word to one before. Police were the dreaded enemy. The filth.

I said, 'I'm sorry you're involved.'

She said, 'I thought something was going on, but not this.' She cried.

'Lenny, they'll kill me. You don't know how bad they are.'

I said, 'They hide behind fences and ambush two young cops, execute them in the back.' I stopped talking because I felt my voice about to crack. I didn't want either girl to see me cry. Sally sobbed.

I paused to gather myself. Tears rolled down Fran's cheeks as she sat in silence. Fuck it. Through tears and a cracking voice I forced the words out, 'They parked a stolen car in the middle of the road, they left all the doors open and when Damian and Steve leant in to check out the car, they stood up and shot 'em, shot 'em in the back. Then they walked up, removed their revolvers from their holsters and shot them again. I can't get the photos out of my head.'

Sally cried, 'I hate 'em more than you Lenny. They've killed more people than that.'

I said, 'We need your help. They trust you.'

Sally said, 'In 1986 I was in 'B' Annexe in Pentridge Prison with Kath. We were having lunch. Kath stood up and said to everyone, "Who in here has fucked my sons?" I won Lenny, coz I fucked Victor, Trevor and Dennis.'

I said, 'Fran knows, you do this and we will look after you. New name, new address, new life.' With half a laugh I said, 'Look at the positives, you'll never be able to buy heroin again in Victoria, probably Australia.' We all stopped crying enough to laugh.

Wiping her tears away she said, 'It would be quicker and less painful if you just shot me now. Lenny, I can use this to help me stop using.'

I said, 'Exactly. Hold your right hand up and swear after me ...'

Sally put her little hand half up. ' ... I swear, I will do everything in my power to make Lenny look good.'

She smiled and repeated the words.

I said, 'Right, you're in.'

Fran said, 'You gunna call her B1, then you got yourself a right couple of bananas.' Fran explained to Sally what that meant.

A veneer of laughter temporarily hid our deadly serious tones. We chatted away. Inside that big tough, rough exterior was a frightened little woman. She had nothing in the world. Nothing. No family, no friends other than Fran. But of course she always had heroin.

I asked Sally, 'What do you want to do, jump in all the way or just help Fran?'

Sally said, 'I'll go along with it, but I don't want to get in the witness box or nothing like that. I'll just be around to support Fran.'

'Sweet, that's what she needs.'

It's like being a little bit pregnant. A little bit of an informer is an informer. She was in on the giggle, up to her neck. No matter what her past was like, she had the potential of being a great witness. I believed this because Sally, much more than Fran, was really one of them, a real crook. The biggest problem was, she was also a junkie. From my experience junkies can never be trusted. My job now was to make sure I could corroborate everything she did.

I said, 'Deal.' I passed her my mobile phone number. 'Any time, day or night.' I went on to explain that if anyone needed to know, Lenny's an old friend she met through Fran. I stressed that whatever happened, Lenny is a crook; that other cops were not to know about Lenny. I told her I knew she was 'hot' – meaning wanted. I told her that I couldn't protect her if she committed any more crime.

Sally asked, 'How come you can be a drug trafficker?'

I said, 'I'm allowed to be a criminal, I'm a cop.' The girls broke up laughing.

I said, 'I've indemnified Fran as well. Now I'll be indemnifying you. It means that you can traffic drugs with me, just and only me.'

I had now switched into 'professional mode', Lenny the caring, typical drug squad investigator. I said to Sally, 'This is the most important thing – never tell any other cop what you're doing or who I am. Next, if you commit any crime at all from now on, you completely jeopardise the whole operation.'

Sally said, 'I understand. Lenny, I keep thinking that we've met before.'

I said, 'Can I try and help you get some kind of job. Have you ever done any work?

Sally replied, 'Yeah, I still do a bit.'

I asked what.

She said, 'I work in a brothel. I'm the receptionist.'

I burst out, 'Who the fuck does all the work in those joints?

Everyone is always the receptionist. How much do you charge?'

She said, 'Hundred bucks for half an hour.' We all laughed.

I said, 'So if you're with a client, and his phone rings, will you answer it?'

Fran and I laughed so much we started to slide off our chairs.

With a smirk Sally said, 'If I'm in a position to.' Then added, 'If I haven't got my mouth full.' We had started to bond.

I said, 'When this is all over, I'm going to write a book: *Lenny and the Receptionists*.'

Fran said: 'Nah, it sounds like a band.'

There was something about Sally that was very attractive. She was like a naughty little kitten. A kitten that could easily catch its own rats and eat them alive. Sally added something that Fran and I desperately lacked: criminal credibility. She was now on board our leaky little ship.

I said, 'Well, times are going to get tough. If you need a break just tell me.'

Sally said, 'Can I have a break?'

'No.' I leaned over the table and gave her a little punch on the shoulder and said, 'Look on the bright side. Your life has just changed forever. Sally's life of crime is over, forthwith. After today you can't afford to ever go back inside.'

Sally said in a sad sarcastic tone, 'Great, I feel better already.'

We all knew that if she went to prison again, after the Pettingills found out what she'd done, she'd be dead. In a loud confident voice, I said, 'Trust me girls, I'm an undercover cop.' They laughed.

Sally asked, 'Fran, are you sure he's a cop?'

Fran replied, 'Yeah, he's not smart enough to be a crook.'

I said, 'Remember, I'm a cleanskin, never been arrested. I'm just too fucking smart for those dumb-arse cops. I better go.'

We stood up. The meeting was over. As we left the pub, Sally mentioned again that she had been in jail with Kath in the high-security annexe of Pentridge. She used to exercise with Kath every morning over seven months. Then Kath was transferred to Fairlea Women's Prison.

Thirteen months later, Sally was transferred to Fairlea where she again met up with Kath every day. But she said they were never really friends.

As we got to Fran's car, I asked Fran for her handbag. I sat in the back seat and opened it up and removed all its contents. Sally laughed. Fran said to Sally, 'Don't worry, there's no fucking privacy when it comes to Lenny.' I opened up the tape recorder that was concealed in the bottom. I changed the tape and the batteries. I quickly stuffed all of Fran's private belongings back inside. Handing the bag back, I said, 'Remember, luck has got nothing to do with it.'

I touched Sally on the arm and said, 'What a team, two receptionists and a bug catcher.' We all laughed. I am a funny bastard so I can laugh at my own jokes. I stepped out of Fran's car and walked off. I'd gone a few steps when I heard car doors open. Then Sally said, 'Hey, Lenny.' I turned. Sally and Fran had stepped out of the car. Together they lifted their tops, exposing their naked breasts at me. I stood there, slightly embarrassed and looked around to see if anyone else could see. They called out laughing, 'See ya, Lenny.' I just shook my head and walked off thinking, 'A fireman, that's what I should have been.'

As I drove home, I thought, 'Remember Lachlan, this is another world, not your world. Remember, remember, remember, you're only visiting.'

Flashing their tits was to become a regular event. Especially when saying goodbye. It didn't matter where we were. They were just old-fashioned girls.

On May 29, 1993, at 6.15am I drove into Fran's driveway to say hello. I was sitting at Fran's kitchen table drinking coffee when Sally walked in. She had on a black totally see-through teddy. I said, 'That's your receptionist's uniform, is it?' Sally ignored that comment. She was happy and talkative. We started chatting about old and new crooks. Crimes and times.

Sally was half the size of Fran. She was always bright and sparkly. She had distinctive Slavic facial features, and was slim with largish breasts. They had a slightly unnatural pertness to them, and were shaped like ski jumps. I must have a thing about ski jump-shaped tits, I thought.

Fran suddenly laughed and said, 'Hey Sally, tell Lenny what you told me.'

Sally said, 'I spoke to a friend of mine that just got out of Barwon (prison). He reckons Fran's Butch wants to kill a bloke named Lenny.'

Fran laughed. 'Butch reckons Lenny's been fucking his wife and giving her drugs.'

I said, 'Bullshit, Butch's wife's been fucking Lenny, and causing poor old Lenny to take drugs, more like it.' We all laughed. What else could we do? We were all caught in the same deadly game of make-believe. That old saying they reminded us of at detective training school sprang to mind: 'What a tangled web we weave, when first we practise to deceive'.

On May 30, 1993, Fran received a phone call from Indian John. John said he had spoken with Kath and he had three quarter-ounce bags of speed for $230 each. He added that HJ had a further four ounces of speed for $850 each.

Fran rang me and we arranged for John and HJ to come over at 6.30 that evening. I asked Fran to go down and see Kath and ask her what John and HJ were like. Fran grabbed her expensive handbag and paid Kath a visit. This was really just to get more evidence on Kath. Kath told Fran that they were 'good people'. If they were good, I'd hate to meet some of her bad ones.

Kath said, 'Your bloke Lenny will get rid of it, just make sure I get some money.' Fran was not sure where Kath was going to get any money from, so she just left.

I briefed my detective sergeant, Steve Cody. We decided that Lenny would sit this number out and send his number one man to act as a courier. We chose 'Dave'. Dave was a trained undercover operative and resident David Boon look-alike. He was at the squad on a three-month secondment. Dave was a stocky tough bastard and the crooks loved him.

At the time I was flat out being in charge of Fran. It was a constant struggle to lead her down the path of evidence collecting. I didn't want to get sidetracked. Lenny wanted to meet Kath.

I updated Fran. With her handbag locked and loaded with a fresh tape, it was soon time to do the business. Right on 6.30pm Indian John arrived at her front door. John was with a new player named Rod. Dave arrived, meeting Fran for the first time. John had a can of Victoria Bitter in his hand. Dave explained that Lenny had sent him. John pulled at the can; it had been cut in half and then pushed back together. He removed a red-coloured balloon and handed it to Dave. Dave checked the package and gave John $690.

A few minutes later, a car pulled up outside. From the kitchen window Dave could see a very tall male walking towards the front door. A dark-haired female remained in the passenger seat. Fran opened the door. The tall scruffy-looking bloke introduced himself as HJ. Dave looked at him and Fran. Dave thought he recognised him to be another detective from the drug squad.

HJ held out his hand, Dave reluctantly shook it. Something

was very wrong. Fran sensed it. As far as Dave knew, the detective was not an undercover operative. The policeman was normally very well presented while HJ was not.

Anyway, with Dave spinning out totally, HJ carried on and said he wanted to see the money. He then walked outside and spoke to his wife Maxine. Maxine seemed to be struggling around in the front passenger seat.

HJ came back inside saying, 'Maxine will be in in a minute. She's having trouble'.

Dave looked out the kitchen window. Maxine had her right leg up on the dashboard and was reaching around in her crotch. She had lost his five ounces of speed. Everyone was serious for a while, then they began to laugh. Fran said to Dave, 'I'm glad you're buying that shit – I'm not touching it.'

Dave felt like he had been sucked into a bad B-grade movie. Then Maxine appeared in the entrance to the kitchen. She said, 'Where's the bathroom?' Fran and Dave pointed up the hall. Maxine had dirty thick black hair and was slightly stooped over. She slowly waddled up the hall and slammed the bathroom door. Dave said, 'She must need more room to operate.'

Dave said to Fran, 'This is the last fuckin' time I'm workin' for Lenny.' Sally and Fran were laughing away in the lounge room.

A full five minutes later, a very pissed-off Maxine stomped into the kitchen. She said, 'Who wants this?' She held up a beige-coloured package. It was the same size and shape as a baby-size football. Everyone present simultaneously pointed to Dave and said, 'He does'.

Dave hadn't thought that far ahead. Where was he going to put it?

He carefully opened his right jacket pocket with two of his fingers. Maxine dropped it inside and stomped out to the car. Dave handed HJ the $3400. HJ handed Dave a piece of paper

with a mobile number on it. Dave said, 'I'll give it to Lenny.'
There was a knock at the door. It was an old crook called Bill
and an old tent boxer called Fred, who had plenty of form. They
both came inside.

Fran said to me later, 'Lenny, what have you done to me? Me
house was full of fucking drug traffickers.'

I said, 'It's okay, Fran, you're a drug trafficker and so am I'.

Bill and Fred then asked Fran if she or her bloke wanted to
buy half a pound of choof. She told them she would speak to
Lenny. HJ was still in the kitchen talking with Dave. HJ went
on to offer Dave top-quality 'hammer'. He also called it 'slow',
this of course being heroin.

The drug talk continued for a while. Eventually everyone
began to leave.

About ten minutes after everyone left there was another
knock at the door. Fran called out. 'Who is it?' It was a bad
neighbourhood. Two voices called out, 'Fred' and 'Bill'. Fran
opened the door.

Fred asked, 'How well do you know this Lenny bloke?'

Fran said, 'I know him, he's all right.'

Fred said, 'Well, we want you to organise a big drug deal
right, and then Bill and me are going to rob him.'

Fran couldn't help it, she laughed. 'You want to rob Lenny?
Why?'

Bill said, 'Coz he's got lots of money and we want it.' Ask a
silly question.

Bill told her, 'We've got a gun.'

To help sell the plan and as a bit of an afterthought Fred
added, 'We'll give you a whack of it.'

Fran said, 'Fellas, it's late, I'll think about it. Just leave Lenny
alone and I'll get back to you guys.' They were happy with that
and left.

Seconds later, my phone rang and Fran said, 'Don't you ever do this shit to me again.'

'What?' I asked.

Fran replied, 'We had cops, robbers, drug dealers, speed stuck up fannies, the fuckin' lot.'

I said, 'What happened?'

Fran said, 'But do you know the best bit?'

'What?'

She told me, 'Bill and Fred want to rob ya. They've got a gun and they want to rob ya.'

'Seriously?'

'Yeah, said Fran. 'They know you're the money man. They want to hide in me bushes or something, organise a big drug deal and get you with a heap of money, then rob ya.'

I asked, 'And what did you say to that!'

'I told them I would think about it.'

'What?' I said.

Fran said, 'They want to give me some of the profits.' She laughed and said, 'I'm serious.'

She was serious. On top of everything else, two 70-year-old crooks, each with at least one foot in the grave, wanted to rob me.

She went on to give me the full rundown. Dave rang me to talk about HJ. Computer checks revealed that HJ was in fact the identical brother of the detective. What are the chances of that ever happening?

If this was a crime fiction book, you would think this was a very corny unbelievable coincidence and chuck it away. So there you go: Truth **is** stranger than fiction.

As one truish crime writer once said, 'Fiction writers are bound by the restrictions of what is believable while true crime is about the seemingly unbelievable'. Something like that.

It was the old story all over again. One brother going down the evil path and the other up the path of goodness.

The baddie had in fact three full pages of prior convictions. He had been convicted of trafficking drugs twice before. He and his wife were addicts. Hence his wife's not-so-secret compartment.

The following day the other undercover, Dave, handed me the five-ounce package of speed.

I said, 'Mate, that's got to make your eyes water.' Well, it certainly made the courier's eyes mist over when she had to recover the package from its dark hiding spot.

Dave said, 'Mate, that was a fucking circus out there'.

THE detective with the twin was a friend of mine and a top bloke. We never considered for a second that he would condone or in any way have anything to do with what his twin brother was up to. He was a good copper and it wasn't his fault his brother went to the dark side. Shit just happens. As professional golfer Graeme Marsh once said to his brother, Test cricketer Rod – I am not my brother's keeper.

We decided not to tell the detective about his brother. But the fact that Kath Pettingill had just organised me to buy five ounces of speed from a drug squad detective's twin brother did concern us. It caused our whole crew to become tighter, and more security conscious.

The good brother was a detective senior constable at the drug squad. He was heavily involved in a very large investigation codenamed *Operation Afghan*. He lived halfway between the drug squad office and my home. I would often drop him off after work and pick him up. On one occasion I was driving him home when his bad twin rang me on my mobile. I pushed the phone hard against my ear to stop my passenger hearing his brother's voice. He knew I was in the middle of a large undercover job. He didn't need to know who or what I was doing. I must say, I found the whole thing quite hard. At the time it was a very difficult situation.

The following day, I asked Fran to go over to Kath's home for a chat. Fran knocked on the front door and had the following conversation with Kath, according to the statement she later made:

Kath said: 'Come in love' and I said, 'Hi, Kath, how are ya?'

I then followed Kath into her son's, Victor Peirce's bedroom. She sat at the head of the bed with one leg on the bed and she had a small clear plastic bag containing white powder and about six silver aluminium foil strips. She was using a small plastic 'Whizz Fizz' spoon to put the powder into the foils and then she folded them ends first, the bottom up and the tops down. Each foil looked like it would hold a gram of white powder. She then put these foils into a small plastic sealable bag. I believed at the time that the powder was speed. I was sitting on the end of Victor and Wendy's bed while she was doing this. I then had the following conversation with her.

Kath said: 'Not bad, love. How'd ya go last night?'

I said: 'Pretty good, actually.'

Kath said: 'Were there any hassles? No...'

I said: 'No, they were pretty good actually. HJ was packin' but he was all right. He's a bit big isn't he?'

By 'packin' I was telling Kath that HJ had a pistol on him at the drug deal.

Kath said: 'Yeah, he's a big bloke, love. Do you want more?'

I said: 'Yeah ... well.'

Kath said: 'Is your bloke happy with it, love?'

I said: 'Not too bad. He reckons if it was a bit better he'd be able to make more money.'

Kath said: 'What? Complainin', complainin' about it?'

I said: 'Yeah.'

Kath said: 'Fuckin' kiddin'.'

I said: 'No, no.'

Kath said: 'We'll look after ya love, don't worry.'

I said: 'That's all right. I had fuckin' more blokes in my house than hot dinners last night.'

Kath said: 'I made twenty eight hundred bucks last night, love.'

I said: 'Did ya?'

Kath said: 'Mmm.'

I said: 'Where's my money?' Laugh.

Kath said: 'We'll look after you, love.'

I said: 'Oh, grouse, I'll catch up with ya.'

Conversation continued regarding domestic matters. At the end of those conversations, I left Kath's home.

As I was walking, I said to the tape recording in my handbag, Nine minutes past nine o'clock and I'm just getting home from Kath Pettingill's on May 31, Monday night, and I'm turning the sticky tape off, bye.

Fran always called the recorder in her handbag 'sticky tape' so no-one would hear her use the words tape recorder.

As it turned out, I had asked Fran to ask Kath about buying more speed. Kath had purchased the speed from somewhere and supplied it to HJ. HJ then did the deal. This was a surprise to us, but it proved that Kath was doing more than we knew about behind the scenes. Kath had also got Fred and Bill to come over to Fran's to sell the half pound of cannabis.

CHAPTER 3

Hooking Kath

The listening device was
being hampered by a
canary. It sang its little
bloody head off all day,
every day.

ON June 3, 1993, at 10.35am, I was at my office. My mobile
phone rang. It was Fran; she asked me to hang on a second. I
started walking as quickly as I could toward an interview room.
The drug squad was full of detectives swearing and joking. I
sensed that Fran sounded strange. Next second there was an
unmistakable voice on the other end of the phone. I recorded
the following conversation.

This conversation was included in my official police
statement:

Kath said: Hello, love.

I said: How's it going?

No introductions necessary.

Kath said: Not bad.

*I said: I've been speakin' to Fran and I want her to speak to
you about prices and shit like that.*

Kath said: Well, I don't like speakin' over the phone love, you know.

I said: Well, that clothing, I'm the same. That's cool.

Kath said: I'll be able to do it again in a few days, I'll speak with Fran.

I said: Sweet.

Kath said: See ya, and handed the phone back to Fran.

That was it, my first conversation with the inimitable Kath. Back at my desk I explained that I had just spoken to Mary. It wasn't much but it was a start. I was rapt – my first contact with the main target. I wasn't pushing for a meeting with Kath. The last thing I wanted was to be seen to want to meet her. I was prepared to wait.

On Saturday, June 5, 1993, at 8am, Fran was getting ready to take her children to visit her husband Butch in jail. As Fran walked out her front door, she met Kath in her front yard. Kath wanted to know if 'your bloke Lenny was still complainin' about the quality'. Kath also said, 'I'm sick of getting the run around by middlemen, I'm sick of givin' people tick (meaning credit). Money up front talks all languages love. Speak to your yuppie bloke'. That meant me. Kath then said, 'A thousand bucks will get him an ounce of real good stuff. You only get what you pay for, love.' She wanted the dreaded credit. Fran told her she would ask her bloke Lenny.

Here I was, torn between wanting high-quality speed from Kath and giving her the (to be avoided at all costs) credit. I spoke with my boss and controller, Steve. Steve was always calm and cool. Nothing was ever a problem. Later that day while we were still deciding, Kath arrived on Fran's doorstep again. Again she asked for $1000, insisting that this was the best way to get better speed. Kath told Fran to get the money from her man Lenny. We finally gave in. Just on the off chance that we could trust Kath Pettingill, which wasn't something many people did. I drove over to Fran's and handed her the grand. Fran, handbag on her arm, walked over the road and gave it to Kath.

The following day, June 9, 1993, Kath walked over to Fran's. Kath explained that there was a delay in getting the gear. Kath said, 'Listen love, I've given the money to my people but they haven't come back.' On June 10, 1993, Kath again walked to Fran's stating, 'There's a few days' delay. My people almost got pinched, the cops are after them. Tell your bloke Lenny not to worry. If your bloke Lenny gives you a hard time I'll fill him in, all right.' I didn't like the sound of 'fill him in'. Neither did Fran.

We had been ripped off. Yes, that's what happens when you trust the untrustworthy Kath Pettingill. I felt like a fuckwit. Only joking, it wasn't my grand. She had in fact ripped us all off – the whole of the taxpaying community.

By this stage we had been monitoring Kath's home phone and had a listening device in her house. Her phone was full of domestic-related crap. She spoke to her sons every day. As you can imagine, they didn't discuss Einstein's theory. It was all about shoplifting, old crooks dying and who was ripping off whom. What was for dinner came a close fourth. Kath got all excited one day when she was approached by some filmmakers. They were in the process of making a television series called *Janus*.

Kath was most upset because they were going to call her 'Granny Evil'. Her son Trevor Pettingill said, 'That's all right Mum, you've been called worse'. Our surveillance followed her to a meeting with some of the scriptwriters. The whole TV series was loosely based on a family identical to Kath's.

But over the phone there was no mention of my $1000 at all.

Victor Peirce would ring her from jail. We listened as she told her son Trevor Pettingill all about her new neighbours. She said, 'I'm doin' a bit of bizzo with Fran and her yuppie bloke Lenny; they live over the road.' One day she said, 'I don't know what it is but I don't trust that Fran sheila'. She should have trusted her instincts. But to old Kath and to all of us in the drug squad, 'Money talks and bullshit walks'. Kath always needed an easy 'earn'.

Now, to her listening device. The listening device was being hampered by a canary. It sang its little bloody head off all day, every day. The dominating high-pitched whistle was incessant. After several weeks something had to be done, so *Operation Tweety Pie* was born. This of course is a mythical operation. Even so, the real names of those involved shall remain unspoken.

Intelligence arrived at the drug squad that only the male canary sings. As unlikely as it might seem, the females of the species remain silent. A small highly-trained group of detectives were selected. Based on up-to-date current intelligence they knew that Kath's premises was briefly empty. During this window of opportunity, Detective X entered the kitchen area at the rear of Kath's home and took several intimate photographs of the target canary. Detective X then exited the premises. Armed with several photographs, a disguised Detective X attended several pet shops. After selecting an apparently identical 'non-Tweety Bird' Detective X re-attended Kath's home. After several squeaks and squawks and one 'the fuckin' thing bit me', Kath's home fell silent.

Soon after, Kath was heard in the rear of her home talking to a bloke about buying speed. In the middle of this conversation Kath said, 'Hang on Brian, something's wrong with me bird'. Kath started whistling again and saying, 'It must be sick, it used to whistle all the bloody time. Victor and the kids love it whistlin'.'

Now the detectives listening to the device were driven mad by Kath trying to teach the bird to sing again. More proof that you can't win.

On June 23, 1993, Fran saw Kath walking past the front of her house. Fran grabbed her handbag and turned it on. Fran asked Kath about the $1000 worth of speed she was supposed to get. Kath said, 'Just don't worry about it, I've got me boys out looking at the moment and we're going to blow their heads off.' She went on to say, 'It's just a lousy $1000. As soon as I get it back, I don't want to do any more business love. That's it. Ring Lenny now, and I'll tell him.'

Fran rang me at 10.32am. She handed the phone to Kath.

Kath said, 'The blokes have just disappeared on me.'

'Have they?' I said.

Kath was blunt, and to the point. She sounded upset. 'I've got the boys out lookin. They'll get it back and I'll give it to ya. But I don't want to do any more business any more, mate.'

I said, 'What's going down?'

Kath said, 'What's going down?'

I said, 'I only gave it to you because you asked for it. You said it would make things easy, you wanted to do business.'

Kath said, 'Yeah, well all right, I'll put you back to Fran.'

Well, work that out. We ask for some better quality speed. Kath then tells us off for complaining. Then she pushes and pushes us to give her credit. We reluctantly give her credit and she rips us off – then abuses us for complaining. Kath should have trusted her instincts in not trusting Fran. I should have done the same thing when it came to giving Kath credit. As it happened, me giving Kath credit gave her a reason to have a falling out with us. Kath just went along doing her thing ignoring the fact that she owed Lenny the grand. Kath probably thought Lenny would never do anything about it anyway.

My position was, how hard should I or we, the drug squad, push Kath Pettingill? We didn't want to be seen to be a soft touch, and we didn't want anyone to get killed over it either. The Pettingills would kill for much less than a $1000. Kath's son Dennis Allan once killed a bloke for turning down his stereo, shot him seven times in the back. Dennis then got his mum Kath to clean up the bloody mess as good mums do. Hence we decided to tread softly.

At dawn on July 7, 1993, all was quiet in Wedge Crescent, Rowville. The silence was shattered by the sound of breaking glass and splintering wood. Five detectives ran inside over the remains of Fran's front door. When the screaming, 'Police don't move' finished echoing down the street Fran was lying face down on her bedroom floor handcuffed. Sally, however, was putting up a great fight in Fran's backyard. Fran had been safe in the knowledge that she would never get raided by the 'jacks' with her trusted friend Lenny protecting her. Sally was the opposite. She was wanted and never felt safe anywhere. Sally had been asleep, naked, in her bed in the spare room at the rear of the house. At the sound of the front door exploding, she opened her window and dived out.

Back door Charlie, (police term for the poor sucker who goes around the back and guards the back door, thus missing out on all the action inside) got far more action than he expected or needed. He tackled Sally to the ground. Covered in nothing but a sprinkling of prison tatts, Sally tried to scratch and pinch her way to freedom. She lost.

I was incredibly proud of the way Fran remained staunch. She didn't give the game away. As I've said before, there was too much at stake. We could not risk telling any of the local police what we were up to, including the local CIB. Fran gave me the full story over the phone. They searched the house from top to bottom. With Fran's help, they failed to locate the tape recorder in her handbag. Somehow the local CIB received information that Sally was living in Fran's house. They took her away and charged her with numerous burglaries and car theft.

Fran was very upset. I explained to her that I couldn't contact the police who arrested Sally. One of the first things I did was arrange for a new front door. I arranged that from my home. Then I drove straight over and helped her clean up the mess. Her children had finished crying. They were used to this type of life, having been through several raids. The armed robbery squad didn't muck around when it came to arresting their father.

While all this was happening, I received a message to ring the boss at the drug squad. As you do, I panicked and wondered what I had done wrong. I rang him. The boss explained that he had just spoken to the principal of a primary school in Rowville. The principal had said that one of the students had told his teacher that his mother was dealing drugs with a policeman from the drug squad. The policeman was a bloke named Lenny.

Another 'spot fire' that had to be put out. Not good. Unbelievable. What made it incredibly dangerous was that Wendy and Victor Peirce's children went to the same school. I assured the boss that I could handle the situation. I wasn't as confident as I hope I sounded.

I sat down with Fran. The children had found out I was a cop. Fran had somehow told them and she was keeping it a secret from me. When I asked Fran how they found out, she said, 'Lenny, when you have kids you'll find out they don't miss much! They might be young but they're not stupid'. Fran and I had a very deep and meaningful conversation about everything.

I explained to her that there was nothing that she couldn't tell me. Good, bad, whatever. I just had to know.

A new problem, a serious problem. This job was getting harder every day.

To the kids, Lenny their friend, was still the same bloke, but was now much more exciting. I told Fran's boy what I had just found out. He said, 'Lenny, can you come out and show me your car?'

I followed him out the front door. He stood back, stopped and looked at my white Berlina, parked in the driveway. With great thought he said, 'It doesn't look like much of a cop car. Can you show me your blue light?'

I stepped forward and wanted to put my hand over his mouth. I knelt down and whispered into his face. 'Mate, buddy, you really must understand this is not a game. If anyone, anyone at all ever finds out I'm a cop we will be in big, huge danger. You can't tell your friends, your teacher, no-one at all. Come inside and I'll show you something.'

I walked back up several steps and back inside the house. The kid followed. We sat down on the couch. I said, 'I'm going to show you something. From now on we have a big secret. If you ever want to say anything about me being a cop you don't have to. Just look at me and touch your nose like this.' I held up my right index finger and tapped the right side of my nose. 'Do this.' He copied me, touching his nose. He said, 'So I just tap my nose like this?' I said, 'Yep, this is our special secret. When you tap your nose that means you and I have a big secret. I'll tap my nose and look back at you. Just never ever say anything. Do you understand how important it is that you tell no-one?

He sat in deep thought. He said, 'Mum said I can't tell Daddy.' I said, 'That's right, when you visit Daddy you can't tell him. If you did tell him, you would put him and Mummy, you, Sally and everyone in big danger. It's the biggest secret ever. You can do it, big buddy.' With a big smile he said, 'I like secrets. Mum said I can call you Uncle Lenny'. I said, 'That's fine, big buddy.' We looked at each other smiling and practised tapping our noses. I added, 'No-one else will know our secret.'

As he skipped off up the hallway, I put my head in my hands. My safety, everyone's safety revolved around maintaining lies. At that moment I was totally convinced this job was the hardest thing I had ever done and was ever likely to do.

How wrong could I be? I was way off the mark. Years later, I actually wished I could be back in the relative safety of Kath and her clan.

ANYWAY, back to the story. One of the best parts about being an undercover cop was that I got to answer the phone like this. Ring, ring, ring, I answered with, 'What!' It was very therapeutic. It felt great. It was like saying, 'What the fuck do you want?' Without the swearing. The first reason I said it was that it was fun. The second reason was to stop myself ever picking my mobile and saying, 'Drug squad, Senior Detective McCulloch speaking. Can I help you?' My brain going into automatic mode could have been very dangerous indeed. Anyway, it suited my image. Remember, I was a smart-arse, half-baked yuppie drug dealer.

On July 15, 1993, Sally rang me. It was 4.57pm and I was very busy transcribing tapes from our operation. The last thing I needed was more players, but someone else wanted to play. Sally told me, 'There's a bloke in our lounge room wanting to sell us speed, cocaine, smoko (cannabis) and guns. But what he really wants is a Beretta automatic 9mm pistol with a silencer.' I didn't really need this shit. So I said, 'Sally, I don't really need this shit.'

Sally said, 'Fine, I'll tell him to piss off then.'

'Hang on, where the fuck did he come from?'

Sally screamed from the kitchen phone across the hall to the lounge room, 'Hey, whatsyaname, Lenny wants to know where the fuck did you come from?'

I heard a male's voice scream out, 'Frankston, I'm from Frankston.'

Sally screamed out again, 'Not where you live, Fuck!'

A male voice screamed, 'I'm David.'

Sally said, 'Didja 'ear that?'

'Yes, thank you, Sally,' I said in a calm and totally pissed-off voice. 'Sally, please just talk to me now. Why is he at your house, why?'

Sally said, 'He just parked his Redi Hire truck in our driveway and knocked on our door.'

I said, 'Oh, he's one of those truck-driving door-to-door drug and gun dealers. Where I live I only get God botherers and Foxtel salesgirls.'

'Lenny, we're drug dealers, we deal in drugs.'

I said, 'Yes that's right.' I was losing it, my voice started to slowly rise to a scream. 'But we have to keep a fucking limit on it. We can't buy drugs off every fuckwit that comes along!'

Take a deep breath Lock, Lenny, who ever you are. Breathe in … breathe out. Relax.

Sally said, 'Lenny, you need a holiday. Let's all go to the Sunshine Coast.'

I calmly said, 'Could you please suss him out for me and ring me back when he's gone? Don't make any promises to him about anything for fuck sake.'

Sally said, 'You swear much more than you used to.'

I said, 'Could it be the company I keep?'

Sally snapped back with a laugh, 'Fuckin' oath.'

During the call I could hear Fran and the 'bloke' laughing in the background. We did not need any more targets. It was hard enough doing a proper job on the crooks we already had.

Later that evening I became Lenny again and drove to Fran's. I sat in the kitchen and they told me all about David.

Fran handed me a piece of paper with the following written on it:

David (full mobile phone number)
Speed, cocaine, choof or guns.

I could not believe it. Yes, he wrote that on a piece of paper. Truth is stranger than fiction. Next minute the phone rang. It was David. Fran said, 'Hey David, my bloke is here. Do you want to speak to him? Fine.'

I said, 'Hello, David.' We spoke. I invited him over for a chat.

Fifteen minutes later, he drove his Redi Hire truck into the driveway. He was about 25. He was what I would call a 'blow-wave wog' – Italian, young, smart-arse. He gave me his full name, David F. He had seen far too many movies. He spoke of large amounts of every drug and boasted close friendships with all the main mafia figures in Melbourne.

I said, 'So you sell guns but you want a gun from me?'

David replied, 'If you can get it, one of my relatives wants the same gun that Mel Gibson used to shoot at the helicopter, you know off the balcony in the *Lethal Weapon* movie. It's the 16-shot, 9mm Beretta automatic pistol. He needs it with a silencer. He works in the fruit and vegetable market business.'

I said, 'It holds sixteen in the mag and one in the breech. So it's seventeen shot. Mel fired two full clips at that helicopter but it still flew off. If your relative really hates helicopters, he should try something with less bullets and more punch, like a .357 magnum with fully jacketed rounds. You get much more penetration.'

David gave me a puzzled look and said, 'No, he doesn't want to shoot helicopters. Protection, he wants it for protection.'

I said, 'Aw, okay. A mate of mine has two with consecutive serial numbers. Perfect pair. He brought them in from America. He works in a gun shop. What looks cool is when he bought two shoulder holsters and wears them both under a jacket.'

David said, 'Wow, cool, that's cool. I can pay in speed, cocaine anything you want.'

'I'll get back to you,' I said. 'You can get me a sample of your best gowie.'

David reached into his pocket and removed a small clear bag of white powder.

He said, 'That's the speed, free sample. I can get as much as you want.'

I gave 'David the wanker' my mobile number. I had the speed sample tested and it was crap. It was about two per cent speed. Typical street-level crap. We decided to put David away for a rainy day. He had no prior convictions at all. Just a wife, three kids, house, huge mortgage, a poor attitude and bad taste in films.

During this operation the neverending amount of things to do kept getting bigger. The inspector in charge, in other words Steve's boss, wanted to know how our statements, were going. He was informed that we hadn't really started that stage of the operation. We had made mountains of notes and tapes and they could later be used to make our statements which would form the bulk of the evidence brief against all the bad guys.

That didn't work. I was eventually ordered to start obtaining statements from both Sally and Fran. Statements pertaining to all meetings, phone calls, tapes and so on. This also included me making my statements. Paperwork. What a nightmare. At first the girls would talk only to me. As I type with two fingers, very fast mind you, there was only so much I could do. We were given a couple of laptop computers and off we went.

At every available opportunity I would try and lasso the girls and force them into a motel room, lock the door and off we'd go. Sue, our analyst, was conned into typing with me. Fran in one room, Sally in the other.

Other lucky police were given the highly prized job (not) of taking Fran's children to the movies or to an amusement parlour. Those cops only ever did that job once. I never did it of course but from what I heard, that job was above and well beyond the call of duty. I had witnessed them in Sizzler.

Steve would often call in and say hello to the girls. They loved him. He would have a chat and then quickly leave. The girls would always give him the mandatory flash of their tattooed tits as he left. Sue was the classic innocent young 'girl next door'. Never in her wildest dreams would she ever swear. Needless to say she found the girls interesting, to put it mildly. It took Sue a few days just to understand what the girls were on about, let alone what they were actually saying.

The following conversations occurred while I was in the middle of a large family gathering. It was at the home of my 82-year-old grandparents. I had caught two huge crayfish while scuba diving in Bass Strait the day before. All was well. The family thought I was acting a bit strange. Then I answered a call on my mobile and quickly retreated into the beautifully kept backyard directly outside the window next to the dining table. My family could see and hear every word. The neighbours could hear too. I didn't realise that I speak about three times louder when I talk into my mobile and ten times louder when I'm annoyed. Not good.

On Sunday, July 25, 1993, at 1.55pm my mobile phone rang. I said, 'What!'

Voice, 'Hello.' The unmistakable voice of Kath.

I said, 'How's it goin'?'

Kath said, 'Not bad, love, not bad.'

I said, 'That's good.'

Kath said, 'Listen, I'm droppin' these off to Fran.'

I said, 'Yeah, how many?'

Kath said, 'There's five here, love.'

I said, 'Yeah?' I'm thinking, 'What is she on about? But of course I'll take whatever she wants to give me. It's bound to be illegal, so what the hell.'

Kath said, 'Yeah, it's $18.50. It you want them, if not I'll take them out for you, all right love?'

I said, 'Not a drama. If Fran reckons they're good, I'll take them.'

Kath said, 'No worries.'

I said, 'All right, when do you want me to pay?'

Kath said, 'I'll tell Fran to fix me up in the morning.'

I said, 'I'll fix you up for the washing machine.' That was the only code I could think of. To make out to Kath that I was being careful talking over the phone.

Kath said, 'Good one. Sweet.'

I said, 'See ya, I'll be there in the morning, I'll drop it over.'

Kath's voice changed – from nice, to deadly serious. 'No, no, love, I'm busy. You do it the way we've organised.'

I said, 'Okay, I'll give it to Fran.'

Kath said, 'Bye love.'

I said, 'Bye.'

Well I tried. Kath wasn't going to have a bar of me. She had put me right back in my place. She just stamped the words 'nobody' across my forehead. Kath was prepared to talk to me over the phone but that was it. I was incredibly offended. There I was, a detective senior constable in the drug squad being

Lenny Rogers the drug dealer and Kath didn't trust me because I wasn't a good enough criminal. She just didn't know me well enough.

I rang Fran straight away. 'What the fuck did I just buy? Five what?'

Fran whispered, 'She just left. She came stormin' in here with an esky. Wanting to know if you wanted to buy five ounces of choof.'

I said, 'How much do I owe her?'

Fran said, '$1850.'

I said, 'Where's my discount? Our $1000 that she owes us? She is a fair dinkum witch.'

Fran said with a giggle,' I think she's forgotten about it.'

I said, 'She's red hot. A bloody criminal. I'm going to go down in history as the only person to have ever trusted Kath.'

Fran said, 'Listen, for some reason while Kath was here, she reached into her knickers and pulled out a pistol. It was one of them pen pistols. It had gold plating on the top of it. She showed Sally and me. She even opened it up, unscrewed it and showed me the bullet inside. It was loaded.'

I said, 'No use having a pistol if it's not loaded.'

Fran said, 'She called it her little toy, but it ain't no fucking toy.'

Kath obviously wanted us to know she was a serious old granny who could do the business if required. I thought if Kath wanted to get serious, why didn't we? Lenny had been dicking around long enough.

I telephoned and updated my controller Steve, and two of my crew. That took another hour. I took a deep breath, got rid of all traits of Lenny that I could find and became Lachlan McCulloch. I tried to leave Lenny in the backyard. Then I opened the sliding glass door and took my seat at the dinner table again. Just a normal family gathering.

Silence. I looked around the table and saw that big fat pregnant pause written all over their faces. My wife's face was the worst. It had aged ten years·in the last few minutes and it had 'keep away from me, don't look at me, don't talk to me' written all over it. It was as if I had done something wrong. All I did was become Lenny, but Lachlan must have brought a bit of Lenny back into the house on his shoes.

I thought, 'What am I, who am I and what have I become? For Christ's sake, I'm just a normal person being a horrible person. The wrong bloke was just in the wrong world. They were my worlds.' I looked around the room. 'I really shouldn't let Lenny out, not here. This job is too important to fuck up. If I drink more, I won't think so much.

'What I do is way more important than this gathering anyway. Lenny, just smile, keep your cool. Assimilate. Assimilate. Breathe. Can I smoke more than one smoke at a time? More alcohol.' An hour or so later I was fine. Not. But at least everyone was talking to each other. I made a mental note to tell my father what I was doing. One day.

Stomping up and down in the back yard, swearing at the top of my voice into my mobile, talking about drugs and guns within the full view and hearing of my whole family. This became known as 'The Crayfish Incident'.

AT 7.15 that evening Fran rang me. 'Lenny, Kath just came to me door and demanded your full name and date of birth.'

I said, 'Good, that's good.' I had trained Fran and made sure she remembered my details.

Fran said, 'I told her and she said she was gunna check you out. She said, "When I find out, I'll tell ya all about him".'

I wondered who she was going to check with, to find out who Lenny was. I didn't have to wait long. Kath went home and rang a Sydney number. She left a message for someone named Steven to telephone her back. We don't know where she went then but she did not use her home phone. All I know is that later that night I received a phone call from my controller Steve. He informed me that Kath had given my details to Roger Rogerson in New South Wales.

My first reaction was, '**The** Roger Rogerson?'

'Yes.'

This was not good. Rogerson was the ex-detective sergeant from Sydney implicated in many serious crimes. But the one that had me concerned was he had been charged with hiring the hit man who shot an undercover policeman called Michael Drury.

This undercover cop was shot through his kitchen window while he ate chicken noodle soup with his wife and two kids. He was shot with a .45 automatic and only just survived.

This information was received via our organised crime squad. Rogerson was now working as some type of unofficial private investigator. As it happened, Rogerson somehow checked me out and told Fran that I had never been to jail. To Kath it just confirmed that I was a nobody.

We found out about the check by coincidence. One of the detectives assisting our crew was married to a detective at our organised crime squad. He had told his wife about Kath's enquiry and she had contacted my controller Steve. Small world. Sometimes too small.

This highlighted the need for total security in an already difficult job. All it really did was make sleeping that little bit harder. I made a mental note to give up chicken noodle soup.

The next morning I drove into Fran's driveway. I looked at the esky of cannabis that was waiting for me. I didn't take it because I wasn't going to pay for it just yet. I would put Fran in too much danger if I took it and held back on payment. Before

I left, I sat down with Fran and Sally. I explained that if Kath wanted to play games, let's play games. I told them that I was not going to give Fran the money just yet. Fran and Sally weren't impressed with my new plan.

'I've waited for nearly a month for Kath to fix us up with the $1000,' I said, trying to sell my new plan. 'Now she's got to be testing us. Why would I pay her full price $1850 when she owes me a thousand?'

Fran asked, 'Can you tell her that?'

'Tonight, if you haven't already seen Kath, can you go over there and tell her I'm not happy? Tell her she owes me, Lenny, the $1000.'

Sally said, 'Now it's getting interesting. Can I watch?'

Fran spat, 'Watch the gun shots.'

'Now get Kath to meet me. Talk her into it. We've dicked around long enough. She can sort it out with me. Tell Kath that when we have sorted this shit out, Lenny wants some smack.'

'Why now, why do you suddenly want heroin?'

'I need money, the ski season, I'm selling shitloads up the snow. Plus there's more jail time in heroin,' I said, trying to push the point. 'Tell her Lenny can't get enough from his supplier. Tell her straight out I can get heaps of cut, jumped-on crap. Some of the smack I've been buying has been cut so much you could put it on your fucking cornflakes. Tell her I'm only interested in rock, or nothing.'

Fran said, 'Why now?'

'Fran, I'm the boss, trust me. We're ready now. Time to do the business.'

Fran said, 'Oh, I get it. Is my house bugged as well? Can you hear me fart and stuff like that?'

I said, 'Fuck Fran, we've got enough to do without listening to you fart. Your house is not bugged.'

'Go on, say it: "Trust me, I'm an undercover cop",' Fran said sarcastically.

My sergeant and I had decided to stop fucking around with Kath. Obviously she wanted to keep in total control. She seemed to sell drugs when she felt like it, whether we'd ordered drugs or not. Kath was like one of my mates, Paul. When he'd ring me up, I was never sure whether he was really late returning my phone call, or if he was just ringing me up out of the blue to say hello.

If Kath wants to play and sell us heroin, she can. It's all up to her. I was relying on the saying, 'Money talks all languages'. Especially Kath's.

On Monday, July 26, 1993, I drove around to Fran's. When she answered her front door, I said, 'Fran, what the fuck is going on with Kath?'

Fran said, 'So you've got the money, I hope?'

'Yes, is she coming over?'

Fran said, 'Not while your car is parked in the driveway.'

I had forgotten. I was a nobody. If I was to meet Kath I'd have to not let her know I was there. I said, 'Fuck, I'll move the car.' I backed out of the driveway and parked in a back street. I quickly snuck back into Fran's. It was all a waste of time anyway. Kath didn't show.

Fran and I had a good chat and caught up with all the gossip. It always got back to Kath. I said, 'Fran, can you grab your bag and go and see her and say that Lenny is still owed a thousand fucking dollars. Why the fuck am I going to pay full fucking price when she owes me? Kath's logic just doesn't work.'

Fran said, 'Kath reckons it pays well.'

Fran appeared rather upset. I knew that when she said, 'I'm not happy. I'm not taking the handbag, I look too suss.'

I said, 'You fucking well smoke too much, you're paranoid.'

Sally said, 'Is there a tablet or some kind of drug you can take to get rid of being paranoid?'

I screamed, 'No, it's the drugs that make you paranoid.'

Sally looked at Fran and said, 'Looks like you're stuck with it, then.'

I said, 'All right Fran, wear mine.' I removed my recording device. After fucking around I had it all ready. I grabbed gaffer tape from my car then helped Fran wire herself for sound. Sally ran over to every window in the house and pulled down the blinds, yelling at me, 'Show the neighbours why don't you – stereophonic Fran.'

I said, 'Where do you want to tape the microphones?'

Fran said, 'You're the expert, you do it.'

Fran tucked the recording device in the front of her pants. I said, 'Just tape the two microphones in there.' I pointed to her cleavage. I added, 'You could fit a whole fucking surround sound system down there and no-one would see a thing.'

Fran removed her top revealing two huge breasts being supported by a highly stressed bra. She grabbed two pieces of gaffer tape off me and stuck the microphones between and slightly underneath her breasts. She put herself back together. I wished her good luck.

As I was leaving Fran said, 'If I die, at least I get to tape the fucking murder, you bastard.'

I said, 'If you die, just make sure Sally hears the shot and Kath doesn't hit the recorder. Seriously, I'd much prefer a murder brief against Kath than drug trafficking.' We all laughed, but not for long.

We all looked at each other. There was an awkward silence. In a feeble attempt at a show of support I touched Fran on the arm and started to leave.

All of a sudden the whole thing had become very unfunny. It

often seemed like a game of cat and mouse but these were real people.

Later, Fran made a statement that was presented in court and given in evidence. It went like this:

At ten minutes to ten on ... Monday, the 26th day of July, 1993 I was in my kitchen when I turned on a recording device which I was wearing. I then said, 'It is ten to ten on the 26th of July 1993 and I'm on my way to Kath Pettingill's house.'

I then heard a knock on the front door. I said, 'Hang on.' I then turned the recording device off again. I opened the front door and found it was the cat from next door. I then walked out the front door onto the street. At this time I was with my friend Sally.

As I was halfway across the street, I turned the recorder back on again. I said, 'Back again, it's me. It's now seven minutes to ten and I'm on my way up over to Kath's.'

Kath Pettingill lives at 30 Wedge Crescent, Rowville. As I walked up to the front door I saw Kath Pettingill looking at me through the frosted glass window next to her front door. Sally stopped and waited in the driveway next to Kath Pettingill's gold Ford. Kath said, 'Hello luv.'

I said, 'Hello. Are you spying on me?'

Kath said, 'It's fuckin' ten to ten. What are you doin'?'

I said, 'I thought you'd come down to my place.'

Kath said, 'I'm waitin' to hear from you.'

I said, 'Oh, me guy come over. He didn't have all the money with him so I didn't want to give him all the gear (cannabis in the esky) *you gave me coz you would have gone off the cruet at me.'*

Kath said, 'Ah, you did the right thing, luv. Well, has he got the money now or what?'

I said, 'No.'

Kath said, 'No!'

I said, 'I wouldn't let him take it.'

Kath said, 'Ay, listen luv, I want me gear back then. What's goin' on? He's supposed to take it, and pay for it.' I said, 'Well, I don't know.'

I was starting to get very scared of Kath Pettingill. She was getting very angry.

Kath said, 'I could have had it sold. See luv, this is the problem.'

I said, 'Well he said he was takin' it, but he fucked me around. I don't know. Fuck!'

Kath said, 'Well, you tell your bloke something from me, luv. I don't want to do business with him any more. I either want me gear or the money first thing in the morning.'

I said, 'See, he's dirty, when he's ... Um, well, without the thousand fuckin' dollars.'

Kath then leant down and picked something up behind the front door.

Kath said, 'Here y'are, take this, take this for the lousy $1000.'

Kath then gave me a clear plastic snap lock bag which was full of 'Mull', which is marijuana. This marijuana is what I call manicured heads and I knew it to be good quality. I took it and said, 'What is this?'

Kath said, 'It's just a bit of green, luv. Give him that.'

I said, 'A bit of green, eh. All right.'

Kath said, 'Tell him from me to fuckin' shut up.'

I said, 'Really.'

Kath said, 'About his $1000.'

I said, 'All right. Fuck, I thought you might've come down. He was sittin' there. He wanted to fuckin' meet ya.'

Kath said, 'What for, luv? I don't like getting involved with people I don't know. This is the thing, luv.'

I said, 'Yeah, I tried to tell him that. Fuck.'

Kath said, 'What's his name again?'

I said, 'Lenny.'

Kath said, 'That's right Lenny, Kenny Rogers.'

I said, 'I don't know, fuck. I didn't know what to say to him, he wanted to meet you to pay for the gear and all that shit. I'll just give him that. So now you just want your gear or the money in the morning.'

Kath said, 'Well, it's like this, luv. I could've had it sold, you see.'

I said, 'I know.'

Kath said, 'And I'm bein' fucked around by him. I don't even know the bloke.'

I said, 'You might know him, he was the little blond kid in the Bug Catcher ad years ago – remember the blond kid that snuck around the back yard with a Bug Catcher and said, 'Aaahhhhh, Gotcha!'

Kath said, 'All right, luv. I'll catcha in the morning.'

I said, 'I'll tell him. I'll tell him to stay there.'

Kath said, 'I'm tryin to fix this fuckin' curtain.'

I said, 'Oh, right.'

Kath said, 'I'll see you in the morning then, luv.'

I said, 'All right, I'll bring it over. If he doesn't bring the fuckin' money I'll give him this bag, and tell him to get fucked and he won't get the fuckin' Esky.'

Kath said, 'Well that's it luv, I'm gunna fix this and have a fuckin' smoke and head off to bed.'

I said, 'Yeah, I'm sick of this fuckin' bullshit. I'm gunna have a smoke meself. Sorry, eh. Fuck, you know. See ya.'

Kath said, 'See ya luv.'

At this time I was inside Kath's front door watching her trying to fix the curtain in the main bedroom over to the left of the front door.

I said, 'You can shut it, are you right to shut it?'
(I was referring to Kath's front door)
Kath said, 'Yeah luv, yeah.'
I said, 'See ya.'
Kath said, 'Bye luv.'
I left Kath's house. As I walked past her gold Ford, Sally joined me in the driveway. I said into the recording device: 'Ssshhhh (to Sally) ... It's ten past ten still on the 25th of July, 1993, and I'm turning this fuckin' thing off.' I then realised I made a mistake and turned it on again and said, 'Fuck, it is actually the 26th day of July, I'm with Sally and I'm finished'.

Statement taken and signature witnessed at 2.29pm on Tuesday July 27, 2003, at Melbourne.

Kath paid up for the $1000 only when she really had to. The other thing I noticed was that the bag of cannabis was right there at the front door, ready to give to Fran.

Sally did not walk up to Kath's front door. She stayed next to the gold Ford in the drive. Sally knew that she could not go any further. Strange unspoken rules apply to junkies. Sally obviously went along to help support Fran, knowing there could be trouble. But she could not go into Kath's personal space. Nothing was said, they both just knew. Kath could see Sally, standing alone in the driveway and said nothing. No 'hello', no 'come over here luv'. Junkies are just as dangerous to real crooks like Kath as they are to fake crooks like Lenny.

Fascinating stuff. Sometimes I felt like I was some sort of scientist studying bugs. Other times I felt like I was one of the bugs being studied. Reality always brought me back. I forced myself to always remember that this was their world and I was only visiting. There was never any fear that I would get too comfortable, want to stay or anything like that. My fear was that when it was all over and Lenny left, he would take some of their world with him. Lenny could be stuck with their warped unethical reasoning, their beliefs and language.

What I did want to rub off on me was Fran's strength, her incredible self-belief and confidence.

She was like the Alpha male without the male bits. She was totally happy with being Fran. Nothing put on. She didn't act tough. She just was.

What I never forgot during this job was that Fran was doing this for everyone – the community. She was introducing an undercover cop to Australia's worst crime family because she could, not for any reward. She hated Kath and all she stood for. She believed two of Kath's sons were involved in the execution-style murders of two young cops. She hated Kath for all the misery and death she had caused. I was beginning to see the real Fran. What was exciting was the fact that this job had just begun.

When Fran got home, she rang me and said, 'That is the last time I am ever going to do your dirty work. Kath was filthy at you, no more business with you, she said.'

I said, 'What? What have I done wrong? If she is organised crime, then we are all safe. She has to learn to give a bit more, all she wants to do is take! With her it's all one way – her way.'

Fran said, 'That's why she is queen of the criminals. Listen Lenny, she gave me a big bag of 'mull' to 'shut Lenny up!'

I said, 'What, a thousand bucks worth?'

'Yeah, maybe,' Fran replied.

I said, 'So what now?'

Fran said, 'Well, you still owe her for the dope in the esky, $1850. You better have it in the morning or I'm givin' the gear back. She was filthy on ya.'

'Okay, Fran, I'll bring it over in the morning, about six o'clock. I'll walk down and give it to her.'

Fran said, 'Are you faster than a speeding bullet?'

I said cautiously, 'What?'

Fran said in a serious tone, 'You don't get it, Lenny. She'll fucking shoot ya.'

I said, 'Okay, that was plan A. Plan B is I will give you the money in the morning and you can give it to Kath.'

Fran laughed, 'Good plan, Lenny.'

I added, 'See, I would deliver the money to her but I'm allergic to bullets, I break out in a rash.'

I then heard Fran scream out, 'Hey Sally, Lenny's allergic to bullets.' The girls were laughing away.

That last meeting with Kath was the first and the last time Fran was to wear a recording device in that operation. Now, I don't know much about bras, but I do know they are supposed to stop breasts from bouncing. Either her tits or her bra were broken, because on the tape, every single step or movement, created a *katcha katcha katcha* noise as Fran's breasts bounced and rubbed the microphones. Very funny but very annoying. It made for great courtroom humour when the tape was played in evidence. But that court case was light years away from the present.

The following morning I drove over and parked in Fran's driveway. Gave her the $1850. Fran grabbed her ever-ready handbag and off she went. I weighed the bag of mull Kath had given me – 50 grams exactly. There are 28 grams to an ounce, so we got about an ounce and three-quarters. Kath was selling an ounce of choof for $370 so we got about $700 worth, if that. Fran was back about a minute later. It had been a month since we had given Kath the $1000 in cash for an ounce of better quality speed. Serves me right.

Henceforth, from this date onward let it be known that Kathleen Pettingill should not be given credit during a drug deal. Here endeth the lesson. Trust me, I'm an undercover cop.

Killing time … the Richmond clock face riddled with bullets. Some claim local police were the culprits.

The scene of the crime … the car park at the back of the Russell Street building.

A parking officer claimed he was fired upon while issuing parking tickets to detectives' private cars.

Me when I was a fresh-faced detective ... before I went undercover as Lenny Rogers.

When I told a senior officer I would bust an amphetamine lab that weekend he said he would stand on a drug squad table in a pink tutu if I did …

... he lost the bet.

**Andy Dang near the Yarraville Railway Station
… a high-level heroin dealer.**

Every step took him closer to arrest, court and finally prison.

Football Head under surveillance just before one of the early heroin deals.

Football Head (above) was deflated after his arrest. Trust Me (right) … should not have worried about looking behind. The trouble was right in front.

NCA officer Peter Vujanic with Trust Me and his mullet.

Trophy photo … drug dealer Bill Chan smiles for the drug squad camera after he is snipped for heroin trafficking. I am clearly happy with the result.

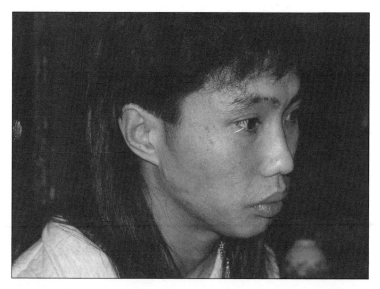

Trust Me Le. He has just been busted after selling me an ounce of heroin. He ordered the suckling pig – instead he got jail porridge.

Drug trafficking emergency gear … standard issue for major dealers. Make war not love.

Strictly cash. Almost $1million in undercover money. We carried it in a sports bag. It wouldn't fit in a wallet.

Me pointing to where we found heroin during a raid on a major Romanian dealer.

Me hitting the phones in the old drug squad … we worked in shit, investigating shit for a community that didn't give a shit.

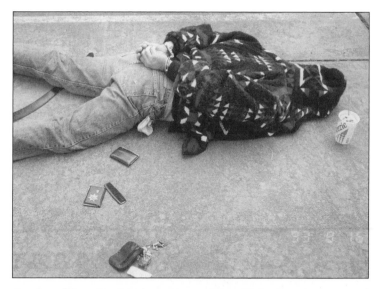

Stacker bites the dust courtesy of the SOG. He went horizontal but his slurpie stayed upright.

A different sort of stack … hidden compressed cannabis found during a drug raid.

I used this stubbie holder to hide money during a drug deal. I didn't see that it was a police footy club stubbie. Sometimes I frighten myself.

CHAPTER 4

Guns and money

You have no idea how
close you are to death,
mate. You'll be dead
before you hear the
gun shots.

IT was 4.18am on July 29, 1993. The street lights in Wedge
Crescent barely lit the footpath. Above the faint hum of distant
traffic was the crunch of footsteps on frozen grass. Then
silence.

Smash! Fran's kitchen windows exploded. Half a brick
caught the curtains inside, ripping them off the wall. Smash!
The lounge room window exploded.

When Fran and Sally woke, it was all over. They met in the
hallway. The children screamed. Fran grabbed the phone.

No good news comes from a 4.20am call. I crashed my way
from bed to dressing table, found the phone and screamed,
"What?"

Fran was hysterical. I reassured her, grabbed Lenny's clothes
and drove off. I called the police and said my girlfriend's
windows had just been smashed.

By the time I arrived, there was a cop car in Fran's driveway.

There was glass everywhere. Fran gave me a filthy look as she told the police it must be a drug-related domestic related to the previous tenants. Fran said the old tenants were drug dealers.

I frowned hard at her. Why would she be talking about drug dealers? Fran tilted her head several times toward her front door. I took the hint and had a look at the door. In bright red spray paint were the words 'DRUG DEALING SLUTS'.

The cops left and we started to clean up. Then we had our own drug-related domestic. A real one. Fran was in the kitchen sweeping up glass and swearing. Sally echoed each sentence with, 'She's right you know, Lenny' or 'We're only doin' this for you, Lenny'. The girls weren't happy.

I said, 'Girls, you're not blaming me, are you?' They said sarcastically, 'Oh no, no way.'

To change the topic I joked, 'I think "Drug Dealing Sluts" is a bit rough – you're not real drug dealers.' No reaction. So I added, ' "Drug-dealing receptionists" would be more accurate.' They did not see the funny side. There probably wasn't one.

I waited until 8am before ringing the drug squad and speaking to Steve. He authorised payment for new windows, security lights and deadlocks. I organised for the windows to be fixed.

By lunchtime it was almost fixed. Now I had to fix the girls. Steve organised some money for me to take them and the children out for a lunch at Sizzler in Knoxfield.

The children weren't what I would call highly disciplined. It had been a big day. I decided to have a few beers, so I threw Sally the car keys.

Over lunch I asked Fran for the tenth time, 'Who do you reckon smashed the windows?' Fran declared, 'Lenny, I don't care any more. I'm movin' out. We're going back to Frankston.'

She was serious. We'd made contact with Kath. We had to leave the area soon anyway. Wendy Peirce was about to come home.

When we finished terrorising the restaurant we left, to the relief of everyone else there. Sally seemed to have difficulty sitting in the driver's seat. Fran side-stepped into the back seat rather awkwardly. Then I saw why. They laughed and they produced bowls, plates, all types of cutlery, salt and pepper shakers, two vases ... and a big framed water colour.

It was my turn to go right off and for them to laugh at me. I said, 'For fuck's sake, we're not thieves.' I went on about how stupid it was. It was too late to take the stuff back now. I started to collect everything.

When we got back to Fran's I packed all the stolen gear in a cardboard box. I could not believe they could steal so much under my nose. I taped the picture to the top of the box. I labelled, dated and signed it. In big letters I wrote 'To be returned to Sizzler, Knoxfield.'

This action would cover me just in case someone saw them do it.

The girls didn't understand that I could not be involved in any theft. We were indemnified under Section 51 of the Drugs Act 1981 to traffic and possess drugs, but not theft.

But Sally and Fran saw Lenny as a crook and expected him to behave like one. I had to become more like them, not less. For Lenny to be successful, he had to blend in.

I HADN'T told Fran, but I knew Wendy Peirce, and she knew me. About two years before, when I was a detective at Carlton, I answered a call to assist an off-duty policeman detaining a man for shoplifting. I was working special duties in scruffies (plain clothes) looking for burglars.

It was at a 7-Eleven Store in North Melbourne. About ten Asian males were holding someone down on the footpath. I flashed my badge and cleared them away. What was left, lying on his back was a very frightened Victor George Peirce. I grabbed my revolver and told him to lie face down.

I had never met him before, but I knew him because he had only just got out after being acquitted of the execution murders of Constables Steve Tynan and Damian Eyre in Walsh Street, South Yarra. His face and that of his brother, Trevor Pettingill, were burnt in to every police officer's mind.

As I cuffed him, I told him he was under arrest. I wasn't sure what he'd done, but I was sure he was guilty. I searched him and found the problem – a little jar of Nestle coffee worth $1.66. What a loser.

The sight of a little girl crying, trying to hug her daddy was pathetic. It was young Katie. She was only five. Katie was of course named after her grandmother, Kath. What a thing to saddle a little kid with.

Katie was crying and wanting us to leave her daddy alone. What she didn't understand was that we were never going to leave her daddy alone. Her daddy had forfeited his right to be left alone when he and his crew executed two young police at Walsh Street, South Yarra.

As we picked Victor up, he kept saying, 'Stay next to me, Katie, stay next to me.' He wanted Katie for protection. He thought if she stayed close, there would be less chance of us shooting him.

Victor spoke to me with a 'Please' and a 'Thank you, officer' at every opportunity. He did not like being under arrest and was petrified. Word of his arrest got out. I found myself protecting him from other police who were calling in to say hello.

I interviewed him with Constables Martin Hardy and Narelle Fraser. Victor said, 'With respect, I would like to answer "No comment" to all the questions.' I was happy with that. But he still managed to incriminate himself.

I found it hard to be in the same room with him. He wasn't criminally insane, just criminally stupid. After the interview there was a commotion outside. It was Wendy. Victor and she deserved each other.

Wendy was convinced we were about to shoot Victor or had already shot him. She used language that would make even Kath blush. She made poor young Katie cry even harder, the way she carried on.

Wendy supposedly fell out with the Pettingill clan when she decided to give evidence against Victor, father of her children. Just after Victor was arrested with his brother Trevor Pettingill over the Walsh Street murders, Wendy turned crown witness. She made statements and video interviews about how Victor had admitted being one of the shooters. He had told her he had plotted and planned the murders, had helped park the stolen car used as bait, left the doors open, then jumped up and shot the cops in the back.

Wendy had been put in witness protection. While there, she had fallen in love or lust with one of the policemen protecting her, and had even got his nickname tattooed on her arm.

After almost twelve months of protection Wendy flipped again.

This time against the police. She came back and made up with Victor.

'For the sake of the kids,' she said. At the double murder trial she denied her previous statements and was partly responsible for the prosecution failing. It all seemed very convenient, as a lot of the prosecution case had been built around her evidence.

Anyway, I left the interview room from Victor, only to be confronted by Wendy. She was loud, bombastic and rude, crude and aggressive. We kicked her out.

We then bailed Victor out and set him loose to find Wendy. They deserved each other, but young Katie deserved better.

MEANWHILE, I was busy running the girls, trying to stop them committing crime, transcribing tapes, organising surveillance, doing drug pick-ups and was in and out of undercover operations, pretending to live at Fran's, keeping exact and endless notes of everything said and done, keeping a log of all written and taped notes.

My crew was on 24-hour rotation manning listening devices, telephone intercepts, transcribing relevant tapes regarding all evidence, updating evidence logs, briefing papers, typing affidavits for search warrants, mission statements, information reports, surveillance applications, money applications, target profiles and folders, phone checks, address and name checks. Once or twice a week we all got locked in motel rooms to make statements.

While all that was going on, we often had to drop everything and help out other crews with arrests, buy busts, house searches, surveillance. Occasionally, I had time to go home and see my wife.

On August 5, 1993, at 4.05pm, Kath Pettingill knocked on Fran's door. Fran lit up a smoke from her handbag as she opened the door. Kath had come over for a cuppa and a bong, as you do. Fran made the tea; Kath loaded the bong.

Fran said, 'My sugar-daddy bloke (meaning Lenny) has heaps of money, but has been getting shit quality gear and he really wants much better gear.'

Kath said, 'Yeah, what do youse want?'

Fran said, 'Speed.' At the same time Sally said, 'Smack.'

Kath said, 'Well, which one is it?'

Fran said, 'Both, he wants both.' (Fran had meant to say 'Smack'.)

Kath said, 'You get onto your bloke and I'll organise it.'

Fran tried to ring me. For some reason my mobile phone wasn't working. While Kath was in the lounge room, Fran was on the phone in the kitchen. She finally rang the drug squad and asked for Lenny. Luckily, the receptionist knew I was Lenny and put the call through. Fran didn't want to ask for Detective Senior Constable McCulloch while Kath was there.

I HATED answering my work phone. If I did, I would put on a fake voice. I was starting to become paranoid. I picked up my desk phone and growled, 'Drug squad, can I help you?'

Fran whispered, 'I need to speak to Lenny.'

I said, 'It is Lenny. What's the matter?'

Fran said, 'I've got someone here that wants to talk to ya.'

I knew it had to be Kath and I'm on my desk phone in the drug squad office. I covered up the mouthpiece and screamed out, 'For fuck sake, I've got a U/C (undercover) phone call – not a sound, please!' Everyone froze.

Next second Kath said, 'G'day luv.' Like we were old friends.

I said, 'How's it goin'?'

No names. Kath's house and phone had been bugged for years and she was not dropping her guard now.

Kath said, 'What do you want, a slow car or a fast car?'

I said, 'Slow, very fucking slow, as slow as you can get.'

Kath said, 'Sweet, here's Fran.'

Fran took the phone. In the background I heard Kath say, 'I'm going to head off now and make a few calls. Speak to ya later.'

I covered the phone and said, 'That was Mary. Mary's getting us some heroin. She's going home now to make some calls. She calls heroin a "slow car".'

I said into the handpiece, 'Fran, are you there?'

She said, 'Yeah, you happy now?'

I said, 'Fran you're a legend. Has Mary gone?'

Fran said, 'Yeah, to make a few calls.'

I said, 'Fran, you do know that all these months of pain has come to this. This is what we wanted. Heroin has serious jail time attached to it.'

Fran said, 'Look, Kath is putting us onto some bloke called Stacker. Sally knows him.'

Then Fran went on about how Kath might have bugged her home. Fran was paranoid again. My paranoia was safety induced. Fran's was drug induced. Anyone that uses lots of cannabis or speed becomes paranoid just after use. They think everyone is following them, listening to them, or both.

A computer check revealed 'Stacker' was Stephen James Clive MacKinnon, born 01/04/1960 and first convicted for burglary at 12. He'd had more than 40 court appearances for 132 offences, including thefts, burglaries, car stealing, serious assaults, trafficking and possessing drugs of dependence, carrying weapons and assaulting police.

Like the Pettingills, he was an old Richmond boy and had a deep hatred of police.

Why the name Stacker? We did some research. I wished we hadn't. Baldrick found out he got his nickname because he kills people and 'stacks' up their bodies. I had been hoping he used to stack his bike or something.

The boss walked past. Baldrick covered Stacker's target profile. If one of the bosses found out about Stacker's past, Lenny might not be authorised to meet him. No boss wants to lose an undercover cop in the line of fire. Bad for the resume.

ON August 5, 1993, at 5.56pm, Kath Pettingill called her criminal associate Donato Corsi, a 35-year-old drug trafficker. Donato was an associate of Kath's son Trevor Pettingill and of Stacker.

The phone conversation later formed part of the evidence against Kath. It was a long conversation but they ummed and aahed and tried to talk in some sort of half-arsed code about slow cars and fast cars.

'Slow' meant heroin and 'fast' meant speed. The transcripts drag on so I won't bore you with it all.

On and on it went. They were cautious talking on the phone, but this was a great call because it showed us Kath was keen to help buy heroin. My problem still was that Kath wanted Sally to do the drug deal.

I couldn't understand why on one hand Kath hated junkies, yet when it came to doing the actual deal she only trusted Sally the junkie.

Somehow, Kath believes the more criminal you are, the more you can be trusted. Weird. These are the things I had to work out to infiltrate this criminal family. I had to learn by experience. That could get dangerous.

On August 6, 1993, I pulled up in Fran's driveway about 4am. I made a coffee and read magazines for a while. Fran and Sally eventually dragged themselves out of bed. We all had a coffee in the kitchen.

Fran said, 'At about 6.30 last night Kath rang. She asked me to send Sally down to her place.'

Sally said, 'Yeah, Lenny. She met me out the front. She said she was in a hurry coz she's going out to bingo with the girls. Then she asked me what time could I meet Stacker. I told her some time in the afternoon would be good.'

I said, 'Do you know this bloke Stacker?'

Sally said, 'Yeah, I met him when Kath, Stacker and me were at the Office of Correction in Carlton, in 1987. We were on the same pre-release prison program together.'

I said, 'What's Stacker like?'

Sally said, 'He's big and unpredictable. Lenny, he's fucking mad. But we get on well together. I asked Kath if I could bring Lenny along and she said she won't deal with people she don't know. If there are any men involved she won't do business. I've told Stacker that it would be just you.'

I said, 'Well, it's my money, so we'll just have to wait and see what happens.'

I opened the curtains. We had a clear view of Wedge

Crescent. My car was in the driveway. I said out loud, 'I think Kath can smell my cash.'

I said, 'Fran, how's the tape going in your bag?'

Fran called out, 'It's fine, I should have a couple of hours left.'

I said, 'Can you check?'

Fran said, 'You've never asked to go through my handbag before?'

I emptied her bag and opened the recorder concealed in the bottom. The tape had finished. She must have left it on. I opened the bum bag I keep around my waist. No spare tape – and Kath was coming any minute.

I rang Steve at the squad. He organised the fastest courier service in town – a marked police car. I jumped in my stock standard Holden Berlina and sped toward Brandon Park Shopping Centre. I asked for the cop car to park outside Safeway and leave the tape on top of the rear driver's side tyre. I got there first and waited. They placed the tape and walked off. I grabbed it and hammered back to Fran's like a typical hoon would. I changed the tape and we were set for Kath.

I decided to have a shower. Sally called out, 'Hey Lenny, do you want me to wash your dirty bits?'

I called out, 'No, it's all right. I'll get Lachlan to do it.' Sally walked off up the hallway singing, 'Lenny's a poofter, Lenny's a poofter.'

When I finished, I sat back in the lounge. I called out, 'Here she comes, Fran.' Fran went into the hall, reached for a smoke and opened the door. Her magic handbag recorded the conversation.

Kath walked in. Fear took my breath away. My mouth dried up. I slowly got to my feet and tried to say something. I nodded. It didn't matter. She ignored me.

Fran said, 'Kath, this is Lenny.' Kath hesitated and said, 'G'day.' I said, 'G'day.' I was petrified. She looked away and continued her conversation. She didn't need to meet me. Maybe it was just as well she wasn't too interested – the last time I had seen her I was in full uniform, just out of the police academy. It was June 1984. I had opened the front door of the Richmond Police Station and she had abused me for not knowing who she was. At the time Kath was reporting twice a day for possession of a machinegun and trafficking heroin. Things hadn't changed much in ten years, except I hadn't yet seen her machinegun.

Kath was full on. She demanded attention. She was not the grey-haired old lady you see on the news, defending her sons against persecuting police. That was the person she wants everyone to see.

This was her in her true element. She was a criminal queen and knew her power. She scared the crap out of me.

I sat down again. We all lit smokes. Kath stood in the middle of the room and started raving about her son Victor. She was putting on a show, making sure I knew who she was. She walked straight past me to a bookshelf and grabbed books. She said, 'Fran, Victor wants crime books. He loves true crime books. That's all he reads.'

Fran said, 'Big Victor or young Victor?' Kath was looking after her grandchildren, Victor Junior, Chris and Katie.

Kath said, 'My big Victor in jail. He loves crime books.'

Fran said, 'What, like Chopper Read?'

Kath said, 'Fuck him.'

We all had a laugh. What Kath didn't know was that her Victor would end up dead and at the time of writing Chopper was very much alive, but anyway.

Kath said, 'Well youse can all watch me on TV again soon. I've just spent the whole day Tuesday down at Channel 2. I'm goin' back again.'

Fran grabbed Kath's right hand and started to look at some of Kath's rings. One had a huge diamond.

Fran talking about the ring, 'Did you make that, have it made?'

Kath said, 'No, Dennis did.'

Fran said, 'That's grouse.'

Kath then said: 'Look at this.' It was a big gold medallion on a gold chain around her neck. She held it out and said, 'I got this from Dennis when he was in hospital. I've got a lot of other stuff hidden away.'

Fran said, 'What's this about TV?'

Kath said, 'They're gunna do a film about a family like mine. On Channel 2, Fran. I'm the researcher. They've gotta find a person that can play me.'

Again we all had a laugh.

I said, 'Is there money in it?'

Kath said, '$40 an hour as a researcher.' Fantastic, I thought. The ABC, alias Australian taxpayers, was paying family of cop killers top dollar to 'help' make a television series about them.

The conversation got back to Stacker and Donato.

Kath said, 'Yeah, well he bumped into my son Peter in jail, and my son Peter flogged him. He's been belted twice in jail over my kids.'

I said, 'Who's this?'

I was losing track of who was who. Kath said, 'Oh, just a bloke.' To her I still did not officially exist. Sally was nice and said, 'Stacker.'

Kath then said, 'Stacker shit.' She looked at me and added, 'He was going with this girl, Laurie, and I nicknamed her Laurie load of shit.'

Kath changed the subject to Wendy and Victor's house, where she was living to look after the kids. 'Look, she hasn't got a light fitting in the fuckin' house. She's got nothing.'

Fran said, 'Really?'

Sally said, 'Nothin'.'

Kath said, 'All the old carpet, the rugs and that, are what I gave her years ago. They've fuckin' had it. I can't be bothered pinching fuckin' rugs and that.' She laughed.

Sally kindly offered, 'Oh, we'll go with ya.' Fran laughed.

Kath said, 'No, I go one out.'

Sally said, 'I can see ya walking down the road with a rug.'

Kath snapped back, 'I done it at Dimmeys.'

Fran said, 'In Richmond?'

Kath said, 'Yeah, years ago.'

Trying to join in I said, 'Yeah.' Kath ignored me. I thought, can't we talk about crime a little bit more substantial? This was a glimpse into the life and crimes of Kath Pettingill – but only shoplifting, so far.

Kath said about pinching the rug, 'Yeah, fucking oath I did. This fat tart was with me. She said, "Ya pay for it over there." I said "Yeah" and called out "I'll see ya at the car." I just walked out.' Kath was proud at not being caught shoplifting for years.

Kath picked up her smokes and went to leave. I gave Fran a sort of look that said to ask about the drug deal. Fran said, 'Righto Kath, what's going on?'

Kath said, 'I better go.'

Sally said, 'What's happening with Stacker?'

Fran said, 'What is it with this guy? I'm going to have to get the money from Lenny.'

Kath said, 'Who's Lenny?'

I said, 'I'm Lenny.'

Fran said, 'My darling here, my money bags.'

Just when I thought I was 'in' Kath made sure I knew I did not exist. I had nothing to lose but my life and reputation. so I said, 'So is he cool; is he cool to deal with, is he?'

Kath turned, gave me a filthy look and said, 'Fancy you asking me that?' She was not happy with Lenny the upstart.

I said, 'No, well I don't know the bloke.'

Kath said, 'Well I'm doing it through Sally. Sally knows him.'

I said, 'Sweet.'

Fran said, 'So he'll come here?'

Kath said, 'I don't know what's going to happen till he rings.'

Fran said, 'We'll wait, shit happens.'

Then Kath looked at Sally and said, 'But I just said, "I won't be doin' this." It will be you and Stacker, no-one else. Just you and him.'

Kath was making sure Fran and I would not be involved in the deal.

Kath added, 'He won't deal with anyone else.'

Fran said to me, 'Well, you will just have to give the money to me.'

Kath said, 'Sally.'

I said, 'That's fine.' It wasn't. I just thought I better say that.

Kath was laying down the ground rules.

Kath said, 'I don't know what area you're going to have to go to, or anything like that. It will be coming from the slopes around Footscray.'

As Footscray is an inner suburb and snow-capped mountains are few and far between, I took Kath's reference to 'slopes' to mean Asian dealers.

Fran pointed to one of Kath's diamond rings and said, 'I want that one.'

Kath said, 'Actually, I got that one off Stacker, I dudded him. I give him a spot for that.' Kath turned and held up her hand for me to see the ring. The diamond was huge. Kath added, 'It's not for sale.'

Fran had a look at another ring on Kath's other hand.

Fran said, 'A bit of sucking for that one?'

Kath said, 'Oh well, that's nothing.'

We all laughed. Fran meant sucking up to someone. Kath was on a different wavelength. In her younger days shoplifting wasn't her only way to get a quick 'earn'. She was a well-known sword swallower.

Kath said, 'I better go and get this phone call.'

I said, 'I don't like talking on the phone.'

Kath said, 'No, that's it luv, we don't.'

Fran said, 'I'll get you that rug. I'll bring it over in the morning before I go.'

Kath said, 'OK. See you all later,' and walked off out the front door.

We waited until she got over the road. Fran said, 'She's full on, eh?'

I said, 'What a classic. She scared the hell out of me. I got used to her after a while.'

Sally said, 'I've seen some of the toughest crims turn to jelly when they go near her. Lenny, it's what she's capable of that scares 'em.'

Fran said, 'You can wake up dead if you cross her.'

I telephoned Steve at the squad. Gave him the full update. 'Steve, she's bloody scary for a little old woman,' I said.

As usual, Steve said, 'You'll be right, buddy.'

I said, 'Fran, what's the go with this rug?'

Fran said, 'Mind your business.'

I said, 'Seriously, what's going on?'

Fran said, 'Kath wants me new rug. She wants to take it back to her house in Venus Bay. I paid $704 for it.'

I said I'd pay her for the rug in cash, so we could give it to Kath in the morning if the drug deal went ahead. I said, 'Where is it?'

Fran fetched the brand new rug. It was still rolled up. I said, 'You paid for it?' Fran and Sally laughed.

Fran said, 'Lenny, Kath reckons we stole it; Sally and I say we paid for it. Who are you going to believe?'

I snapped back, 'Kath, definitely Kath.'

Fran said, 'Fuck off.'

I said, 'The receipt, where's the receipt?'

Fran laughed and said, 'I lost it.'

I should have been a fireman.

KATH was busy organising our heroin. That evening at 6.12pm, Donato Corsi telephoned her. Little Katie Peirce answered the phone, then got her grandma. The conversation was pretty jerky, but they knew what they were talking about.

Donato: I've got that organised for you.

Kath: Yeah, all right. I think they've gone out shopping at the moment.

Donato: Yeah.

Kath: Don't say anything over the phone.

She said we had $12,000, and told him to deal only with Sally. She immediately rang Fran's house. One of the kids answered and Kath wouldn't say who she was. Then Fran got Sally for her and Sally said it was all organised to do the deal with Stacker next day. Kath reminded her to bring the carpet as payment for setting up the deal.

I spoke to Fran and found out tomorrow was to be a big day. I was to get to Fran's home nice and early to take the rug over to Kath. Then I was going to help Fran shift back into Frankston. Kath was also busy packing ready for her move back to Venus Bay. The street only had two days until the lovely Wendy Peirce came home.

Kath Pettingill hated the way Wendy had been spouting off how she was going to fix people up, bash them and so on. Wendy apparently wanted to bash a few people in her street because she thought they had assisted the police and had helped Victor go to jail.

Kath was also concerned about Wendy going back on the drugs. Apparently she had a problem with valium. Kath told Donato's wife Nella that Wendy would get on the valium and not feed the kids properly. Kath accused Wendy of giving her children toast for dinner sometimes. It just goes to show, everyone has a mother-in-law.

That night I didn't sleep much. About 4 am, I thought of how I was going to mark the rug before giving it to Kath. The next thing I was worried about was how I was going to prove to a court that Kath was organising us heroin and not a real 'slow car'.

Up until now she could quite easily beat any trafficking charge by saying she was only organising Sally, Fran and Lenny a cheap automobile. I knew I had to do something. I just didn't know what.

I couldn't say, 'Excuse me, Kath, but when you say "slow car" do you really mean heroin?' I didn't want to fall at the last hurdle.

About 6.30am I got up, had a shower and started to become Lenny. I was set to leave home when my wife called, 'What are you doing?' I peeped into the bedroom and said, 'Sorry, I didn't mean to wake you. I'm just going off to work.'

She said, 'It's Saturday. Haven't you got something planned?'

I said, 'Yeah, I have to pay a crook for organising me some heroin.'

She said, 'Do it tomorrow.'

I said, 'I can't, I'll ring you later.' I gave her a kiss on the head and left.

She was obviously not happy but what could I do? As I drove off, I was thinking of Kath, tape recordings, Fran, Sally and the whole job. Then when I was almost at Fran's, I thought I better start my recorded notes. I started my tape and said, 'My name is Lachlan McCulloch. I am a Detective Senior Constable stationed at the Crime Department drug squad. Today the, um, August 7, um, um. Shit!' I stopped the tape. The seventh day of August is my wife's birthday. I rang home. No answer. Shit.

When I got to Fran's, I called again.

'What do you want?' my wife said. 'I'm sorry, I forgot. Happy Birthday, darling.'

'Is it?' she said. I was in big, huge trouble. A thousand promises later I got back to work.

I sat down with Fran and Sally, unrolled the rug and photographed it. On the underside I wrote YNIT. Fran said, 'What is that?'

'It's the name of your dog Tiny backwards. I have to mark the rug so I can prove we gave it to her.'

The phone rang. It was Kath, demanding the bloody rug. She didn't trust us.

I made her wait. The tape recorder was activated and B2 and I walked down to her house, carrying the rug. The conversation was tape-recorded and later admitted in evidence.

Kath took the rug from me and leaned it against the wall. We followed her to the kitchen. As I walked into the kitchen, I saw danger. I was so tied up with meeting Kath that I had forgotten all about young Katie Peirce. Katie was now about seven years old. She was sitting in a chair to my left. It had been two years since I'd arrested her father Victor in her presence. But I knew what kids' memories were like. It's like they have a new disk in their head – they can remember everything.

'Hi Katie, I'm Lenny,' I said. I kept my face turned away as much as I could. How could I have forgotten about Katie? I told myself to forget Katie and get back to my job. I tried to make small talk with Kath.

She started to walk towards the front door. Now and then she would put her right hand down into her crotch and fiddle around. Just like I have to do sometimes when my jeans are a bit tight. But Kath was adjusting something a lot colder, thinner and harder than I did. In fact, she was adjusting her pen pistol.

I was running out of time to get her to say something incriminating. I said, 'I've got to pay Fran 700 bucks for that,' and pointed at the rug I had just given her.

Kath said 'Bullshit!'

Fran said, 'He's already paid me.'

Kath: She pinched it.

Fran: I did not.

Kath: Didn't ya?

Fran: No, I paid for it. I bought that.

I cut in. 'That's why I was going to give it to you afterwards.'

Kath said, 'No, I can't because I got to go out too, to the jail to see my big Victor.'

Kath said either she got the rug or got 'a whack' out of the money from the deal.

I said, 'I thought I was going to give you what, fifty or a hundred bucks every time I got an ounce off him or something.'

'That all works out the same way,' Kath said.

I was on a roll. We were all talking comfortably. Do it now, I said to myself.

'Does he – he's talking about slow-moving cars?' I asked.

'Yeah,' she said.

'Smack?"

'Exactly … mmm.' Kath nodded her head.

I thought, 'Yes, she is gone.' I had slipped the word 'smack' in and she'd answered before she realised what she was saying. Everyone knew smack was heroin.

'Sweet, I just wanted to make sure,' I said.

Kath: 'But I said to him, you're only to deal through Sally.'

Fran: 'Well, Stacker wants to meet me.'

Kath: 'Yeah, all right, but it's a bit dodgy with a bloke.'

McCulloch: 'But, I just, it's my money, I want to be there when we … '

Kath cut me off. 'No, no, it's not like that.'

I said, 'No?'

Kath looked straight at me and said 'Can't trust you, gotta be patted down and …'

Fran started to laugh as if this was a joke. Kath's face changed. In an instant she was very upset. She screamed, 'Hey! That's my rules.'

I laughed. Just a nervous reaction. Kath made it clear that we were not allowed to laugh during a drug deal. This was her life we were laughing about.

'My fuckin' oath it's my rules!' she screamed. She was a lot of things, but in her world she was not stupid. She knew something was wrong.

She started patting down my chest. She opened the front of my T-shirt. I stopped laughing. She rubbed her hands under my shirt all over the front of my chest. She searched right down to the top of my jeans.

Fran came to the rescue. She grabbed my groin with her left hand and said, 'You can't have that.'

Kath said, 'I don't mean it like that. You've gotta take your clothes off, or you get nothing.'

I started to pat myself down hoping that might help. Kath knocked my hands away as if to say, 'Stop being stupid, I'll do that.' I did not want to take my pants off.

Looking back, there were a lot of funny things I could have said or done. But at the time it was too frightening. Not so much physically, but the whole job depended on what happened at that moment.

I had pushed it to the limit and was paying for it. Trying to sound calm I said, 'Okay, pat me down, yeah.'

Kath finally stopped rubbing her hands all over me. She seemed satisfied I wasn't wearing a 'wire'.

Kath again fiddled around with her crotch. I was too much of a gentleman to comment on what was obviously some sort of intimate dilemma. I wondered, is the pen pistol facing forward or backward, up or down? Would Kath even know?

I wanted to say, 'Trust me,' but she'd probably heard that one.

I just wanted to get the hell out of there.

As quickly as Kath became angry, she became almost nice again.

'Ya just worried about it's going to be cut and stamped on?' she asked, meaning was I worried about being sold diluted heroin.

I agreed. She said, 'Well, it won't be.'

I mentioned all the cash I would have, as if I was nervous about being ripped off.

Fran piped up, 'He (Stacker) won't do a bolt, the Harold Holt?'

Kath said, 'Nah, he'll just have to pat you down.'

Just as things had calmed down, Fran fired Kath up again, trying to make a joke.

'I can guarantee there is nothing on him, ha,ha,ha.'

In her most serious voice Kath said, 'Yeah? But you can't, you can't. Nobody's guaranteed.'

I agreed. I just wanted to leave. Kath pointed her finger at me and said, 'Dennis (her late son) never trusted me 100 per cent, and I never trusted him 100 per cent, and he's my son!'

'Yeah, I know,' I said soothingly.

We talked about the rug. I said I owed Fran $700 for it and Kath fell in to the little trap. 'Yeah, but you pay her off a hundred a thingo,' she said. 'That's seven deals.'

Fran and I left. As we walked to Fran's I said for the tape, 'That was a meeting between Kathleen Pettingill, B2 and Detective Senior Constable Lachlan McCulloch, alias Lenny. The time is now 9.32am on Saturday, August 7, 1993. I'm now turning this tape recorder off.'

I gave Fran a hug. We laughed and relived the highlights. I said to her, 'I'm going to have to go, it's my wife's birthday and I forgot. I have to buy a present.'

Fran said, 'You're kidding. You didn't.'

I thanked Fran again. I said, 'I'm completely stuffed. You did really well in there, mate.' She laughed. She had taken the whole meeting in her stride. Fran said, 'Don't ever do that to me again though, Lenny.'

I said, 'What, which part?'

Fran said, 'When you said "smack" Kath's face changed and she stripsearched you.'

I said, 'Fran, we weren't there for fun. I had to clarify that the slow car was heroin.'

Fran said, 'She didn't like that. Clarify when I'm not there next time, would ya.'

I had to go. On the way home I bought an $800 dress for my wife. She hated it. I said, 'I gave Kath Pettingill a $700 rug today, and do you know what? She said "thanks".'

NEXT day (August 8, 1993) at 5.40pm Fran and Sally drove out to Stacker's flat in Reservoir. Fran got a cigarette from her handbag and turned on the tape recorder.

Stacker said he would try to get a sample of rock heroin, which would cost eleven grand an ounce. Then he said, 'Look, tell your bloke that it's $12,000 an ounce and make a grand on the deal.' He said the deal would go down in Collingwood or Yarraville next day.

The girls rang me when they got back. Stacker seemed fine to deal with, Fran said.

Next night I drove Fran out to see him. I waited while she went in and paid him $50 for a small sample. We later analysed the sample and found it to be 12 per cent pure. Better than normal street quality, so I was happy.

Three days later, Kath telephoned her son Trevor Pettingill and spoke to Stacker, who was there. The conversation was recorded and later used in evidence.

Stacker said he was waiting on his contact (to get the heroin) and Kath demanded a spotter's fee for referring Fran and Lenny. But she also warned Stacker to stripsearch both of them.

Kath's voice became loud and serious. 'I said, "If you're wearin' a wire or anythin' I said fucking bad luck. If you don't take your fucking clothes off you get nothin".'

Stacker agreed. Kath went on to say he should 'work' only with Sally because she had 'been in jail' and so could be trusted.

This call proved we were not dealing with the Salvation Army. So much for not speaking on the phone. There were no code problems with that call because they didn't use one. Kath and Donato Corsi had huge code problems. Organised crime – but not very.

At 9.15am on August 12, 1993, Stacker rang Fran's home. Stacker said he had it all organised. He apologised for not being able to organise the heroin the previous day. He wanted us to meet him near Trevor Pettingill's flat in Collingwood. Stacker finally agreed to do the deal on the corner of Johnston and Hoddle streets at 1pm. This was about 500 metres east of Trevor's home.

I DROVE to Frankston to pick up the girls. I found Fran putting on her lipstick. Her dress showed off her massive cleavage. Sally appeared in a see-through, black lace teddy. I had suggested they wear something that might distract Stacker, and they had taken it to heart.

Unfortunately it also distracted several truck drivers on the freeway who almost ran off the road looking down at the girls' breasts. This hazard was not helped by the fact they both pulled their dresses down as low as possible and squashed their assets against the window.

I screamed, 'Those tits are going to get us killed,' as I wove the Berlina through a sea of truck tail lights. The word had gone over the truckie radio system and they were all looking for the travelling peep show.

I was late to meet Steve from the squad. He gave me the $12,000 cash we needed for the buy and asked why I was late. When the girls flashed him, he understood why I was having trouble.

They were a handful. He shook his head and wished me luck. I parked my vehicle outside a bank in Collingwood, as arranged. We were all nervous. It was important for this deal to go down. An ounce of heroin from Stacker meant an ounce of heroin against Kath. But I felt confident.

Fran saw him first and jumped out and walked across Hoddle Street to see him. Her trusty handbag recorded the whole thing.

'Sit down Fran,' Stacker said. He was edgy, and no wonder.

'I was comin' around the corner here,' he said, indicating a laneway, 'and this dude, a bloke with a camera, right, a big one ... was takin' photos and he was with another bloke with headphones on and shit ...'

'Bullshit,' said Fran.

'I swear, they're around the corner. The one with the camera had a purple shirt,' said Stacker.

Fran handled it. 'We'll go for a walk and have a look,' she said. 'Hold me hand, Stacker.'

From the car I could see this, but not hear it. Something was obviously wrong, but I had no idea what.

I had to make sure Fran was safe. I did a U-turn and drove into the laneway. As I did this, Stacker took Fran to the exact location the unknown men had been.

Stacker was telling her, 'He was standing right there behind the fence, takin' a photo of something right over the road at youse ... there was another bloke come around the corner with headphones, a microphone. Seriously.'

Fran: 'There's no one there, mate ... come somewhere else if you're getting paranoid ... he's got the money in the car.'

Stacker: 'Oh, I'm fuckin' paranoid. The two blokes with one camera and headphones and shit make ya fucking paranoid!'

I drove into the laneway and stopped next to them. Stacker backed away from me and seemed upset. I wound my window down. Fran was obviously nervous.

'Stacker seen some blokes,' she began. Then Stacker looked

at me and said, 'There was two blokes up at the vacant lot right there, right? One with a camera over in the corner taking photos. He had a purple shirt on, over there (he pointed) and one other with a microphone type shit. They're "jacks" for sure, mate.'

I had told my colleagues doing surveillance to keep away from all areas between Trevor Pettingill's flat and the drug deal location. But no, they had put themselves behind a wooden fence with their backs to a laneway that led straight to Trevor's flat. Stacker had come up behind them, stood there and watched them while they were looking at and photographing my white Berlina.

Cunning plans are in the air, everywhere. You've got to grab one and run with it.

'Oh shit,' I said. 'Well let's get out of here now. Jump in.'

'Okay,' said Stacker. 'Yeah … let's fuck off … look for a bloke with a purple shirt …'

We drove off up the lane.

'Turn right up here,' said Stacker. I asked him if he wanted to warn his mate about the "jacks". He said he wanted to ring him from a phone box.

I drove around a few back streets to check we weren't being followed. Stacker liked that touch. I shook hands with him – a good, hard shake like I meant it.

I said, 'Sally, can you turn around and make sure we're not being followed. Just in case we do get pulled over, girls … the usual. I won this twelve grand at the races. I've even got receipts.'

Stacker then sprang a surprise. He told me to drive to Footscray (the other side of the city) to do the deal. He was still agitated. His stale cigarette and body odour almost over-powered Fran's cheap perfume. He was looking all around, inside and outside the car.

He was wearing a black leather jacket, black jumper and

black pants with a belt. He sat behind me to my left. I glanced at him at every chance. He kept sitting forward between our front seats. It all spelt danger.

He directed me to Footscray. All the way he spoke of a lack of money and about being a good friend of Trevor's.

He spoke of Kath and how he had to give her a hundred bucks after today.

Every now and then, he would turn around and look for "jacks".

He said, 'If you see blokes with cameras and microphone things, that's not bein' paranoid ... that's seein' blokes with cameras and things.' A fair point – but not one I wanted to hear just then.

'Stop here,' he said. 'I'll just go see me mate and work out what's going on.' He walked out of sight. I quickly tried to call Steve at the squad, but he was out of the office.

I was suffering from a bad case of undercover syndrome. This is when you think you are the most important person in the world – and you are. Stacker was walking back toward us. When he got back in, he ordered me to drive to the railway station car park.

Fran wanted to look at Stacker's belt buckle. Fran undid her seat belt and turned around and started to wrestle with Stacker in the back seat. I was getting very upset. I yelled at Fran that it wasn't a game.

'They think it is a game, don't they?' Stacker said. For a moment it was Stacker and me against the girls.

Stacker told me to park again. He said he was going to go to see the heroin supplier. I complained about how long it was taking and he promised me again he'd be quick. Stacker walked off.

Again the girls went mad. I tried to calm them down. This time I quickly rang a pager service then quoted Steve's pager number and left an urgent message to turn his phone on.

I looked around but could not spot any of my surveillance team. I had no idea if there were cops covering me or not. I had no contact with my controller and everything was upside down.

I lit my 100th cigarette and reassured the girls. They'd had enough and wanted to go home. Then Stacker appeared and climbed into the back seat.

'You got the gear?' I asked.

'No, just drive up here a bit and turn left,' he said.

I parked in a short-term car park next to a large brick wall. In front was an open area leading to the station. To my right was a small grass area and a big car park.

Stacker ordered me to turn the car off and give him the money. 'What?' I said.

'He can't give you the gear without the money,' Stacker said, almost politely. 'I'll only have the money for about twenty minutes.'

I could not believe what I was hearing. I thought, 'Keep calm, negotiate, be firm and polite to this fucking idiot.'

'I don't blame you for asking,' I said. But I made it clear I wasn't keen on letting twelve grand out of my sight without seeing the gear.

'No, no, no. Listen to me mate, right; I'll have the gear by half past two, right? I may as well be sittin' in the car with you right, it's that safe.'

'No, mate,' I said. Fran said to Stacker, 'But what are you gunna do with the money?'

I was reaching deep to muster every bit of sincerity I could find. I wanted Stacker to know that I was not going to give him the money for one second, let alone twenty minutes, without first getting the heroin.

'I'll show you the money. You can look at it, but I'm not letting you take it anywhere without me getting the gear first,' I said.

Stacker: 'Mate, that's fair enough, fair enough.'

I was being reasonable to an unreasonable person. Keep negotiating, I told myself.

Stacker: 'Fair enough, I want you to trust me, mate. You'll have the gear at half past two. Right. I'm not gunna lash ya. They (Fran and Sally) know where I live.'

'I know what you're saying,' I mumbled.

Stacker: 'I need the money to get the gear, that's what I'm sayin'.'

Me: 'I'm not letting this money go anywhere.'

I opened up the centre console, grabbed the bag of cash and showed Stacker. For twenty minutes we continued this circular debate on how the deal was to happen. Stacker stuck to his 'trust me' line. Then he asked me to show a 'little faith'.

Stacker called the heroin supplier 'the Asian bloke'. This Asian and I had the same problem: we couldn't trust Stacker with the heroin or the money.

I wanted to do many more deals in the future. If I let the money run this once, he would expect it every time. Eventually I'd be ripped off.

Stacker was getting tired of me not giving him the money. Normally, I would have given it up. But I needed the ounce of heroin against Kath.

All of a sudden Stacker had an empty glass Coke bottle in his right hand. He started slapping it into the palm of his left hand. Fran had put that bottle on the floor at her feet and it must have rolled back. An obvious threat.

I looked into his face. He was losing it. As I tried to calm him I reached under my seat and armed myself. I pushed my 9mm Beretta pistol down the front of my pants. I pulled my shirt out so he couldn't see a thing.

I made sure Fran and Sally had no idea when I was ever going to be armed. They knew I was prepared to be stripsearched by Stacker, so I probably wouldn't be armed. No one was going to stripsearch me now.

Stacker ranted about how he was not going to rob me. The girls suddenly went against me, telling me to give him the money.

'It's not your money so shut the fuck up,' I told them. Then I said to Stacker, 'It's a lot of money and I worked hard for it. Drug deals don't work your way. They work money for gear. That's it. Money up front sucks.'

We kept arguing. I'd had enough. So had Stacker. The girls kept on wanting me to give in, which was making it very hard for me. I gave Sally a dirty look. She looked very worried, and put her right hand into the shape of a gun. Stacker never saw Sally's action, but Fran did. While Stacker was talking, he casually pushed his jumper down behind the butt of a small automatic pistol.

I grabbed my pistol from under my shirt. Mine was much bigger. I secretly pointed it at Stacker's chest. Even though I would be shooting from my hip I couldn't miss. It's funny what goes through your head at times of extreme stress.

I was conscious of not shooting my left arm. I kept it up out of the way. I thought of the incredible noise it was going to make in the car.

I said to myself, 'If he grabs that gun I'll give him a quick two shots, as close as I can to the middle of his chest. BANG BANG all over.' But if I shoot him, the job's off. No more evidence on Kath, no Trevor Pettingill. All gone. I could see the headlines: Another Victoria Police shooting.

Okay, so don't shoot Stacker. Not now. Stacker is not worth wasting this job.

Stacker dropped the Coke bottle on the floor and pointed his right index finger at my face.

'I'll tell you something now mate, right,' he said. 'Just do it. Do the fuckin' deal.' He was desperate. The more he argued, the more he needed some of the heroin I wouldn't let him buy. In a calm voice I said, 'You're asking too much, mate.'

This went on and on. Stacker drew back his top lip and said, 'I should just fucking' put ya in the boot, right, take the money right, go and get the dope.'

I was disappointed that the deal had come to this. I kept saying to myself, 'Control, control yourself.' Then I said to him, 'You just don't do business this way, mate. You want to sit there and threaten me – or do the business?'

He gave me the evil stare. I said to myself, 'Right, give him all eight shots in the chest, can't miss. Shit, the gunpowder's going to burn the side of my stomach and put a hole in my shirt. I can cope with that. War wounds. I just really need to shoot him now.'

The others had no idea I was pointing a pistol at Stacker's chest. I thought, 'You have no idea how close you are to death, mate. You'll be dead before you hear the gun shots.'

We eyeballed each other. Stacker stepped out of the car and paced up and down the footpath. Sally said: 'I'm goin' home. This cunt's packin' (carrying a gun) and you're fucking 'im around.'

'I know what I'm doing,' I said. 'Relax.' I was calm. It was the worst situation I'd ever been in, but I felt in control. In my mind everything slowed down.

Later, I found I had to pay for such bravado, with sleepless nights and endless dreams. Adrenalin-pumping undercover action is like junk food – feels good at the time, but it's not healthy.

Stacker had walked out of sight. Fran went after him. I rang Steve. This time I got him.

Fran walked back to the driver's window and told me the gear was around the corner with an Asian dealer. She asked me to give her the money to do the deal. I told Steve: 'He's got a gun and threatened to shoot me and put me in the boot. He's fucking mad.'

At first Steve wanted me to hang in there and do the deal

with Stacker alone, to keep the evidence strong. I told him the Asian didn't trust Stacker. I also told him Stacker had spotted the 'dogs' (surveillance crew) in Collingwood.

Steve said, 'Let the money go. You're doing a great job.'

Then the Asian came into sight – Andy Dang, a well-known heroin dealer.

Andy was only 24 years old. I had worked on him a couple of times. His mother was the madam of a brothel. His family were linked to several drug-related murders.

I first saw him when I was covering one of my undercover colleagues during a deal. After the deal, I was driving back to the office and as I pulled up at a set of lights, Andy drove up in his Mazda MR2 and stopped next to me. I hadn't been as invisible at the drug deal as I thought. He actually followed me for several blocks. He was a good dealer who knew what he was doing. This time he waited with his hands in his pockets about 30 metres from my car. Fran was in deep conversation with Stacker off to the left. Sally sat behind me.

Stacker came back and said: 'He's right to do it.'

As he stood behind Fran I could clearly see the handle of a small automatic pistol sticking out from his pants. His jumper was tucked in behind it.

'I'm giving the money to Fran now,' I said. 'Then I'm going to step out of the car and stay well back here.'

'I'll call you over when I want the money,' he said. As he walked away, he pulled his jumper out to cover his pistol. He only wanted me to see it. Stacker walked back to Andy.

Fran warned me: 'He wants to fuckin' shoot you, Lenny.'

This deal was going from bad to worse. I rang Steve again and told him Stacker wanted to shoot me and take the money. 'At this stage the deal is going ahead,' I said. 'Get the "dogs" in close, but tell them to be very careful ... here he comes.'

Steve told me I was doing a great job, buddy. I was getting tired of hearing that.

As I was doing this, Fran said, 'Do you know what he said? "I'm going to knock him, take his money, and we can all run".'

Stacker walked around the corner and straight up to Fran's window. He had his hands in his pockets.

I told him Fran could take the money and do the swap.

Stacker said, 'No, forget about it. We got followed over there – by the coppers.'

'Well, do you want a lift back or are you right to go?' I asked.

Stacker knew he had seen cops at Collingwood and now here. I told him I hadn't seen any. So did the girls. But he said, 'Believe me. My mate spotted them. He told me to just go. It's off, get out of here.'

Andy Dang's brain is not clouded by years of drug abuse. His police radar runs flat out. Stacker's desire for heroin, and money for more, causes him to take risks Andy wouldn't dream of.

'Hey, Stack,' I said. 'One more try.'

Stacker said he would speak to Andy one more time. He went to call him from a phone box. While he was gone, I called Steve and told him what was happening.

Stacker came back, got straight back into the back seat and asked if I could drop him off in Collingwood?

I drove off. Stacker was speaking quietly, obviously trying to hide his anger. It was as if he spoke too much he would explode.

I drove flat out. I wanted him out of the car. The girls were excellent. They could feel the tension. Sally kept on giving him a cuddle. My gun was tucked into my pants. My theory was if I drove fast he was less likely to shoot me. I had my rear-vision mirror so I could see him clearly.

I kept trying. Stacker was only stupid to a point. He said, 'It's important to do the deal, right, but it's more important to be safe. We could have been pinched now. We've been lucky.'

Everything I said seemed to irritate Stacker. First I bagged the 'gooks' for attracting police attention and he told me they were his mates. Then I said something about Kath he didn't like.

The tension was getting worse by the second. Stacker said something strange. 'My finger, it's itchy.'

I looked in the rear-vision mirror. Stacker was shaking, sweating and upset. He was hanging out for heroin and angry. He was scratching his right index finger with his left hand. I drove even faster. Sally picked what was going on and started rubbing the back of his neck and whispering to him.

Stacker was telling me that his trigger finger was getting itchy. He wanted to shoot me – now! The feeling was mutual, but I had to drive.

The girls laughed and carried on until Stacker directed me down the last couple of streets. He asked for my phone. He rang Trevor's flat to tell him he was about to arrive. As I stopped to let him out, I said, 'I'm sorry about getting a bit aggro before, but we're all safe, that's the main thing. I'll hear from you then. We'll find a safe place next time.'

As Stacker got out of the car, he said, 'Lenny, just hang in there, hang in there … it'll happen, right?'

The second the door closed, I drove off. We all let out a sigh. Fran yelled, 'For the record, I quit.'

I thanked the girls for an incredible job. They were so sure that Stacker was going to shoot me. I couldn't tell them I was armed and almost shot him. We all agreed never to deal with Stacker again.

I parked behind Fran's car and gave them a big cuddle. I removed the used tape from Fran's handbag and put a fresh one in. We had lived though two hours and 35 minutes of hell. We promised to call each other again that night.

There was nothing else to say.

As I drove back to the office for the debrief, I thought, 'All we just need is another cunning plan, a Stacklerless cunning plan.'

CHAPTER 5

Earthquake

We had a rare chance
to lock up some good
crooks. Crooks who
killed good police.

I PARKED my vehicle in an office car park off Lygon Street, Carlton. I put on a cap and big sunglasses and lifted up the collar on my coat. My old shoulder bag hung low off my right shoulder. Lenny the drug dealer had transformed into what appeared to be a mature-aged uni student.

Looking down, I shuffled through the old McKenzie Street car park and up the stairs of the old Victoria Police Club. With a brass key I opened a large steel door, walked down a hallway through what had been a kitchen. The air was damp and stale. I stopped in the doorway to the main bar. I recalled drinking sessions I'd had when this place was alive. Some of the funny crook-catching stories.

Then I recalled the face of an old mate who died driving home drunk from this very room. I walked down a rusty staircase to my last locked door. Opening that put me into the driveway of the underground car park and the safety of Russell Street police station.

Up another three flights of stairs put me in the foyer of the drug squad. I was sick of walking in and out the front door of Russell Street heavily disguised. Research led me to the hidden entrance. After leaving undercover jobs I would often have to dive onto the floor of unmarked police vehicles and get driven into the police complex. I had crushed two sets of expensive sunglasses during these dives. This way was safer and cheaper.

Baldrick had bought a pair of Olympus 2 sunglasses – the glasses that the big, bad and cool black guys wear in the American TV show *Cops*. They were wraparound glasses with a thick gold band along the top and very dark glass. I couldn't have a crew member cooler than me so I bought a pair. Next minute all of our crew was wearing them. Anyway.

I found that the rest of my crew had just arrived back at their desks. They all laughed, saying things like, 'You had a good time with your new mate Stacker did you?' and 'Come on, it was only a drug deal'.

I flopped into my chair and said, 'I've been "Stackered". He is a nightmare. Did Steve tell you Andy Dang was the supplier?'

Steve walked into the room and said, 'You survived.'

I said, 'Don't worry about your phone, Steve, it's not like I'm doing anything dangerous!'

Steve just laughed and mumbled something like, 'You'll be right, buddy'. Several of the 'Dogs' (surveillance police) walked in. We laughed at each other. Curly, a short bald Dog, said, 'You had fun today, did you Lenny?'

I said, 'Only because of your purple shirt. Thought you'd spice up my drug deal did you, fuck?'

Curly said, 'What, I'm invisible.'

I said, 'It's a bit hard for me to deny you exist when Stacker's standing there behind you. He stood there watching you and your purple bloody shirt photograph me across the road.' Putting my feet up on the desk, I added, 'And who was the radio microphone man next to you?'

Vag, standing next to Curly, gave me a guilty smile, and turned away.

I proclaimed, 'You're burnt and I'm burnt five minutes before the bloody drug deal.'

'Yes, that was most unfortunate,' Curly said guiltily.

'Unfortunate!' I could not think of an expletive that would adequately describe my frustration. I quoted one of my favourite poems: 'Into the valley of death rode Lenny Rogers'.

Baldrick said to Curly, 'I've got a yellow shirt with big pink dots you can wear at his next deal.' Curly ignored the attempted joke. It had all become unfunny. It was one of those rare moments when black humour fell flat. We moved into the conference room and started the debriefing.

We went over what had happened. There was no blame. The Dogs do an incredible job under extreme circumstances. At one point I said, 'Stacker and I were going to shoot each other. You guys had to be close and you got burnt. I wouldn't have been there in the first place if you weren't covering me.'

The mood was quite sombre. I said, 'It started badly and ended badly.'

Baldrick added, 'With bad shit in between.'

I continued, 'You guys should hear the fallout over the telephone intercepts and listening devices. The last thing Stacker said to me was, "Watch your back!"' I paused, putting my face into my hands, and said, 'I need to lie down. That meeting drained the shit out of me'.

I was to learn that some of my undercover drug deals were so easy that they made me believe the job was a walk in the park. It never seemed to matter how much I was buying. What mattered were the little things that either didn't happen or almost did. The 'what if' questions would creep into my thoughts whenever I had time to think. Keeping busy or drunk stopped them. For a while.

Someone said, 'Bobby McGee's is big on Thursdays.'

I agreed, 'At times like these we need Bobby McGee's.' It was planned. Twelve of us planned to meet at 6.30pm in the biggest nightclub in town.

It was a brief debriefing. We walked back to our desks, discussing our next move. In particular, my next move. Baldrick's mobile phone rang. His voice took on a serious tone. At 4.23pm Kath Pettingill telephoned her son Trevor Pettingill. Stacker answered Trevor's phone. The following conversation was contained in the police brief and admitted in evidence:

Kath: What?

Stacker: Hello.

Kath: What's going on?

Stacker: Yeah, I went to do that. Right.

Kath: Yep.

Stacker: And I went to meet 'em down near Hoddle 'n' Johnston Street, right.

Kath: Yeah

Stacker: And there's a vacant lot down there, right, and I seen these two blokes there, one with a camera, an' one with like a listening device, right.

Stacker spoke with great intensity as he dissolved months of hard work. With all the drama fresh in his mind, he told Kath of the day's events.

Kath: Yeah.

Stacker: With ear phones on his head and a box, right.

Kath: Yeah.

Stacker: And I spoke to that Fran, I called her over. I said: 'There's blokes around the corner here with a camera taking photos of youse and that, Fran.' And she said, 'Ay, it's paranoid, we went and had a look and they were gone.' Right.

Kath: Yeah.

Stacker: They ... they kept telling me I was paranoid, right. Yeah, we went over to Footscray, right.

Kath: Yeah

Stacker: And uh, me little mate seen the same blokes with the camera and that over there.

Kath: Oh, why. What did you do?

Stacker: Oh, we left.

Kath: You didn't give her nothin'.

Stacker: Nuh.

Kath: Good. Yeah, 'cause I don't know whether I trust 'em.

Stacker: Mmmm

Kath: Give it a miss.

Stacker: Yeah, that's right. I told Trevor I nearly got pinched.

Kath: You've gotta be paranoid.

Stacker: You know ... somethin' is goin' on, isn't there?

Kath: Yeah, fuckin' oath, because I told her if he's wearin' a wire, if she's wired as well?

Stacker: They're fuckin' unreal, aren't they?

Kath: Give it a miss.

Stacker: Yeah, fuckin' trying to set me up.

Kath: That's what, I had an idea, but I didn't know.

(Trevor Pettingill then took the phone)

Trevor: Mum, what's going on?

Kath: What?

Trevor: Well, you want to find out who that bloke is.

Kath: His name is Lenny, Lenny Rogers.

Trevor: Fuckin' with that Fran sheila. And Lenny was to tell you, that it didn't happen.

Kath: Not to tell me? I was wary of him. I said, 'If you're wearing a mike or anything', I said, 'You've had it'.

Trevor: Mmm

Kath: I said, 'If you don't take your clothes off.' He took all his clothes off. She must have had it then. You don't trust Sally, anyway.

Trevor: All right then.

Kath: I've got what I wanted anyway.

Trevor then put his four-year-old son Jamie on the phone to talk to his grandmother. Trevor and his wife Debbie named their son Jamie after Trevor's brother Jamie Pettingill, who died of a heroin overdose at the age of 21. This of course doesn't stop them both selling heroin.

MY whole crew and I sat there numb. Dead; the job was dead. I said, 'Steve, if it wasn't hard before, it's hard now.'

Laurie said, 'They won't go near you again.'

Baldrick said, 'To kill him they will.'

The crew started talking about finishing up the job. Then they started on the amount of evidence they had on Kath and several of the other crooks. To them the job was over.

I looked at Steve and said, 'Stacker might be home by now'. I grabbed my mobile off the desk and walked into one of the interview rooms. Steve followed, closing the door behind him. Steve and I went through what I was going to say to this lunatic. I rang Fran. I thanked her for the fantastic job she'd done. She was still upset. She told me that Stacker had rung her from Trevor's. She said Trevor was talking in the background. They must have left Trevor's and used another phone line as

Trevor's phone had not been used. Stacker had accused Lenny of being a copper.

Fran told me, 'Lenny, Stacker told me, "If that Lenny is a copper, I'm going to knock him".'

I calmed Fran down, or tried to. She was very upset. During the call I heard her suck in smoke from a bong. We'd all had a bad day. I assured Fran that everything would be all right. Fran asked me to hold the phone because Sally wanted to talk to me. Sally then informed me that Stacker wanted to kill me. Sally said, 'Lenny, Stacker said that you're a "jack" and I said you're too fucking stupid to be a jack.'

I laughed and said, 'Thanks, Sally. I find it hard to act stupid. I'm a good actor, aren't I?'

'No Lenny, I'm serious.'

I said, 'All right. I don't act that stupid, do I?'

She said in all seriousness, 'He wants to kill you. He told me he'll "cut Lenny's fuckin' throat".'

I again thanked both girls for doing a great job. Sally gave me Stacker's phone number. As I hung up I said, 'Steve, Stacker wants to cut my throat and add me to his stack.'

Steve laughed and said, 'You'll be right, buddy.'

I said, 'I'm going to ring him and give him a blast. You watch how tough I can be now. Steve, if he punches me through the phone you're my witness and we've got him for assault.'

Steve just sat there shaking his head at my behaviour.

I said, 'How dare he accuse me of being a copper. I'm way too stupid.'

As I took a deep breath, I became serious. Becoming serious was always easy, it was the laughing that was getting harder. At 6.14pm on August 12, I rang Stacker's home. He was short and straight to the point. He told me that he had spoken to his Asian mate (Andy).

Stacker: Yeah, those coppers are watchin' you mate, I'm tellin' ya. Listen, my mate (Andy) described the same bloke I seen today. Remember, I seen the bloke in Collingwood, now he seen the same bloke in the purple shirt right, in Footscray Railway Station.

McCulloch: Well that's fucked, look mate.

Stacker: No you look behind ya. They were watchin' youse and takin' photos of youse.

McCulloch: Okay, I take your word. If you reckon that's the go we'll just leave it then. I want to do business but ...

Stacker: If you see 'em, see if you can follow 'em, right.

Now Stacker wants me to follow the cops that are following me. I need a holiday. There was something I wanted to clear up.

McCulloch: Apparently, you reckon, you said to Fran that I'm a jack and you want to knock me.

Stacker: I didn't say that. I said you might be a copper.

That was it. Now Stacker doesn't trust me! I attacked. I clenched my teeth and made sure Stacker understood I was livid.

McCulloch: I'm rooting Fran for fuck sake. You mean to tell me, you could sit in a car for three fucking hours with a jack! Piss off you couldn't, you're too good for that. You can pick a copper a mile off. You've got a jack radar or something.

Stacker: Yeah, okay, right.

McCulloch: You look at a jack in the eyes, mate, you can tell. You can smell 'em. You looked me in the eyes.

Stacker: Yeah, well, right. You're right. Youse work it out.

It was all a bit much for Stacker. There was too much thinking going on.

McCulloch: You tell me why they want a photo of me if I'm one of them? Talk to me!

Stacker: All right, all right, all right.

I took a deep breath and relaxed. Stacker had backed off. I relied on appealing to Stacker's anti-cop radar. Crooks like Stacker always think they can pick a cop a mile off. I was fighting an uphill battle against his first impression of me. First impressions in this business are everything. Me being burnt by my surveillance team just before our first meeting crippled a good first impression.

McCulloch: Thanks for spotting them, Stack. I'm sorry I got you involved. Are you all right?

Stacker: Yeah, I'm right. You just see, you're gettin' followed.

McCulloch: I'm putting on some security, I'm gunna piss off my car. Get a new one. I might need you to help me spot the jacks, see if I'm clean. I'll pay ya.

Stacker: Yeah, I can do that. I know who I'm looking for, I seen 'em.

Stacker seemed very happy with that idea. We crapped on for a few more minutes. I told him that I'll sort myself out and speak to him in a few days. We finished on good terms. Maybe.

As soon as I hung up, Fran rang me. As usual, I recorded the call on my mini tape recorder. She was very upset. She wanted to make sure I didn't organise another drug deal because Stacker would shoot me. As I spoke to Fran, Sally called out, 'Don't let Stacker manipulate you, Lenny.' Sally grabbed the phone from Fran.

Transcription reads:

Sally: He goes, 'Leave it for three days and just open your eyes. Just look around ya'.

Sally was very concerned. She insisted that she knew Stacker and what he was capable of.

Sally: I don't feel right about this. Um, even I can tell he's changed in talking to me, Lenny.

I told the girls we were going to have a few days off. I finished up by thanking them for everything they did today. At 7.06pm I finished the call. The day of August 12, 1993, was a day I'll not forget.

Moments later I grabbed a texta and wrote my home address on my inner forearm. My plan was, when this drinking session was over I wouldn't be able to speak. Not English anyway. I could just pull back my sleeve and show the taxi driver. Tonight required excessive drinking.

The following day the rest of my crew informed me that I'd had a good night. They said I'd had a great time. Apparently Stacker got a few mentions. Baldrick said that I spent most of the night talking to women being either Neville Sponge, deep sea diver, or Rex Dexter, dolphin trainer. I think I had a good time because I had no money and I smelt like an old hotel carpet. My brain was sore and it felt a bit mushy.

I arrived at work about lunchtime. Steve and I had a chat. I was concerned about the girls. They needed a break. Steve took that to mean I needed a break. He spent a few minutes in the boss's office. Steve came out and said, 'The boss agrees, the girls need a break. Tell them they can go off into the country or somewhere. The boss is giving them both $400 for expenses and we're paying their motel bills for three nights for B2, G6 and the kids.' This was excellent. They would love it.

I told Fran that we were all very proud of how well they were doing. Fran asked me to come along. I explained that this was a chance to get away from me, drug deals, the lot. Fran and Sally believed the job was doomed. All over. I kept telling them that there were cunning plans out there that we hadn't thought of yet.

When I got off the phone, Steve and our whole crew had a chat. It was decided I'd ring Stacker and tell him that I was taking a few days off. We agreed to plan a much smaller deal when I got back. This time we'd let the money run a bit. The plan was that I was going to Falls Creek skiing. Steve and I went off to an interview room and I made the call.

Stacker agreed to give it a break. I told him how when I got back we'd try again. This time I'd trust him with some of the money. Stacker seemed happy with that. I left the office and headed home. I started to plan several fishing and scuba diving trips over the next few days. I was fine until Kath decided to make another phone call. I'd been home just long enough to fall asleep on the couch. The phone rang. I was notified of this call.

At 4.03pm on August 13, Kath Pettingill telephoned her son Trevor Pettingill at his home:

Debbie: Debbie's hotline.

Kath: Yeah, where is he?

Debbie: Yeah, hang on.

Kath: Yeah, put him on.

Kath sounded very angry.

Trevor: Hello, Mother dear.

Kath: You don't fucking mother dear me …

Trevor: (inaudible)

Kath: What are you up to?

Trevor: What?

Kath: What are you up to? You've got a wife there that's pregnant and Jamie and you're pissed off all hours of the night with those rats again.

Trevor had been out on the town with Stacker, Donato and a friend Eddie Fiorello.

Trevor: What happened?

Kath: You heard me.

Trevor: All right, Mum.

Kath: If I don't see you tomorrow morning, Trevor.

Trevor: I'll speak to you … All right, Mum.

Kath: You'll get all right Mum.

Stacker was in the background saying, 'I want to speak to her'.

Trevor: Do you want to speak to Stacker?

Kath: Yes, I do.

Stacker: Kath?

Kath: What?

Stacker: The bloke rang me again before, right? Like yester-day the bloke, Lenny, didn't want to leave the money out of his sight, right?

Kath: Yeah.

Stacker: Now today they wanted to give me the money.

Kath: No, don't have nothing more to do with them.

Stacker: What about just taking the money?

Kath: No, that's what Victor got into trouble about, for taking the money?

Stacker: Yeah? At the market.

Kath: What if it's marked?

Stacker: They won't get it back.

It's not enough to want to shoot me and put me in the boot of my car. Now he wants to rob me. All the while believing I'm a cop. I started to seriously wonder if I could ever trust Kath or Stacker again. Stacker had really worked himself up and felt like he needed to tell Kath everything. After all, Kath had introduced this cop to him. And another thing, where had the code gone? The slightest sign of trouble and the code, if you could call it that, went straight out the window.

Kath: No, but what if it's marked and then they jump on you the minute you take it? That's what they'll do.

Stacker: Yeah.

Kath: I wish I could say yes, but I ... I don't know ... don't think it's worth it. I don't think, Stacker.

Stacker: I might get the money, right, and get out quick and see what happens. See, I was supposed to meet them today.

Kath: Yeah, well I went over the road 'cause Victor has got a mate that moved in over the road, Fred Rose, and he's already declared them.

Old Fred had declared us as informers and cops and he too wants to rob me. I must have come from another planet. On my planet, drug dealing is dangerous enough without robbing people who you think are cops. In their sordid world money comes before personal safety and freedom every time.

Stacker: Fair dinkum?

Kath: Right, I knew this might be on.

Stacker: Mmm.

Kath: If you want a way to get the money, well do you know what the best bet would be?

Stacker: 'What?'

Kath: If you had Donato down the end of the street on his motorcycle.

Stacker: Yeah.

Kath: Drive to Donato, just throw the money to Donato and go, go for it like hell.

Stacker: Yeah?

Kath: That's the only way you're gunna beat the jacks.

Stacker: Mmm, yeah.

Stacker was warming to the plan. For me it was like listening to two little boys playing with action figures in a sandpit. Both are heavily involved in the heat of a mythical battle with flying monsters, laser beams, explosions and endless guns. Both perfectly tuned into the same imaginary world. A world without grown-ups, logic or any reality. I had to keep telling myself that this was real, they were real and they were talking about me.

Kath: Throw the money at him and go for your life … jump on the back of the motorcycle with him and piss off as quick as you can.

Stacker: Yeah, But they will still get us.

Kath: Who?

Stacker: The jacks, the fucking jacks.

Kath: Yeah, but what with?

Stacker: Nothin'.

Kath: Nothin' exactly. You'll have the money!

Stacker: What, with assault and robbery charges. That's nothin?

Kath made the charges sound like the least of his problems. Again Kath put money first at all cost.

Kath: Knock him on the chin. I'd take the money and go too.

Stacker: Because, that's what I'm thinking about, you know.

Kath: I'm sorry I even sent them. I told old Fred over the road, he used to fight in Sharman's Troupe (a travelling boxing tent show) and he said, 'I've just declared them dogs. I said, 'Oh, God'.

Stacker: Yeah.

Kath: Now they've moved out to Frankston, they'll be hounding you now.

Stacker: We'll see what happens, I might get 'em to bring a heap of money.

Kath: Don't let Trevor go please.

Stacker: No, he's not part of it. Well … see you then.

Kath: If you can get away with the money.

Stacker: Yeah, I'll try.

Kath: Maybe in a lane or something, where Donato's … standing still … standing start. Because I don't think the jacks will jump on you as quick as you can get on a fucking motorbike.

Stacker: Yeah, that's right, we'll see what happens.

Kath: Yeah, yeah.

Stacker: All right, here's Kath ... um, Debbie.

Kath: Do your best.

Stacker: I'll try.

Kath then spoke to Debbie about how Wendy was giving her the shits. Kath went on to say how upset she was that Trevor was not being a good father. Kath asked Debbie to put young Jamie on the phone.

Jamie: What?

Kath: Jamie, I'm coming down tomorrow and I'm gunna bash your father.

Jamie threw the phone down.

Debbie: What ... Oh, he's a beast. What did you say?

Kath: I said, 'I'm coming down tomorrow to bash your father.' And he just threw the phone, did he?

Debbie went on to tell Kath how Trevor's back using heroin. Kath is most upset.

Kath: Yeah, well he can go back to fucking where he come from ... what's it called ... Odyssey.

Debbie: Odyssey ...you're kidding? He's going backwards, not forward.

Kath: Wake up to himself.

Debbie: Doesn't he want to be around to watch the police get charged ... go under for the murder blue. Ask him!

'Murder blue' refers to the blue form that the charge is printed on.

Debbie: Yeah (to Trevor in the background) ... your mother said you want to wake up to yourself. Don't you want to see the coppers ... um ...

Kath: Go under.

Debbie: Go under for the murder charges.

Kath: What did he say to that?

Debbie: Nothin', he's sitting at the table like a zombie.

Kath: Yeah, that'd be right.

Not only did Kath want to rob me, believing I'm a copper, but she used the fact that seven police had recently been charged with murder as an incentive for her son Trevor to stop using heroin and stay alive for their conviction. Seven police had been charged over the shooting of Graeme Jensen. This shooting was the reason Victor Peirce and his mates shot Tynan and Eyre in Walsh Street, South Yarra. Charges against five of the police were dropped and the remaining two were acquitted.

WHAT caused a human being to become like Kath Pettingill? How can a human think this way? Kath of all people knew heroin killed and destroyed. She'd had three children die from heroin overdoses. Yet she organised the sale of heroin. One of her few living sons was currently addicted to heroin, yet she sold heroin. She hated and didn't trust junkies, yet she sold heroin. On top of all that she trusted non-criminals or 'cleanskins' even less.

I have no doubt that Kath in her own way had been and was a very loving mother. I do question however her right to have remained one. Her mothering philosophies, methodology and teaching skills had repeatedly failed. Over many decades our community allowed her to mother. It seemed that mental, moral, physical and sexual abuse committed within a criminal clan was acceptable **because** they were criminals.

Our Social Services Department obviously didn't have anyone willing to try to remove any of Kath's kids, who regularly witnessed heroin trafficking, serious assaults, sexual acts and even murder. Kath brought up her babies and children in brothels. Yet no-one went to their rescue. No-one tried to remove these born victims from the clutches of Kath's criminal clan. Our community allowed it.

There I was, an undercover cop. In a small way, I was supposed to understand this behaviour. Not only understand, but live in it, be part of it. Well, only if I wanted to be successful, of course. Thank Christ, I was only visiting. Normal decent human beings don't need to know about this shit. I'm talking about me, the real me. The one deep down inside. I tried to keep the real Lachlan separate. Lenny was exposed to all this bad shit. I tried to protect Lachlan. That way I could get rid of Lenny after work and become a nice person. I was conscious of wanting to become normal again after this job. I thought there were two of us.

I recall Dad asking me one time when I was young, 'What do you want to be when you grow up?' I said, 'A gentleman.' They all laughed. I didn't want to be a gentleman in a top hat and tails. I wanted to be a gentle man. To me a gentleman was everything that was good. Things hadn't changed. I think most of the time I am a gentleman. I felt like it might be harder to be one after being exposed to all this crap. Each time I washed Lenny off, it seemed to take a little bit of me with it, and it worried me. These conversations, combined with my interaction with these people, gave me an insight into a world that should not exist. It exists through learned behaviour. Kath's strong character assured it. Decency is replaced by greed. Kath's world was all about today and now. Take what you can get with no thought of cost. How could she ever pass on or teach her siblings empathy when she had none? After everything going wrong with Stacker, I was determined for this operation to continue. We had invested too much to allow this investigation to fold. We had a rare chance to lock up some good crooks. Crooks who killed good police.

Listening to them interact with each other gave me an insight into their irrational, illogical mentality. I had to focus. I wanted evidence more than ever. More cunning plans were needed. They needed to be in prison eating porridge and we'd better hurry up with it because they were still breeding.

I spent the next two hours on the phone talking to Steve and Baldrick, all the while working hard on my drinking problem. Mostly chardonnay – after all I was a gentleman. Most mornings I'd wake up around one or two o'clock. In the dark, sitting up on my couch, with the TV off. I would always be fast asleep before tipping my glass of wine over myself. I'd stand and take off my wine-soaked shirt and pants. Climb into bed and close my eyes.

My wife had given up waking me. Apparently, when she did, I'd jump up swearing and throwing punches. And they call it giggle-juice.

I think I felt safe sleeping. I had endless nightmares but I did always wake up. My most common were running out of ammo in a big shoot-out or having the wrong bullets for my gun. Another one was, while peeping through a crack in a door I'd be stabbed in the stomach by a sword. Don't analyse this one but I once had a dream that I was a zebra. I was walking into a cave. It turned out to be a lions' den. Here I was with all these lions creeping up to eat me. I stood there and convinced them that I was not a zebra, I was in fact a striped lion from a country far away. The lion king said, 'Oh, no worries, have some of this.' He then handed me a big chunk of zebra to eat.

Sleeping was fine. It was being awake that was really dangerous. Trying to stay asleep was a full-time occupation. I would lie there thinking, 'If I say this, then they would say that and I would say this' and so on and so on. I would spend most of every night trying to think like them. I would have to think like them to catch them. Drug dealing is one of the very few offences where we, the investigators, can create the offence. Once we had proved these crooks were in the business of drug dealing we could create a crime for them to commit. Somehow we had to do it safely. Sleep was precious stuff.

THE next morning Fran rang me. She had packed up Sally and the kids and was heading off. She had no idea where – just away. At least Fran was happy. They got as far as Marysville over the Black Spur, in the ranges east of Melbourne. I found out later that the girls just had to buy some 'smoke' before they left. Fran and Sally drove to Trevor's at 11.15am on August 14. I only found this out when Kath rang Debbie to say hello. Debbie told Kath that Sally was about to arrive. Kath went right off. Kath repeated the words, 'I don't want her there' several times. At first Kath thought Sally was buying heroin from Trevor.

Debbie: Trevor's just gone to meet that sheila. She rang up here wanting something.

Kath: Which one?

Debbie: Sally.

Kath: I told Stacker what to do, God almighty why hasn't he fuckin' done it?

Debbie: Choof only.

Kath: Oh, yeah? That's cool. I thought it was the other (heroin). *But if she's apparently got um people on video* (working for the cops) *what's the fuckin' good of having her there, the thing.*

During the conversation Sally arrived at Debbie's front door. Kath screamed, 'Tell her I want to speak to her.'

Trevor kept on calling out, 'Tell her (Kath) I'll ring her back.' Kath's final words were, 'Tell her to get out!'

Kath might not be nice, but she's not stupid. This was another example of learnt behaviour. Kath had taught her son well. She'd passed on her money-first-at-all-costs and safety-last principles.

At about midday on August 14, I slipped into a small doorway at the rear of the Melbourne Museum. I pulled on a curly wig, an old woollen beanie and an old fishing jacket. I crossed over Russell Street, walked into the foyer of the police station, flashed my badge and a young uniformed officer pushed the security door button and let me in. I entered this way when I couldn't be bothered walking around my secret rear entrance. It was funny how no-one ever checked my ID. Maybe they were used to my eccentric behaviour.

As I walked through the old corridors, I took my wig off and changed back into me, whoever that was. I dropped my bag containing several different versions of me onto the floor and pushed them under my desk. I then started removing my tape recorder from my bag, spare magazines for my 9mm pistol from my bumbag, the pistol itself from my shoulder holster, spare tapes from my jacket pocket, mobile phone, pager from my belt, notebook and pen from my jeans pocket and my mini micro-recorder from my shirt pocket.

After placing all of that on my desk I flopped down into my chair. I jumped back up and let out a pained 'aw, shit' as I had forgotten about the two padlocks and several 'lock picks' in my back pocket. I always tried to pick them whenever I got bored. I flopped down again.

Steve arrived at his desk with a cup of coffee. He said in his friendly old cowboy type voice, 'G'day buddy. Why don't you grab a coffee and we can have a chat?' As I went to get a coffee

Steve headed off with his notebook toward one of the interview rooms at the rear of the office. This was our usual hiding place. Armed with my coffee and notebook, I closed the door behind me as I sat down opposite Steve at the interview room table. Steve always sat where the crook would normally sit. I thought this was so I wouldn't get some sort of criminal complex.

I started to brief Steve about the fact that Fran and Sally had gone over to Trevor's flat that morning. I made it clear that I was not happy about this as we had not organised it to happen. Obviously Fran and Sally wanted to test the water after our failed heroin purchase from Stacker. The girls had no idea that Kath and Stacker were planning to rob me. We made sure the girls only knew what they had to know. I felt sure they kept us in the dark about much worse things. We spoke about the fact that the job had hit an all-time low. I tried to remain positive.

Steve asked, 'How are you?'

'Fine,' I said.

Then he said, 'No, how are you?'

Then I realised he actually meant it. I thought, 'How am I going?' I said, 'What's another word for fucked?' Steve sat there silent. He had his serious face on. No more jokes. I had walked the undercover tightrope for a long time. Staying balanced. I had to convince my controller Steve that I was sane and professional enough to do the job. Then he had to convince his bosses I could do it. I had to show Steve I was coping. All the while being totally insane for doing it in the first place. Steve could see I was a touch emotional. 'You're doing a great job.'

I said, 'I'm sure these crooks don't appreciate how hard we have to work to fuck them over.'

I sat there on the edge, just holding myself together. I'm sure

Steve knew. We both sat there silent. 'Don't speak,' I thought. I knew my voice would crack into a sob. Another word by either of us and I would be a crying, slobbering mess. It was at that moment I realised this job had a shelf life. If I couldn't speak to my controller without crying, I wasn't coping. Parts of me **were** falling apart. I drank too much, couldn't sleep and needed a cry. Shit. Best we catch all the crooks fast, so I could go fishing.

A sudden sense of urgency snapped me out of my emotional eddy. This was the biggest job I had ever done and was ever likely to do. So we'd better do it. With a new lease on myself, I looked at Steve and said, 'I've got statements to do'.

Steve smiled and said, 'Let's just walk slowly down the hill to the cow paddock.'

I laughed and said, 'Exactly.'

Steve was referring to the old joke about the young bull and the old bull. The young bull wanted to run down the hill and fuck one of the cows. The old bull said, 'No, let's walk down the hill and fuck them all.'

FRAN and Sally arrived back in town on the evening of August 17. On arriving home, Fran rang me. It didn't matter that it was 11.35pm. They had a great time away from me, so they said. I told Fran to hang on as I was starting my tape. I pushed the record button of my mini recorder with my right hand and held it between the ear piece of my mobile phone and my ear. It was difficult in the total darkness but after the past couple of months I was getting good at it. I said, 'It's Detective Senior Constable Lachlan McCulloch and B2 of 93, it's 11.35pm on 17 August, 1993.'

Fran was full of new news. She started telling me how Trevor, Stacker and Eddie had had a huge punch-up and they had black eyes and were going to stab each other. I said, 'I thought you had been away?'

Fran said, 'We have but we needed a choof so we went to Trevor's.'

I said, 'You are fucking unbelievable. Are you running this operation or are we?'

Without hesitation Fran snapped, 'Me, I am, and Sally. In the background Sally screamed, 'I missed you Lenny, kissy kissy'.

Fran said, 'Lenny, just shut up and listen. I'm telling you something.'

I said, 'I'm in bed, asleep.'

My wife whispered, 'No, you're not' as she pushed me out of bed with both her feet. I hit the floor, smashing my mobile phone and tape recorder into my face. I lay there, too tired to get up.

'Shit Fran, I don't need this now.'

Fran said, 'Hang on a second, someone's at the door.'

I said, 'Someone's at your door, now?'

In the background I heard, 'Stacker, Eddie. What are youse up to?' Sally was laughing in the background. Fran quickly said to me, 'Honey, I ordered two ounces of choof, Trevor said it's $760. He gave me a $40 discount, good ay? I'll ring you back a bit later.'

I said, 'What are they doing at your place, now?'

Fran hung up. I put my equipment back on the side table and climbed back into bed.

After a few moments of total silence, through the blackness my wife said in a flat monotone, 'Honey'. Fran's booming voice had escaped my earpiece and travelled to the other side of our king size bed. I was in big trouble. I paused for a second and said, 'It's an undercover sort of thing'. The next thing I heard was a big thump as I hit the floor again. I felt safe down there. Uncomfortable, cold, but safe. I reached up and grabbed my pillow. As I put it under my head my mobile rang again.

I staggered to my feet, grabbed my phone and recorder and left the room. I answered it as I opened the fridge and hosed some of the cask chablis into a large glass. It seemed a good year for wine in a box. I drank the wine with my left hand and tried to hold my phone and recorder to my ear with my right. Fran said that everything was fine. Stacker and Eddie had come over to smoke some of the choof she had bought from Trevor. It turned out that Fran had ordered two ounces and purchased a quarter ounce. I didn't want her talking to me with them in the background.

I said to Fran, 'Tell Stacker that I want to buy some slow – top quality rock slow on Thursday. That gives Stacker two days to organise it. Tell him I want a quarter ounce, that's seven grams. Get him to get a price and ring me tomorrow.

Fran replied, 'Okay, that's good.'

I said, 'Fran, will you be right to do the deal? I'll give you the money to give to Stacker. We'll see what happens.' Fran was happy with that. I added, 'Fran, save some of the choof you just bought from Stacker.' I let Fran get back to her newfound friends. As I finished the call I said, 'Fran, don't forget, you're a legend'.

Fran said, 'I don't, but you sometimes do.'

I sat on my couch writing down notes into my official diary. When I finished I sat there drinking and thinking. Thinking what an incredible person Fran was. Here she was, risking her life playing cops and robbers for nothing. No promise of money. No reward whatsoever. Sally had charges hanging over her head and was also doing a sensational job but wasn't in the same league as Fran. They would be labelled dogs and maggots by everybody in their world. All she was ever going to get was grief. This was my job. But it was their lives I was fucking with. On top of that there were the children. Fran, what a nightmare. But Christ, what a gal. Fran and I had developed a strong bond. Fran was totally absorbed in the thrill of the chase. She had to win, just like me.

I slowly drifted off to sleep and tipped wine all over myself. Again.

In the middle of all this I was trying to become a sergeant. I was having to study for promotional examinations. The only time I could find time to study was in the mornings. I found that if I left my car at home and caught the train I could read notes and attempt to study to and from work. I would sit there on the train, reading away.

While I was reading I would often pick away at my locks. The more I picked, the better I got. One time I was picking away when this young bloke said, 'Hey mate, you know you're not allowed to have those lock pick things. You could get into trouble'.

I said, 'Today, I'm a locksmith.'

The kid said, 'Oh, you're allowed to then.'

AUGUST 18, 1993, at 8.15am Fran rang me. She said she had saved some of the choof she had bought from Trevor Pettingill. But there was a slight problem. She had hidden it last night before she went to bed but had no idea where.

I explained to her that this was a common problem with stupid bloody drug addicts.

Fran pulled me up and said, 'Don't put me on the bloody drug addict. I just like a smoke.'

I said, 'Pretend you're a cop and conduct a drug search.'

She laughed and called out to Sally, 'Hey Sally, you're probably due for another drug raid by the local Ds.'

In the background Sally screamed, 'I'm naked, I'm ready.' Most conversations quickly went straight down below the belt.

I explained to Fran that we needed her and Sally to come into town for a chat. Her first contact with Trevor Pettingill was very important to us. We needed statements from the girls as soon as possible. I spoke to Steve and received authorisation for the payment of a taxi from Frankston, where they had just moved, to the Melbourne CBD. This would be expensive as it would take about an hour. Then I updated the crew. Again we all spoke about how Fran and Sally would have to give evidence in open court against Trevor. Trevor, the accused and recently acquitted cop killer, was high on our list of targets. A seven-gram cannabis purchase from him was hardly going to put him in jail but again, this operation was not quantity. It was about the identity of the targets. I quickly typed up a money request and walked down to the senior sergeant in charge of the drug squad books. All monies spent in *Operation Earthquake* had to be accounted for.

Each operation had a budget it had to stay within. This included everything from stationery to drug purchase money. All the senior sergeant did was hand us money and then chase us for receipts. He was near retirement. This meant that every time you spoke to him he would talk about how he was going to buy a big boat, live in Queensland and go fishing every day. He hadn't been an operational policeman for many years though he was a good one. He was tuned right into effective accounting practices and treated drug squad money like it was his own. He was affectionately known around the office as 'Duck's Bum'.

Armed with a taxi voucher from the Duck's Bum, Baldrick and I met Fran's taxi outside the Carlton Inn Motel. We booked two adjoining rooms. Baldrick took Sally into one room and I took Fran into another. The girls did everything within their power to make us feel uncomfortable. It took about an hour before the dirty jokes and sexual comments started to die down. These were fun times but it did become incredibly difficult to stick to the task at hand. Five hours and five pizzas later we had signed statements from both girls. At the completion of each statement, the girls read them out aloud on tape. We knew that all charges would be fully contested. Our case had to be as tight as Senior Sergeant Duck's Bum's bum.

Fran handed me her handbag. She had of course turned her bag on and recorded everything. I replaced the tape. Fran had mentioned during her statement that while she was at Trevor Pettingill's flat, Trevor's brother Lex, a bloke named Eddie Fiorello and a guy they called 'Big Al' arrived. Fran said they all sat down together and smoked some pipes of marijuana. Big Al turned out to be Fat Albert. Fat Albert's appearance was at odds with his occupation. You see, he was an armed robber. His problems inevitably began every time he went to work. Whenever witnesses described a 200 kilogram masked bandit he got a visit in the early hours from the armed robbery squad.

Fat Albert had a great sense of humour and a colourful imagination. On one occasion he complained to the police internal investigations department about the treatment he received from the armed robbery squad. He said his home had been raided just before Christmas. Members of the armed robbers had stood him in his lounge room, stripped him naked, handcuffed him behind his back, dressed him up like a Christmas tree and forced him to sing Christmas carols. He even showed them the marks where they had taped a little white angel to the top of his bald head. What a jokester.

Fat Albert was well known for his amusing defence strategies at the County Court. In one trial, he pleaded not guilty to several armed robberies. The basis of his defence was that the real offender had jumped over the bank counter during the robberies. Fat Albert claimed that it was physically impossible for him to accomplish such feats. His case was not helped by video footage of the actual robberies. The offender caught on film displayed the agility of a pregnant walrus. The prosecution case claimed that over the past two years, while awaiting trial, the defendant had attempted to assist his defence by consuming more than his fair share of cream puffs.

Anyway. I got Fran to telephone Trevor to find out about the two ounces of choof she had ordered. Trevor asked her to come straight over. One of my back-up team brought over the $760 for the two ounces and an extra $100 to pay Fran back for the quarter bag of choof she had bought the night before. I told Fran to stop smoking all the evidence. Armed with a new tape, Fran and Sally met Trevor in his flat. Fran explained that the choof was for her man Lenny. Fran mentioned to Trevor that Lenny still wanted to 'do the slow', meaning buy heroin. The girls stayed for about an hour and left. I met them down the road and drove them home.

Later that night, Fran rang Trevor again at home. Trevor said he was going to talk with his mate Eddie. Trevor was always careful when he spoke on the phone. Like him, his code was very basic. Like Stacker, he called all Asians 'gooks'. During this taped call, Trevor told Fran that he was going to meet with the gooks Stacker had been dealing with. He said that Stacker had upset the gooks. I thought the only people who didn't hate Stacker were people he hadn't met yet. Fran said Trevor sounded nervous all of a sudden. It was like he wanted to say something but could not think of a code. In the end he gave up thinking and said, 'I will shoot you if we are followed, right?' Fran knew it was more important for him to get his point across than it was to keep any code. His business always came first, safety second. Fran and I did the only thing we could do. We laughed. There was nothing else to do.

All this talk of gooks caused Fran to follow suit. Needless to say, I soon found myself saying gooks when I was making notes on my mini voice recorder. All my notes were later transcribed and formed part of the brief of evidence. Not a good look for an impartial unbiased witness such as myself.

THURSDAY, August 19, 1993. At 9.05am my phone rang. An excited Fran told me Stacker had just rung. Stacker said, 'the quarter will be 3.5'. That meant $3500 for seven grams of heroin. He told Fran to come, with Sally only, at 3pm with the money. We spoke about how Stacker mustn't know about Trevor trying to make the deal.

Fran had just bought an old Toyota. I told her that I had arranged some petrol money through Duck's Bum. Fran was very happy with that. She said, 'So this secret operation may cost me my life but I won't be out of pocket, eh?'

I answered, 'Exactly.'

I told her how good she was and she agreed. I arranged for the girls to come into town. At 1.50pm we met at a small café in a back street in Carlton. Baldrick and Steve arrived a short time later. We sat there and began to run through what was to happen. I handed Fran the three and a half grand. I told Fran that she didn't have to count it, but she counted it anyway. She added, 'How do I know you're not trying to rip me off?' The answer was far too complicated. I just shook my head.

At that meeting the girls were all excited. Steve gave them instructions. Baldrick and I added our ten cents worth every time Steve took a breath. Fran finished counting the money then shoved it straight down the front of her jeans. As our meeting was coming to an end, I said in a stern, serious tone, 'Girls, this is the first time we have ever sent you to the milk bar on your own. Don't talk to any strange drug dealers or hop off the tram before it stops.'

Fran looked at Steve and said, 'I'm still not convinced this Lenny bloke is a copper.'

Sally said, 'But he is a very strange drug dealer.'

As we left the café, Steve and Baldrick walked to their car and I walked the girls to theirs to give them their final briefing.

I paused for a second as the girls simultaneously turned around and called out, 'Hey, Steve'. Steve was about ten metres away. He turned around just as Sally and Fran lifted their tops and flashed their breasts. They just as quickly pulled them down again and kept walking as though nothing had happened. This action was a ritual, no matter where they were. As we walked along I conducted my ritual. I gave both girls a visual inspection and then patted any unusual lumps or bumps. I stopped when I felt reasonably sure they hadn't stolen any paintings, vases or light fittings from the café.

I gave Fran my mobile phone and told her to keep me updated. I had to grab another work phone from the office. For a few seconds I just stood at Fran's driver's side window. Sally was sitting in the back seat. Sally said, 'Christ, Lenny, you look like you need a smoke.' She leant forward and handed me a smoke. I lit it. We all knew this was our biggest moment. Fran said, 'We've got to go Lenny.' I tapped on the roof of the car and said, 'Luck's got nothing to do with it'. As Fran drove off she said in a voice just loud enough for me to hear, 'Righto Sally, how do I get to Myer from here?'

I rang Steve as I followed them in my car. Our surveillance teams were notified, all systems go. I phoned the OP (observation post) to inform them that B2 and G6 were arriving at the intersection any second. I peeled off and parked two streets away. As Fran saw Stacker standing in the same place where we had picked him up last time she leant across and turned her handbag on. Fran's voice had taken a serious, almost professional tone:

Fran: It's the 19th day of August, I'm B2.

Sally: I'm G6.

Fran: It's ten to three in the afternoon and I see Stacker. Today we're buying heroin.

Sally: We hope.

Fran: We better be.

Stacker got into the front passenger seat and said, 'I couldn't find them blokes'. Stacker directed Fran to drive a few hundred metres over to a twenty-storey block of housing commission flats – 229 Hoddle Street, Collingwood. This building was known as the suicide flats due to the high incidence of flying leaps taken from the top floors. Stacker took the girls up the stairwell to the fifth floor. Stacker walked over to a small laundry just outside the lift area. He asked Fran to stand in the laundry. Stacker said, 'Drop your pants so I can see if you're wired.' Fran reached into the front of her jeans and removed the large wad of money. As she pulled her pants down she said, 'Just don't you rip me off.' Stacker stepped forward and lifted Fran's top. He reached around and checked her back. As Fran pulled up her pants Stacker rubbed both his hands over Sally. He said, 'If you don't trust me, hold my jacket till I come back.' As Stacker handed Sally his jacket Fran gave him the money. Sally put his jacket on. Stacker went up in the lift.

As soon as the lift door closed, Sally started going through Stacker's pockets. As Sally removed a small black address book from one of his pockets, I telephoned Fran. As I asked

Fran what was going on, I heard Sally say, 'We have a lot of names in here'. Sally then started reading out names and phone numbers into Fran's handbag.

I laughed and asked, 'What if Stacker hears her?'

Fran said, 'Relax, we are professionals.' She added as an afterthought, 'He fucking well searched me, pulled my pants down, the lot, thank you very much.'

I rang back five minutes later and Sally was still reading names out. No Stacker.

Fifteen minutes later Stacker came back to the laundry. He was smiling. He opened up his right fist and produced a small parcel with a rubber band wrapped around it. He removed the band and unfolded a small clear plastic bag. He grabbed a small white rock from the bag and put it up to his mouth. With his front teeth he bit off a small piece of rock, which fell back into his hand. He held up the small piece he had bitten off and said, 'See this? If I used this all at once I'd be dead.'

Fran said, 'What's this? Lenny paid for that.'

Stacker said, 'Tax time, Fran.' Stacker placed the large piece back into the bag and handed it to Fran. Sally took it from Fran and opened it again.

Just like in the movies Sally wet the tip of her little finger and touched it on the rock. She put her finger in her mouth and tasted it. Sally said, 'Well, it's not Ajax.'

Compressed soap powder is the most common substitute when crooks rip people off. Fran put the rock back into the bag and shoved it down her pants. The three of them then took the lift to the ground floor. As the girls walked back to their car, Stacker walked in the opposite direction toward Trevor Pettingill's flat.

Both Fran and Sally were to include in their statements that as they walked to their car an Asian male followed them. As they got into their vehicle, the Asian male just stood there and watched. As Fran started her car Sally said, 'Shit, slowly look to your left, it's Donato.' Fran saw Donato Corsi leaning against a tree watching them. He was eating an orange. The girls knew Donato well as they had met him twice at Trevor's flat. Donato was a well-known drug trafficker with strong connections to the so-called Melbourne Italian Mafia. As they drove off, I telephoned Fran. She was ecstatic. In the background Sally was screaming, 'Lenny, we did it. We did it, Lenny.'

Fran said, 'He stripsearched me. We were followed. It was full-on, Lenny.'

I asked, 'Please confirm, you have the gear?'

Fran said, 'It's a little white rock and Sally reckons it's heroin.'

Sally screamed, 'It's rock heroin, Lenny.'

I was parked at the side of a Mobil service station in Toorak Road, South Yarra. As Fran drove up to my car I hung up. Fran and Sally burst out of their car screaming, 'We did it. It worked'. I gave them both a little hug.

Together they proudly presented me the little package. I opened it up. 'It looks like heroin,' I said.

Sally insisted, 'Trust me, Lenny it is.'

I said, 'You guys are the best. Brilliant. From now on I'm doubling your pay.'

Sally said, 'Double nothing is still nothing.'

I said, 'Okay then, here you go, Sally, here's a smoke.'

'You actually bought a packet of smokes!'

I said, 'I had to – you weren't here.'

I pulled one smoke half way out of the packet and offered it to Sally. She said thanks and took the whole packet out of my hand. As she lit her smoke, she put the packet in her pocket.

I said, 'Hey Sally, can I have a smoke?'

She reluctantly handed me one.

I said, 'Hang on a second.' I rang Steve. I gave him a quick rundown including the fact that we were now the proud owners of almost seven grams of what appeared to be heroin. As I updated him, I opened the boot of my car and removed a small heroin test kit. I scraped off a tiny bit of powder and poured on the chemical agent. It turned purple instantly. I told Steve. I was so excited, I was shaking. With tears threatening to run down my cheek, I said so the girls could hear, 'Steve, we've done it. Can you believe it? We're in.' Steve in his unflappable way said, 'Well done, buddy.' Fran grabbed the phone off me and screamed, 'Steve, tell us how good we are.' She went on to tell him the full story. She was assisted by Sally screaming in the background.

The girls left and I headed to the forensic science laboratory. I pulled a few strings and had the scientists test my purchase on the spot. The test indicated it was high-quality rock heroin. I rang Stacker and told him I was very happy. I told him I wanted to do more in a few days. Anyone listening to Stacker and me talk, which there was of course, could have mistaken us for mates. Several days later I was told that my 6.2 grams of heroin was an incredible 91 per cent pure. This meant it was taken straight from a pure heroin brick. Most heroin imported into Australia was broken down into a powder in large coffee grinders, diluted with cutting agents like glucodin sugar and then re-pressed into a hard rock again. They then sell it as 'pure'. Therefore most heroin sold in rock form was found to be between 50 and 70 per cent.

When I arrived back at the office, we all congratulated each other. This purchase was the first good thing to happen in weeks. Steve called a meeting of the *Earthquake* crew. We started moving chairs and desks so the four sliding doors could close around a large table in front of a huge whiteboard. Around the office we still kept our targets secret. Kath was 'Mary', Stacker was 'Psycho', and Trevor was 'Mary's son'. I walked over to the audio visual section and had our latest tape recording put onto a normal cassette.

Graham Cleaves' crew were also invited. Their desk was on the opposite side of the office. They were still working on finding the speed laboratory that was supplying HJ, the crook with the honest brother in the job. The undercover Dave was still doing a great job.

The fourteen of us sat waiting for our boss Inspector Dave Reid to arrive so the meeting could start. He walked in and closed the door. Steve chaired the meeting. The boss explained that due to operational expenses *Operation Earthquake* had to be made into two operations. He asked for a second operational name. Someone said, 'After earthquakes you have tremors.' The boss said, '*Operation Tremor* it is.' For some reason, the pencil pushers within the force required the split for funding reasons. Detective Sergeant Graham Cleaves began to brief everyone on his side of the job. He explained how undercover Dave had made several amphetamine purchases from target HJ. My crew were very happy to hear that they were having heaps of problems with HJ. Security within their job was still tight as his twin brother was still a detective in our squad.

My face didn't show it but I was sort of smiling inside as Graham continued with the following: 'As you all know HJ ripped off Dave on July16 . The only way Dave could purchase speed was to give HJ the money. HJ walked off with our $3500 to meet with his supplier Peter Poniewaz, get the gear and return. He didn't come back. We located him in a motel in Preston. Dave rang him there. HJ thinks Dave's criminal contacts found HJ. Since then HJ has been trying to pay Dave back. So far HJ has given Dave $800 cash, two pieces of carpet, a plasma welder, a Migweld 450 welding unit, two bench grinders, and a light blue trolley. All this was delivered in a blue tandem trailer. So far HJ has committed three burglaries in order to pay Dave back.'

Everyone was laughing by this stage, even Graham. He continued, 'We are currently trying to get him to stop doing burgs and get back to drug trafficking. We're still trying to find the clan lab supplying Poniewaz. We can't seem to get past HJ. He says that Poniewaz doesn't want to meet Dave but we think it's more like HJ doesn't want Dave to go direct because he will lose his cut of each deal.'

Steve asked, 'What are your immediate plans?'

Graham said, 'HJ keeps on talking about selling us handguns and a friend of his wants to sell us an Uzi machine gun. We're also trying to organise a meeting with HJ's heroin supplier. HJ has told Dave that Poniewaz is currently doing a cook and his speed will be ready next Monday.' With that, Graham sat down. I was rapt. By the sound of that, our job was doing better than theirs. At least Stacker hadn't ripped me off. Not yet anyway.

Steve said, 'Thanks, Graham. Our job has had its difficulties.' Someone said, 'Stacker.' Steve said, 'Kath put us onto Steven KcKinnon, alias Stacker, to buy heroin. Stacker has proved to be quite difficult to deal with.' Laughter filled the room.

I said, 'Fucking difficult.' Steve continued, 'Today, B2 and G6 purchased seven grams of rock heroin for $3500 from Stacker at housing commission flats in Collingwood. We hope to identify the Asian supplier shortly. As you all know, surveillance within the flats is impossible. Sally or G6 held Stacker's jacket as security. While he was away she read out his phone numbers into B2's tape recorder.'

One of Graham's crew said, 'How good is that?'

Steve said, 'After their purchase they were followed by an unknown Asian male and watched by a close associate of Trevor Pettingill's, one Donato Corsi.'

One of the detectives present said, 'My husband in organised crime charged Donato Corsi and Trevor Pettingill three months ago with a large cannabis crop in Central Gippsland. Donato is reputed to be well connected with Alphonse Gangitano and his crew.'

Steve said, 'Trevor is trying to get rid of Stacker so he can deal heroin to B2 but that hasn't happened.'

One of Graham's crew asked, 'What evidence do you have against Trevor?'

'Stuff all, I answered. 'He's on the bench at the moment. He wants a game but can't get a kick.'

One of my crew added, 'He'll get a kick.'

Duck's Bum then spoke about how many receipts were still outstanding and how little money they had left. The meeting broke up. I officially handed the drug lodgement forms and photograph numbers from the forensic laboratory to Detective Senior Constable Bigmore, the exhibits officer for *Earthquake* and *Tremor*. It was his job to collate all exhibits and photographs of exhibits. This was important as when it was time for the brief to be prepared and evidence to be given the continuity of all exhibits would have to be proven.

OFF-DUTY cops at parties often get asked stupid questions. The number one stupid question asked by dickheads is: 'What do you do with the drugs after you seize them?'

I have been known to answer, 'We use some, give some away

to friends and then keep it in our pocket or desk drawer until the court case.'

The standard response then was, 'Yeah, I thought that would happen.'

I would then clarify with, 'The drugs are seized, photographed, analysed, locked up in a safe until after the court case then re-analysed just prior to destruction to make sure they haven't been diluted or tampered with then senior officers burn it all in a kiln in front of independent witnesses.'

I then move on.

The fact is the drug squad had a standard procedure, which had to be followed. I would follow it when we either purchased drugs or found drugs at a house search. The procedure was:

I would make a statement outlining all details regarding my undercover drug purchase. This would detail the exact time, date and identity of the person I received the drugs from.

I would hand the drugs to the designated exhibits officer, usually at the drug squad offices. Both the exhibits officer and I would make notes in our official diary and subsequently make a further detailed statement including exact time, date and location.

The exhibits officer would then place the drugs in a sealed bag and enter details of the bag and contents into the drug squad property book. It would be labelled with all the above information including its description.

The drugs would then be locked in a safe by a senior officer and he would make a note in the property book to that effect.

Every day or two a detective within the office would take drugs that needed to be analysed to the forensic science laboratory for testing. The detective would make full notes in the property book and his official diary on which drug exhibits he removed from the safe and at a later date would make a full statement regarding same.

On lodging the drug exhibit at the forensic lab, a lodgement form would be generated and stapled into the drug squad property book to explain where the exhibit was currently located.

Due to the lack of drug analysts, the drugs may take between six months and two years to be analysed. When this ultimately occurred, an analyst's certificate would be sent to the detective in charge of the case.

The drug exhibit would eventually be picked up by a detective from the forensic section and returned to the drug squad where details would again be recorded in diaries and property books.

All the above statements, property book numbers and receipts, analyst certificates and lodgement forms would be included in the brief of evidence. This brief would then be given to the accused.

This process helped us prove continuity of the original exhibit. We had to prove to the court that the same drug seized was the same drug analysed. The above procedure had to be followed whether it was less than a gram of cannabis or multiple pounds of speed. So if you really want to piss a cop off at a party and be a real dickhead ask him or her the aforementioned question. At the police academy we were taught that the most dangerous things we would come across were the three Ps. They were property, piss and pussy. All true, but they got the order wrong. Anyway, back to *Earthquake*.

The following day, August 20, at 2.01pm, Trevor Pettingill

picked up the phone of his next door neighbour. He rang Fran. He spoke openly on what he thought was a safe line. The following conversation took place:

Fran: Hello.

Trevor: Gidday, it's Trevor. Do you still want that gear?

Fran: Yeah, of course.

Trevor: What price were you given?

Fran: Eddie told me $400 an ounce but you said I could have two for $760.

Trevor: Yeah, that's the lowest I can go.

Fran: Sweet, I'll take it.

Trevor: Come over about six o'clock tonight

Fran: OK.

Trevor: See you then, ta da.

Trevor was not making a social call. He was short and to the point. Fran rang me and told me the good news, 'Trevor wants to play'.

'Money talks all languages luv,' I replied.

At this stage we had no idea why Trevor was using his neighbours' phone.

The flat belonged to two young homosexuals. Our surveillance revealed that Trevor would enter this flat several times a day. We started making further enquiries. It was to be another long day. I had started at the office at 7.10am. At 5.30 that afternoon I was sitting in my undercover car with Baldrick. I arranged to meet Fran and Sally in a laneway at the rear of a building at the intersection of Hoddle and Victoria streets, Richmond. This was only about two minutes' drive from Trevor's flat.

Fran pulled up behind me and the girls got into our back seat. At about 6.05pm Sally telephoned Trevor at home. After a quick conversation, she hung up. I handed Fran $800 cash and they left. I said, 'Just get the gear and come straight back here. Fran, I mean it, quick deal this time, no fucking around.'

Fran said the usual, 'It's okay. Trust me.'

Twenty minutes later, Baldrick and I were sitting in our car in the semi-dark. Large street lights faintly lit up the whole lane. Fran's vehicle finally turned into the lane behind us, slowly drove past and stopped.

I said, 'Fuck, something's wrong, who are these pricks?' I could see the outline of Fran driving and Sally in the front passenger seat. There were two blokes in the back of Fran's car.

I ripped my revolver from its holster. At the office I tended to go for the smaller guns. Easy to hide, light to carry yet, being .38 calibre with hollow point bullets, still packing a punch. The gun felt tiny in my hand. It was a Smith and Wesson five-shot revolver with a cut-down handle and only a one-inch barrel. I said, 'Tell me you've got a bigger one than this?' Baldrick pulled out a large standard revolver with a four-inch heavy-duty barrel with six shots in it. I said, 'Okay, you shoot first. I have to wait until I see the whites of their eyes.'

This was a really bad situation. For a few moments all we could see were two unknown blokes looking back toward us through the rear window. I was starting to panic, 'It must be Trevor, it doesn't look like Stacker.'

Baldrick said, 'Do you think they found the tape in Fran's bag?'

'Fucked if I know. They don't look happy.'

Baldrick said, 'Why would they be here? Are you going to get out?'

I said, 'I don't know. Fuck.' There was silence for a minute before I went on, 'One thing I do know is that if they don't kill Fran, I will.'

Fran's door slowly opened and she got out. She walked over to my driver's side window. I wound down my window. As she got close, I whispered, 'What the fuck is going on? Who are they?'

Fran leant down into my window and said, 'It's just Trevor and Eddie. Trevor wants to have a look at you.'

'Have a look at me?'

Fran said, 'He wants you to get out of the car and turn around.'

I wasn't happy. I got out, held my hands out from my sides and turned around. Fran gave me a big hug. She kissed me on the cheek as I kissed her. With her face an inch from mine I held Fran by both arms and said, 'Tell Trevor I don't want to meet him, I just want good gear cheap. Tell him I don't want to meet him. Nothing personal I just don't need to, okay?'

Fran said, 'You can't wait.'

She was right. She reached deep into the front of her pants and handed me a clear plastic bag containing two smaller bags full of cannabis and the $40 change.

I said, 'You okay?' Fran nodded.

'Tell Trevor if it's any good I'll take a pound next week.' She walked off back to her car. I called out, 'I can't believe I got change.'

She laughed and said, 'I bet you will.'

I drove off, asking Baldrick, 'Why'd she say that?'

Baldrick examined the two bags and said, 'There's been a bit of taxing going on in one of these bags.'

One bag looked half-empty. I said, 'How the fuck am I going to make money if she does that to me?'

Baldrick said, 'You're a cop, your pay doesn't change.'

'That's not the point. How's a drug trafficker meant to carve a decent living when every bastard in the world taxes my gear?

Then I've got Stacker chewing on it and Fran fucking sitting on it. I mean, Fuck!'

I drove back to the office. By the time we finished taking notes and putting the drugs through the property book, it was 9.15pm. I spent about an hour talking to Fran about what had happened. It turned out that as Fran and Sally were leaving with the gear they told Trevor that they were going to give it to Lenny. Trevor and Eddie got into the back of Fran's car and started asking Fran a thousand questions about me. Trevor said he wanted to see what Lenny looked like and how big Lenny was. Sally came on the phone and told me that while Fran was over at my car talking to me, he said to Sally, 'Hey Sally, why don't I get out and take the two ounces? I'll give you one'.

She told Trevor to stop joking around. Sally said Trevor sounded serious.

Fran and Sally then started to tell me about what happened at Trevor's house during the drug purchase. While Trevor left the flat to get the two ounces of cannabis, Donato and Trevor's wife Debbie were sitting in the kitchen reading a police brief. They were reading sections of it out aloud. Donato and Trevor were charged with trafficking a large amount of cannabis relating to a crop the cops had found in a small town east of Melbourne. They were particularly interested in one particular witness statement. Trevor returned a short time later with the cannabis. Sally followed him into the lounge room and asked Trevor about the witness who had made statements. Trevor said, 'He's going to be buried in concrete.'

Lots of crooks make idle threats but you had to take this one seriously. After all, the Pettingills were said to have buried one of their enemies under a concrete slab and then built an impressive barbecue on top of it. Fran and Sally again asked me if they were going to be safe. Safe when all this 'blows up' as

Fran put it. Fran said, 'Just wait till Kath and Trevor hear my tapes. I reckon that witness will be safe, they'll be too busy looking for Sally and me.' We all laughed. We always laughed. Despite the fact nothing at all was funny.

I passed on the information about the witness to the informant in the case. I told him exactly where the information had come from. The security of this operation was paramount, but when witnesses' lives are at risk, everything is done to protect them. If word got out that the witness protection program ever failed to protect its witnesses, it would not exist. People like Fran and Sally would not come forward.

The moment the girls collected evidence and made statements, I started to work closely with members of the witness protection program. For ongoing security reasons and because I don't wish to inform criminals how the program works, I am not going to detail operating procedures. Suffice to say that it would have to be one of **the** most professional units in Victoria Police. They leave nothing to chance. I believe Fran and Sally continued to risk their lives during this operation only because they had faith in the way the witness protection operated. Many a time I smiled to myself as I thought, 'The witness protection program is never going to be the same again once the girls arrive.'

Anyway, that night like all the others I didn't sleep much. I lay in bed looking up into the blackness thinking, 'Trevor you're a prick, trying to scare my girls like that. It worked. So Trevor wanted to see me. See how big I was. What I looked like. I don't think he would be all that scared of me robbing him. Not him, not Trevor Pettingill. Robbing me must be on the go. How can I stop him? Make him think there is more money to be made if he doesn't. Just don't give him the chance to rob me. Go to sleep. Worry about it later. Sleep. Sleep.'

A COUPLE of days went by. Days full of questions that had very few answers, heaps of paperwork and hours on the phone to Fran and Sally. On Monday, August 23, at 5.30pm, Trevor Pettingill again walked downstairs and into the 'poofters' place' as he called it. He picked up the phone and rang Fran.

Fran: Hello.

Trevor: It's Trevor.

Fran: How are ya?

Trevor: I've got 'green' for $4800 an elbow.

The word 'elbow' is a common drug term for a pound. It comes from the abbreviation 'lb' meaning a pound. Hardly a code. Trevor was again brief and to the point. He went on, 'I can do the 'white' (heroin) on Thursday or Friday.'

Fran asked Trevor to come over for a chat. At about 8 that evening Trevor Pettingill and Eddie Fiorello arrived at Fran's front door. Fran fired up her trusty handbag and they all sat in the lounge, including Sally. Trevor told Fran that he was willing to sell choof and smack to her bloke Lenny. He told her that he needed some good scales.

Trevor complained that his scales only weighed big stuff. Trevor wanted the little set of electronic scales that Fran mentioned she had some time ago.

Good old Fran said, 'No worries, you can take Lenny's.' Fran went to her bedroom and grabbed my set of scales. I had in fact bought these scales out of my very own money two years earlier. They cost me $420. Anyway. In front of Trevor and Eddie, Fran grabbed a knife and scratched a large 'L' for Lenny of the back of the scales.

Later that night Eddie drove his van home and Fran drove Trevor back to his place in Collingwood. Fran purchased a quarter ounce bag of choof from Trevor for $110. Fran only had $50 so Trevor gave her credit for the missing $60. Before

Fran left, Trevor said that he was the one who sent Stacker to us when we had bought the quarter ounce of heroin. Trevor said from now on we were to only deal with him. He also said that he could do the pound of choof for Lenny on Thursday. Trevor was keen to cut out Stacker. At this stage I was concerned about how Stacker would take being left out of our drug deals. We would have to tread carefully.

It wasn't long before we found out how Stacker took the idea about being left out. On Tuesday, August 24, at 8.15pm, Stacker rang Trevor and spoke about our heroin purchase, which was to happen at 1pm on Thursday – two days later. Trevor tried to tell Stacker that he was going to do the heroin deal. Stacker got upset and called Trevor a traitor for trying to cut him out. Trevor said, 'You keep fucking them around.'

Stacker said, 'If that fucking Lenny bloke tries to buy the heroin from you, I'm gunna hide under your stairwell and cut his fucking throat.'

The next morning, August 25, I arrived at work. Over our morning coffee Baldrick updated our crew about Stacker's latest threats. I hadn't slept much for weeks now. This job was a constant nightmare. I was struggling to hold it all together. This was now, without a doubt, the hardest time in 'the job' I'd ever had. It was also the most important. I kept trying to convince myself that I could do it, and myself really needed some convincing.

The strain must have started to show. I can't recall what it was that I said at that meeting, but it caused Steve to stand and call me into an interview room again. The way Steve spoke and walked off spelt danger. He appeared to be angry and disappointed in my behaviour. The crew fell silent as I stood up and followed. Not 'the room' again I thought. Then again maybe I needed 'the room'.

Steve again took his spot on the crooks' side of the table, but this time he didn't sit. I walked in and closed the door behind me. In a disappointed, almost angry, tone Steve said, 'You can't speak like that out there in front of people. They might think you're losing it.' The moment the door closed behind me, I realised I could not hide what was going on inside any more. The last time I was in this room I needed to cry. This time I had to. Tears flowed. I looked Steve in the eye and said, 'This is the most important thing I have ever done. I've got the girls, I'm trying to keep them on track and happy. We're getting behind in statements from them, then there's my statements, there's Stacker the fucking lunatic and we're so close to Trevor.'

Steve saw Lachlan. Saw a Lachlan who was not coping at all. I continued, 'I can do this. I just need something, I don't know what.' I flopped into a chair. As I sat there, I said, 'I'm the strongest bastard in the world.'

With a slight laugh I added, 'Just ask me, I'll tell you.' After a pause I added, 'I'm not crying, I had chopped up onions for breakfast. I love onions.'

Steve quietly said, 'Lochy, if this job was easy, anyone could do it.'

I thought, 'That's right, I've been chosen for this job.' Well, I sort of chose myself but it sounded better to say I was chosen. Those few words were like throwing me a lifeline.

Trying to excuse my crying, I said, 'I'm an emotional bastard.'

In his quiet way Steve added, 'Let's pick a date we can work toward. A date when it will all end. Sally and Fran can't keep this up forever.'

What a great idea – an end. I laughed and said, 'That's it, we have to think of the girls. They're not as strong as me.' We both chuckled. Steve gave me a reassuring touch on the shoulder.

I said, 'You do know the girls could do this forever?' Steve nodded.

I looked into his face and said, 'They've done a great job, ay?'

Steve said, 'Great job, but we still need more statements.'

Just when I was starting to feel good he had to mention taking statements. They were a huge pain in the arse. I said, 'We've still got heaps to do.'

Steve said, ' September 16. We can all aim at that date.'

I responded, 'I feel better already.'

Steve was bloody good at his job. Without saying it, he had told me that it was all getting a bit much and it had to end. I felt fantastic. An end was now tangible. So was sleep. Steve was the best at what he does, which was control. He had controlled one of the greatest undercover operatives I've met, David Barlow, during the biggest undercover operation ever undertaken by Victoria Police. Steve had confidence in me.

This meeting was almost over. I just needed to know something. I said, 'Now as it stands, Stacker wants to cut my throat, Trevor's sized me up for a robbery and I've got to meet them both at one o'clock tomorrow. Maybe I could do the deal via video link?'

Steve said with a smile, 'There are cunning plans out there we haven't even thought of yet.'

I said, 'I need a meeting, no money, no drugs, nothing. A meet and greet with Trevor and Stacker.'

'That sounds good,' Steve said. 'Do a bit of bonding.'

I went on, 'With Stacker I'll find something, anything you know, that's nice about the bloke and then exaggerate it in my mind.'

Deep down I knew liking Stacker was never going to happen.

I rang Fran. I asked her to invite Trevor, Stacker and Eddie over tonight to her place. Ask them over for a bong or whatever. I said, 'I'm sure you and Sally could entertain them.' My plan was to arrive unannounced.

AT 7.55pm, I arrived at Fran's home. Eddie's white van was parked on her front lawn. I took a deep breath and searched myself one last time. Just to make sure I didn't have anything on me that might give me away. To my relief I was clean. The front door was open. I walked in and found everyone down the back of the house. In a small room at the back of the kitchen I found Stacker, Eddie, Sally and Fran sitting at a small table having dinner. I excused myself for interrupting their meal. Stacker actually seemed pleased to see me. He stood and introduced me to Eddie. Eddie was a short stocky bloke with a huge smile and a large moustache. From the moment I met him he never stopped smiling and making funny comments. I sat at the table and grabbed a chop from Fran's plate.

Stacker towered over the rest of us sitting at the table. His booming voice never stopped. If he wasn't talking, he was laughing at the very unfunny things he was saying. Stacker kept talking about bashing people. Eddie said, 'He's good at bashing his mates.'

Stacker and Eddie spoke about what happened just over a week ago when they all had a fight at Trevor's flat. They had spent the whole day drinking. Stacker said, 'Eddie here, my mate, right, disrespected me so I bashed him, right.'

Eddie said, 'So I dropped him, I won the fight.'

Stacker said, 'I grabbed me knife and slashed all four tyres of his van.' We all laughed.

Eddie said, 'That's not the funny part, right. Me, Trevor and Stacker go off down the street and Stacker found this truck, right. We jack it up and steal the wheels.'

Stacker said, 'We carry and roll all four wheels right back to Trevor's flat and they don't fucking fit on Eddie's van.'

By this stage we were all laughing. Eddie continued, 'So I bashed Stacker for picking the wrong tyres to steal and the whole thing started all over again.'

Stacker said, 'It was almost daylight by the time we'd finished.'

Fran asked Stacker to tell me how he got his nickname. Stacker laughed at the thought of it. Stacker started bragging about how he deliberately overdosed a couple of junkies and they died in his flat. He said that the first couple of times he rang the cops and they came around and he was pissed off because they wouldn't leave. Stacker was laughing as he said, 'Then a while later, right, a couple more people died that I didn't like, right. They were in the bathroom, right. So I dragged them out my front door and left them there. I stacked one on top of the other.' We all laughed. Stacker added, 'But that's not the funny part, then I rang the cops because I couldn't get out of the flat because of the bodies.' We all laughed again.

This was 'over dinner' conversation. Drug dealers talking about bashing people and self-confessed killers talking about body disposal problems. I laughed as I thought, 'What the fuck am I doing here?' But wait – there's more ... Stacker leant forward over the table and in a serious voice said, 'Lenny, do you know anyone that's got AIDS?'

'No, not that I know of.'

Stacker said, 'If you find someone, right, I want you to get a couple of syringes full of their blood, right, so I can infect a couple of people I don't like.'

That stopped me laughing. I said, 'Okay, I'll do that.'

Fran in a serious voice said, 'That's not very nice, Stacker.'

In a matter of fact way, Stacker added, 'I'll pay for them.'

I said, 'No worries.'

I had no doubt he was serious and no doubt one of those 'couple of people' was me. If he was trying to scare me it was working. I thought, 'Look on the bright side, he must trust me if he starts bragging about killing people. Maybe. No, he's just stupid.'

I asked Stacker where Trevor was. Stacker told me he was at home being a good dad. Stacker said, 'Tomorrow, $3500 for the quarter ounce of smack.'

I said, 'I want to do that first, then I'm doing something with Trevor. At one o'clock right. I want it quick. If it all goes well I want a lot more. I can move a lot more shit, it just has to be like the other shit I got.' Stacker held out his hand for me to shake. I shook his hand with a serious firm grip. Stacker smiled and said, 'Just show some faith in me, Lenny.'

I'd had enough for one night. I said goodbye to everyone and started to leave. Eddie said, 'Where ya going?'

I said, 'I have to drive to Tootgarook.' Tootgarook is a small bayside suburb about 45 minutes drive away.

Eddie asked, 'What are you doing there?'

'A bit of this and a bit of that,' I replied.

Eddie said, 'What street?' I felt like telling him to fuck up and mind his own business. Be nice, I thought. With a reluctant tone, I said, 'Melville Street.'

Eddie said, 'I only asked because I used to live in Leopold Street.' Leopold Street runs into Melville Street.

I said, 'Oh yeah, with the boat ramp at the end. When I was a kid I used to go flounder fishing with a spear and a spotlight along the beach there.'

Inside, I sighed with relief. Eddie was testing me out. I thought, 'I nearly slipped up. Lucky I picked a place I knew.

Stop thinking about luck. It's not luck. I can't rely on luck. If I do I could be unlucky.'

As an undercover operative, a small almost insignificant question like that means everything. If Eddie was to find me bullshitting once, about anything, to him I would be a bull-shitter for life. Even if a first impression could be changed over time, I was certainly not going to be undercover long enough to do it. As I was leaving, Eddie told me he would be there at Trevor's tomorrow. I called out goodbye to the girls and left in my car.

I felt really good. The meeting had gone better than I expected. As usual, the best part for me was that it had finished. As I drove toward home, I felt incredibly drained. I needed an emotion transfusion. After a few quiet moments in my car alone, I rang Steve and told him all that was done and said.

Steve said, 'So you feel good about doing the deals tomorrow?'

I said, 'Good? No. It should go all right, though. I think Eddie's on my side. He seemed good. He never said so but I'm pretty sure Eddie is the cannabis supplier.' I didn't hit it off with Stacker but it was the opposite with Eddie. He was easy to like, you know, a sort of nice drug trafficking thug.

Later that night I rang Fran. She was laughing. I could hear Stacker and Eddie in the background. Fran said in a loud voice so everyone could hear, 'Hey Lenny, you've got a new nickname.'

'What?' I asked.

Fran said, 'KGB. Eddie recons you're the secret police.'

I laughed and said, 'Yeah, well, you tell Eddie that if he comes to Trevor's tomorrow I'll arrest him.'

That Eddie was a funny bastard. Too funny, sometimes.

From then on Eddie always referred to me as KGB. The really funny part was that Eddie thought it was a joke. Funny, isn't it? I went home that night and drank and drank and drank.

THURSDAY, August 26. I arrived at work about 8am. All the crew was busy. I asked Baldrick if the money was ready. As usual the money was 'on the way'. In the mess room I found Duck's Bum and asked him about the money. Getting the money on time was a neverending hassle for me. As if I didn't have enough to worry about. We had several briefings with surveillance teams, bosses and our technical support unit. I spoke to the girls about ten times that morning. Just in case you're wondering why I would speak to the girls ten times, three of the calls revolved around what they should wear to today's drug deal. Say no more.

I organised more tapes for Fran and myself. In a flash it was almost midday. The deal was set for 1pm. For the first time I intended to drive the girls right up to the front of Trevor's flat. I wanted to make a good first impression with Trevor. I had thought of a way I could hide the money. I grabbed a Pepsi can out of the bin next to my desk. I quickly cut the bottom of the can off. I then started searching other detectives' desk drawers for a stubby holder. In about the fourth drawer I found the perfect one. It was made of soft blue coloured neoprene and had a large emblem with the letters 'ABS'. Below this were the words 'Auto Brake Service' printed on it. I stuck the can into the can holder. This would be perfect.

It's hard to describe how I felt shortly before a big undercover job. Looking back, I know I would change heaps in that hour or so before the deal. Some might say, not change, just get worse. Before every job I became aggressive, bombastic, pedantic, loud, demanding, talkative and most of all egotistical. I've seen it happen to other undercovers but I think I was pretty bad. Around the office everyone calls it 'U/C syndrome'. For me it was uncontrollable. I think it happened to me because I was about to do something difficult, important, alien, frightening and obviously dangerous. I would become the most important person in the world. I insisted on perfection from those around me.

Everyone else in the office was going to sit in a safe place for the next few hours. Maybe the undercover syndrome was caused by a part of me that wanted all these safe observers to pay. To see what I was going through. The police force often preaches: 'You're never alone'. To which I say 'bullshit'. As an undercover operative I was most certainly alone. I have never felt more alone in my life. At times I think the syndrome was my subconscious surfacing, telling me to fire up. I was about to need and use every life experience I'd had. That is what makes a good effective undercover. So I believed.

I wired myself for sound. I left the office and was driven to a nearby back street. This time I lay on my back and didn't crush my sunnies. I stepped into and drove off in my newly acquired 4WD Holden Pajero. A friend of a friend had a mate who worked in a nearby vehicle auction house. I'd borrowed it for a few days. That was my story, anyway. I picked up Fran and Sally at an auto repair shop in Carlton. Then I parked in a side street. It was seven minutes to 1pm. Fran said, 'What are you doing? Go we're gunna be late.'

I said, 'Fran, I'm waiting for the money.' Fran and Sally started screaming, 'We can't be late. Trevor goes off at Stacker all the time. Trevor hates people late.'

I said, 'It's not me. The money is coming.' I was furious. I telephoned Steve, 'Where's the money? Steve I don't need this shit, mate.' I told Steve that I would not be doing this again if the money was not ready hours early. The money had to be withdrawn from a bank, put through property books, cash books and so on. At five minutes to one o'clock an unmarked car pulled up alongside me and gave me the cash.

I drove off toward Trevor's flat. As I was driving I gave some money to Fran and some to Sally. I asked them to make two bundles. One $3500 for the seven grams of rock heroin and one $4800 for the pound of green. When they finished, I put $3500 into the can. The $4800 was made up of three separate bundles of cash held together with rubber bands. I put them inside my leather bumbag. As we got closer, I asked Fran to ring Trevor and tell him we were arriving. Fran said, 'We're gunna be about a minute late.' As Fran hung up she spewed out the words, 'Trevor said, "Just because Stacker fucks you around, it don't mean you can fuck me around".'

I said, 'For Christ sake spare me grief over one minute.'

Fran said, 'Lenny, not you but they could bash us for being late, Lenny.' I hadn't thought of that. As I drove into Dight Street, I saw Trevor and Eddie leaning against Trevor's front balcony. From this balcony he had a clear view of the whole street. Eddie wore his normal huge smile. Trevor's face looked serious and not happy at all. As I parked, I said, 'Girls, hang on a second, take a deep breath. Let's work together. We can do this.' The girls were fuming mad.

I said, 'Detective Senior Constable Lachlan McCulloch speaking from the crime department drug squad. Today I'm Lenny Rogers and I'm with B2 and G6. I'm outside Trevor Pettingill's home and the girls are leaving my car.' In a sarcastic voice Fran said, 'Hello, I'm B2', and Sally said, 'G6 here, and we're gunna do it right now.' I said, 'Girls, remember, be quick with Stacker, tell Trevor that I don't want to meet him, I just want good gear cheap.' The girls got out of my car and walked toward the stairwell that led straight to Trevor's front door. Above me I heard and saw Trevor calling out to the girls. 'Tell Lenny to come up.'

Fran stopped and said, 'Trev, Lenny wants us to do it.' Trevor changed his tone. 'Tell him to come up here; I want to meet the bloke,' he demanded. Fran stepped back to my car and opened the passenger side door and blurted, 'Lenny, Trevor wants you to come up'.

I said, 'Okay.'

Fran said 'Now, come on.'

I said, 'Fran, this is me trying not to be too keen.'

Fran was sick of me being me and said, 'For fuck sake this is what you wanted, this is it.'

I said, 'Fran, wait. I'm trying to be cool.'

I checked myself for the tenth time. I stepped out of my car and locked it. I mumbled to myself, 'This is a bad area and there could be criminals about.'

I looked up and nodded my head at Trevor. He nodded back. I casually walked up the stairs. There was a hell of a lot of talking coming from Trevor's flat. As I walked up to his security door, I noticed it was made of heavy steel. As I approached, it swung open. A woman of about 30 held it open and said, 'Hello, I'm Debbie. Lenny is it?'

I said, 'Yeah, Lenny, pleased to meet you.' I recognised her from photographs. She was smiling and extremely pregnant. As I tried to get past her and her baby Stacker barged out of the flat. He looked very strung out. He was sweating and shaking all over. Debbie let go of the door and I stepped into the kitchen.

Stacker came in and held out his hand and said, 'I need the money'. I looked at Fran, who was standing behind Stacker. I handed Stacker the Pepsi can that was inside the neoprene holder. Stacker thought I was offering him a drink. I said, 'It's the money, open it.'

Stacker pulled the can and grabbed the money from inside the holder. He handed the holder and the can back to me and rushed out of the flat. I gave Fran a little kiss on the cheek and said, 'Good luck, don't be long.'

To my left Eddie was sitting on a couch in the lounge room. Down a small hallway to my right I heard a toilet flush and another male appeared. He was the spitting image of Eddie except he was much uglier and had short hair. He held out his hand and said, 'Lenny, is it?'

I said, 'Yes it is.'

'I'm George, Eddie's brother. Look, Trevor is just in a meeting at the moment so you can wait in here.' George led me a whole metre into the lounge. Eddie smiled, stood up and shook my hand. I sat down next to him on the couch. We both faced the television. I put the can and its holder on a glass coffee table in the centre of the room. About three metres off to my right were two sliding glass doors, which led onto the balcony. I could see through the curtains that Trevor was standing out there talking to an unknown male. I laughed to myself, 'Trevor's in a business meeting. You're kidding me?'

I sat there watching George. The phone would ring, George would answer it, put the phone down, walk past me and open one of the glass doors. He'd say something to Trevor, Trevor would tell George to piss off and he'd go back to the phone. George needed to go to secretarial school. Sally was talking to Debbie in the kitchen. I sat there thinking at a million miles an hour. I kept telling myself to relax. After about ten minutes, I started to get worried about Fran. Then the male Trevor had been talking to left and Trevor closed the glass door behind him and stayed on the balcony.

George rushed up to the door and opened it. He had a quick chat to Trevor and closed the door. George took two small steps and stood in front of me. He said, 'Trevor will see you now.'

I said, 'Sweet.' I thought this is nothing like I expected.

George slid the door open and I stepped onto the balcony. Trevor was leaning back with his arms folded across his chest like he owned this world and all that was in it. He gave me a smirky smile like he knew more than I ever would and casually unfolded his right arm. We shook hands. I said, 'Trevor, I'm Lenny.' He stayed where he was, leaning back against the rail.

Trevor said, 'What did you think of the …' with two fingers of his right hand he tapped the inside of his left elbow '… that you bought last week?'

He obviously meant, 'the heroin' but didn't want to say it. As we spoke he slowly moved forward and shook my hand. I realised that it wasn't just me that he didn't want to say the word heroin in front of. He had spent his whole life with either his house actually bugged or him believing it was. I said, 'Yeah it was quite good.'

He said, 'What, you've had better?'

'Yeah, I tried to cut it four times but it didn't work. I ended up cutting two to three times depending who I was selling it to.'

He said, 'It was very hard, the stuff you got. It depends how they wash it when they make it. So you reckon you've had better, have you?'

I said, 'Yeah, I'm not complaining. For the price though I reckon it should be better.'

'At $3500 a quarter, you're paying $14,000 an ounce,' he said. You're paying only $12,000 if you want an ounce off me.'

I said, 'At the moment with all the fucking hassles I'm

having with Stacker, I'm only buying quarters. Trust, when trust comes so does the money.'

Trevor smiled and nodded. 'Stacker fucks everyone around. You're far better off buying an ounce for $12,000 than fucking around with quarters.'

We both started to talk about our difficulties with Stacker. We spoke of the aborted drug deal in Yarraville. I was happy to hear Trevor actually blame Stacker for all the problems that day.

Trevor started asking me questions about heroin again. From the outset, I knew I could hold my own in any decent drug dealing conversation. I'd been a trafficker for years. It's just that with me there was a 'twist'. A little 'twist of the wrist' at the end of most drug deals. With Trevor I felt confident to stick with him talking about the technical aspects of diluting, cutting, packaging. I did hold my own for a while. Then he said, 'So how do you cut it?'

I said, 'In a grinder.'

'What grinder?'

'A small coffee grinder.'

He asked me how, when, why, where, and the ins and outs of a duck's bum. I could have said, 'Mind your own business' but that would only have made him suspicious. His barrage of questions caused me to realise who I was talking to. My mind screamed, 'Stop, you can't compete with this guy. He is son of Kath, Trevor Pettingill for Christ's sake. All his life, his whole world has been trafficking heroin.'

I looked at him and said, 'How do **you** do it?' Then I made myself look very interested in every word he said. It was easy because I was – very interested. In a second, I'd gone from swimming upstream without any arms to zooming down stream in one of those New Zealand jet boats. From then on, he would teach me the world of drug trafficking according to Trevor Pettingill.

I am not well known for my listening ability. In fact, I rarely do. But I amazed myself this time. He changed. I found that I was talking to a different bloke. I realised it had all been an act. Trevor wasn't as arrogant as he had first portrayed. When he met me he must have been trying to live up to his name. He suddenly became very friendly and polite. I had my preconceived ideas about what he was like. He must have thought I was going to be different as well.

What helped was we had a common problem. Stacker. I said, 'I am never dealing with Stacker again. I know he's a friend of yours and that, but a good simple ...' here I tapped the inside of my left arm indicating heroin '... deal is just not in him. He can't do it.'

Trevor said, 'If I'd known he was going to take twenty minutes we could have gone and got the green by now and got it over with.'

I said, 'I'm ready when you are.' I patted my bumbag indicating I had the money.

Trevor changed the subject and said, 'You know he was going to get it out in Footscray the other week.' He was speaking about our failed heroin purchase.

I said, 'I'm sure he was but how can I trust a guy who was threatening to shoot me and bash me one second and trust him the next?'

Trevor said, 'Stacker that day was doing my business and knows that I would fix him if he did the wrong thing.' Then he asked, 'What's it with you and the girls?'

I said, 'I fuck 'em and that. I'm trying to teach them how to deal, you know, properly.'

Trevor said, 'I hear Fran's husband wants to kill you.'

'Really?' I said. 'At the moment he'll have to get in line.'

Dangerous game this drug dealing. Trevor's brother Victor Peirce was in jail with Fran's husband. They all must talk.

The comment I made about having sex with the girls was to come back and haunt me at future court proceedings. Can you believe the defence thought it was true? How anyone can find truth amongst so much deception is beyond me. Anyway.

George opened the sliding glass door and handed Trevor a bong. It was already lit. Trevor ducked down below the height of the balcony rail and took a deep breath of smoke. He stood and offered it to me. I said, 'No thanks mate, I want to stay clear, I've got a lot to do.'

Trevor said, 'All right.'

I added, 'That's if Stacker ever gets back.' George took the bong back inside.

Seconds later George opened the sliding door again. He said, 'Shabbo's here to see you.' My heart stopped. I looked off the balcony. It was about six metres down onto a concrete footpath. I thought, 'Two broken ankles but I'll be all right. If Brydon Shabbo walks onto this balcony he will see Detective Senior Constable Lachlan McCulloch from Carlton CIB Branch, not Lenny.' I'd arrested him twice. On both occasions we had to interview him with a firm hand, if you know what I mean. I describe myself as a lover not a fighter. Well, he was the exact opposite.

Trevor dismissed George and said, 'Tell him I'm in a meeting.' There is a God. We'd just started talking again when George came back. He said, 'Trevor, Shabbo said it's real important and it can't wait.' Again I thought, 'I am jumping off this balcony.'

Trevor clenched his teeth and said, 'Tell him to piss off and come back later, I'm busy.' George was obviously distressed at the thought of upsetting Shabbo again with this news. As George closed the door, Trevor laughed and said, 'George is funny'.

I said, 'Eddie's a funny fucker.'

Trevor said, 'One time I was standing here on this balcony with George. Cops pulled up in a plain-clothes cop car.'

I know cars can't wear plain clothes but crooks always call them plain-clothes cop cars for some unknown reason. Anyway. Trevor went on, 'The driver wound down his window and said, "Hey mate, what's your name?" The cop knew me and wanted to know who George was. George was about to tell the copper his name so I stopped him by kicking him with my foot. Through the corner of my mouth I whispered, "Tell them that you know your rights and you don't have to tell them nothin'".

'So George thought that was a great idea. He looked down to the coppers and said, "I know me rights, I don't have to tell you nothin". This pissed the cops right off. I started laughing. It was funny, deliberately getting George in trouble.'

I said, 'I don't think they'd like smart-arses.'

Trevor said, 'They don't mate, so they asked him a couple of times for his name and I'm kicking him and telling him, "Go catch real criminals, I know me rights".

'George said, "Why don't youse guys piss off and go catch some real criminals". So the cops went up and down the street talking to people and that. Then the next morning George comes over to my place and he's all bashed and that.

'I said, "What happened?" And George goes, "The jacks kicked my fucking door in this morning and they kicked the shit out of me. They said, 'This is for being a smart-arse'".'

We were laughing. Trevor laughed so much he could hardly talk. He went on, 'Then George said, "Before they left, they kicked me a few more times and said, 'Give this to Trevor, smart-arse".'

I said, 'You're a bastard.'

Trevor's story was just like my cop stories. He went on to tell me several more. One difference between our stories was that in his, the crooks always won. Except George, of course. Another difference was that he could tell his stories. For once I just listened:

Trevor: Do you know Lenny, I've never done a day's work in me life?

Lenny: Not one?

Trevor: Well, a bloke gave me a job as a waiter once. I said, 'Fuck that I'm not gunna wait on people.'

Lenny: You've never worked ever?

Trevor: Me whole life I've done nothing.

I laughed.

Lenny: Have you ever tried to get a job?

Trevor laughed.

Trevor: Never. Never.

I thought, 'The sentencing judge might find that very interesting.' I was right. That bragging was to come back and bite him.

We were sick of waiting. Trevor said, 'Let's do the green.' I followed Trevor back inside his flat.

I grabbed Sally on the way out. Trevor asked me to drive him down the road to pick it up. He sat in the front seat and Sally jumped in the back. Trevor directed me down several streets and lanes. As we drove, he told me how pissed off he was at Stacker.

He said, 'No more Stacker. From now on, you just deal with me.'

He got me to stop outside the rear gate of a small auto repair shop. Trevor entered and spoke to a bloke in a blue shirt. He walked out of sight for a few moments.

Sally and I had a rushed conversation about Fran, Trevor and what was happening in this lane. Sally was worried about Fran. There was nothing I could do. I said, 'We have to just get Fran and get the fuck out of here. I've had enough.'

Sally said, 'Lenny, just don't trust Trevor.'

'I'm not,' I said.

Sally said, 'Nothing is what it seems Lenny. Don't trust what they say.'

I opened the bumbag and slipped the cash into the Pepsi can. After all it had worked once.

Trevor came into sight carrying a Huggies nappy bag. He stepped back in and said, 'Let's go'. I drove a couple of streets away and pulled over in a quiet side street. Trevor handed me the bag. Inside was a football-shaped object. I ripped a small hole in the side of it. It felt like it weighed about a pound. Once I broke through its side there was a strong smell of cannabis. The object was about a pound of cannabis 'head' wrapped tightly in a large amount of clear plastic wrap. 'Excellent,' I said,

Trevor said, 'It stinks doesn't it?' (meaning it was good quality).

I said, 'Yeah mate, that's fine.'

I grabbed the Pepsi can and handed it to him. He pulled the can out of the holder and removed three bundles of cash. He handed me back both parts of the can. I put them on the console between us.

Each bundle was tightly wrapped in rubber bands. I said, 'Four thousand eight hundred, mate.'

Trevor grabbed one of the bundles and said, 'How much is in this one?' I thought, 'Shit, I have no idea.'

I said, 'There's other bundles there.' Trevor grabbed another bundle. He held it up and said, 'What about this one, how much?'

I said, 'It's all there. I counted it with the girls on the way here.' I felt like an idiot, I should know what's what. As I drove back to Trevor's flat he counted the money. At one point he said, 'Why is most of this money new?'

I said, 'Sometimes I end up with shitloads of small notes like fives and tens. I don't like carrying large lumps of fucking cash so every now and then I go to a bank and get them to give me fifty and hundred dollar notes.'

Trevor said, 'Yeah?' He didn't sound convinced.

I added, 'Can you believe that I've had banks charge me five dollars to count my money and give me larger notes?'

Trevor said, 'Yeah they do, if you give them coins and that as well they charge you.'

I said, 'I always go to different banks so no-one gets suss.'

We were almost back at Trevor's when he said, 'I'll give you another tip, right.'

'Yeah,' I said. I was interested in Trevor's tips. Holding his head slightly back as though he was delivering a sermon, he said, 'When you're doing a big deal always organise it after 4.30 in the afternoon'.

I said, 'Yeah? Why's that?'

Trevor said, 'Because all the banks are closed. If you're being set up by undercover cops, they can't get the money out of the bank.'

I fucking nearly died. He was spot-on, totally correct – at least at that time.

I said, 'Fuck, I never thought of that.' I thought, 'From now on Lenny, have lots of money at the office in our safe and make it all small old notes.'

I thought of a great way to change the subject. I said, 'Fucking Stacker. Never again, that's it.'

Trevor said, 'Fuck Stacker. From now on you want slow or the green you just come to me. I can't believe him. He doesn't think ahead you see Lenny. He doesn't think of your side.'

I said, 'Stacker thinks of Stacker's side.'

He said, 'You're right, Lenny.'

I said, 'I'll ring you. I'll leave it to you to talk to him.'

When we got back, Fran was standing out the front. She looked very upset. As I stopped the car, I said, 'This doesn't look good.' We all got out of the car.

I said, 'You got it?

She said, 'I thought he was going to rape me.'

'What?'

Fran said, 'He pinned me down and was going to rape me.'

'Did he?' I asked.

She said, 'No.'

I said, 'Are you okay?'

'Yeah.'

But she clearly wasn't okay.

Trevor was standing there listening to this. He said, 'Hey Fran, has Stacker got the money?'

Fran said, 'Yeah, course he has.'

Trevor looked like he was furious and about to explode. He quickly walked up the stairs back toward his flat.

Fran and Sally were talking. I looked at my watch. Stacker had been gone for 55 minutes. I said, 'Fran, Stacker's ripped us off $3500, has he?'

Fran said, 'He said he was trying to find the gook.'

I could feel myself shaking with rage. I started to think about my next move. Do I search for him? What do I do? What do I say? I asked the girls for a cigarette lighter. There was a voice directly above me. I looked up and it was Trevor. I thought, 'Christ, I hope we didn't say anything wrong.' Trevor said, 'Here you are' and dropped down a lighter. He said, 'You can keep it. I'm sorry you've been fucked around so much.' Trevor spun around and swore at someone. I heard Stacker's voice. He must have come up the stairs at the back. I heard Trevor say, 'Stacker, speak to Lenny not to me.'

A moment later a very apologetic Stacker walked up and handed me a small clear plastic package. He said, 'Sorry, it took so long, right. The gook was late, right, so I bashed him. He won't be late again.'

I said, 'I don't want to talk, Stacker. You just speak to him.' I pointed to Trevor.

I turned toward my car and said, 'Come on, girls, let's get the fuck out of here.' The girls and I got in. It was over. Thank Christ. I needed to be in a safe place. I turned the ignition key and nothing happened. Fran and Sally were in the middle of telling each other about all the day's events when I said to my vehicle, 'You are kidding me, right?' The car wasn't kidding. The battery was somehow flat. I hit the steering wheel with my right hand and then slumped my head onto it. Looking down at my knees, I said, 'There must be an easier way to make a living.'

All of a sudden Stacker's voice boomed, 'Open the bonnet.' I searched for the catch. Next second I had Trevor, Eddie, George and Stacker all helping me. Worst of all they kept asking me questions. I was sick and tired of everything. I did not need questions. My brain was drained and I just needed out. They were asking, 'Where'd you get the car?'

'How old is it?'

'Can you get me one?'

'Can I have a drive?'

I stopped a passing car and asked the bloke if he could help. The bloke looked at my motley crew and drove off. Second thoughts, I wouldn't help me either. Stacker walked straight out in front of the next passing car. He got their jumper leads. With Stacker, it was more like a robbery than a request for help, but it worked. My 4WD finally started. As I went to drive off, Trevor again apologised and told me to go straight to him for 'anything'.

As I reversed out of my parking spot, Stacker ran up to my driver's side window. In a sickly sucky voice he said, 'Can you give me some of that smoke, Lenny?' I looked into his face and sighed. I needed to lie down. Without saying a word, I reached down to the passenger seat floor and grabbed a small piece of choof from the hole in my pound bag, gave it to Stacker and drove off. As I drove away I was hit by relief, happiness, elation and anger. Fran and Sally were drained. It had been a hard day at the office.

Before these drug deals, I would convince myself that it wasn't dangerous. I believed my own bullshit just so I could do the job required. I'd convinced myself it was safe because I was so fucking good. The more I took risks and got away with it, the more invincible I became in my own mind. I believed every word I told myself. I had to.

We'd been at Trevor's for an hour and twenty minutes. It's hard to describe how draining that short time was. I never really ever got back what some of these meetings took away from me. Some people push their boundaries. I was starting to think that I didn't have any – that I could get away with anything. But the truth is, there's always a price. A scar on the soul.

I rang Steve and told him the good news. We were the proud owners of nearly a pound of cannabis and seven grams, less a nibble or two, of rock heroin. Fran had to tell Steve about how she was nearly raped by Stacker while she was doing the drug deal and Sally gave him a full rundown of everything else. I dropped the girls back at their car. They rambled on about how they were quitting and not going to help us any more. I knew they were kidding and returned to the office. As I snuck in the back way and entered the car park in Russell Street police station, I felt safe again. As I walked up the stairs to the drug squad office, I felt sensational. This was always my best time. I was safe, everyone was safe and I had heaps of drugs. Most of all I had great incriminating evidence on tape. This was a special day because I knew I had nailed Trevor.

I FELT twenty feet tall as I walked into my office. I handed all the drugs to Bigmore and made my way to my desk. Questions came from everyone. A few minutes later, interest had died down and I started to tell Baldrick the finer details. I pulled out the Pepsi can from the stubby holder and asked him if it was his. Baldrick said, 'That's mine. What are you doing with it?'

'I hid the money inside.' I showed Baldrick the cut can. In disbelief Baldrick said, 'What? What did you do?'

I said, 'I handed it to Stacker and he took the money out then I handed it to Trevor and he took the money out. Why?'

Baldrick reached over and snatched the holder from my hand. He said, 'On one side it says, ABS, Auto Brake Service and on the other, in bright red large print it says, 'MELBOURNE DEMONS POLICE FOOTBALL CLUB'.'

I said, 'Bullshit!' and grabbed it from him. I could not believe it. There it was in big red letters. I felt sick. Baldrick laughed out loud. I could tell he was about to tell the whole office. I went right up to his face and said, 'Quick, come with me.' I dragged him into an interview room. I shut the door. I was shaking. 'Mate, if you tell anyone I did that I'm gone,' I said. 'People will think I'm a fuckwit.'

He said, 'You are, you are. I can't believe you actually handed this to Stacker.'

I said, 'And Trevor, and I left it standing there on the coffee table for ages right in front of everyone. I only saw the ABS part.' I sat down and still felt sick.

I said, 'I'd have been gone. If one of them had held it up and said, 'What's this, fucking police football club shit?' I would have just looked at it and died. I reckon I'm good, just ask me, but I don't think I could have got out of that one. I'd have just gone into vapour lock.'

Baldrick said, 'Well at the very least they would have searched you.'

I could not afford for this stupid act to get out. I begged my very good mate, now even better mate, to never tell anyone. I said, 'We keep lots of secrets, right. Well this one has to be on a whole new level. From now on, this level will be called, um, the "stubby holder level".'

Baldrick said, 'Okay, okay, I understand. This can't get out. It'll make me look bad because I'm your mate. You know this is bad, I still can't believe it.'

I said, 'I just thought of it at the last minute. I wanted to look sneaky and professional, hiding the money.' We shook hands. I had to trust him never to tell. We went back to our desks.

Some of the crew asked, 'What's wrong, what happened?' I just spoke about how difficult the drug deals were. I had to get my mind off the stubby holder. It wasn't a healthy thing for me to think about.

I walked over to the next building and met my mate Dale. He was in charge of the audio section. Dale knew all about our operation. He had to. He assisted me to obtain the best sound product I could get. After all, the whole job revolved around evidence obtained by either Fran or myself.

Over the years I'd had many tape recorders fail for many reasons. I needed to make sure this one worked. Dale opened the sound room, took my tape and fired up a wall of computerised sound equipment. I closed the door behind us. No outside noise could penetrate the walls, which were more than a foot thick. Massive speakers and sub-woofers surrounded us as Dale pushed buttons and turned dials. I sat on a stool in the middle of the small room. The second that sound crackled from the speakers I closed my eyes and was instantly flown back into my car. Back with Fran and Sally. I had Dale fast forward the tape and heard Trevor speak. It had worked beautifully. I left Dale to do his job.

My crew wanted to know what Trevor Pettingill was like. They wanted to know all the details. It was an exciting time for me as I was very happy about how I had got on so well with Trevor. It was very difficult for me to talk about getting on well with a bloke who had just been acquitted of executing two of our colleagues.

I found myself having to be very careful about what I said. I was incredibly proud of what I had just done. Trevor was going to do jail time. All I needed now was to get some serious amounts of powders from him. Internally it was difficult for me to like a person I despised so much.

I was having a huge struggle with myself. To buy drugs from Trevor, he had to trust me and I had to trust him. For us to trust each other we had to become friends to some degree. I felt uneasy about the fact that he was easy to like in many ways. Maybe I was just fascinated by his world and his reputation. What helped was my complete and over-riding passion to get him as much jail time as I could.

Driving home after work I couldn't stop thinking about the stubby holder. I recall someone once saying, 'People only pay attention to what they discover for themselves'. I had discovered that I was not as infallibly clever as I thought. I made a mental note to try to outsmart others, not myself.

CHAPTER 6

Trust

This is all he knows.
This is all he does.
I hate drug dealers.

OVER the next few days, our crew was kept busy preparing briefs of evidence against all the major players. We now had a full-time crew of fourteen detectives. Each member was given specific duties. The listening device in Kath Pettingill's home was proving of little use. Her screaming grandchildren drowned out any talk of drug trafficking. The telephone intercepts revealed that Eddie Fiorello was Trevor Pettingill's cannabis supplier. Trevor was also buying something from Donato Corsi but we weren't sure what.

Steve put the pressure on all of us by insisting we get more statements from the girls. Steve rotated the worst job of all – entertaining Fran's children. Anyone who had performed this duty insisted they would happily resign before doing it again. Apparently the kids turned fun parlours into torture chambers and quiet movie theatres into fun parlours.

One of my jobs was to coordinate all of the above. Once the kids were extracted from the motel room, the statements would begin. Fran and Sally were always in separate motel rooms so their statements were independent. These were very difficult and busy times. We detectives were all getting paid. Fran and Sally did this work day after day for nothing. They risked their lives all day every day and received a cooked breakfast and not much more. If Fran was lucky, the drug squad paid for some of her petrol and the odd taxi fare. After months of constant contact and surviving moments of terror together, Fran and I were becoming very close. Her commitment to the operation was inspirational. Sally was doing a great job, but Fran **was** the job. The operation depended on Fran. I felt like a bit player most of the time. I was well aware that it was the girls who made Lenny acceptable to the crooks.

On Tuesday, August 31, 1993, at 8.15am Stacker appeared on Fran's doorstep. He wanted her mate Lenny to buy more heroin. At 8.45am, Fran rang me on my mobile. She put Stacker on the phone. Stacker wanted to know why I hadn't got back to him to buy more heroin. Stacker was his usual charming threatening self. I politely tried to explain to Stacker that he should speak to Trevor. Off we went again. Stacker explained that he was the only one who was going to sell heroin to me. I eventually buckled and put him off till Friday, September 3. I spoke with Fran again. We couldn't say much because of Stacker. I got off the phone and called Steve. Steve and I again tried to think of new plans to avoid this total loser. Stacker rang me four times that day. He wanted me to purchase a half ounce for $6500. I just had to make sure I wasn't going to get ripped off.

At 5.40pm, Trevor Pettingill rang Fran. He asked her for my number. Minutes later, Trevor rang me on my mobile. He wanted to know when I wanted to buy some more heroin. I told him I wanted 'half an ozzie' on Thursday just after lunch. We spoke about Stacker again. Trevor explained to me that he was unable to take over the heroin deals from Stacker. Trevor insisted he would personally make sure that this deal would go smoothly. He had spoken to Stacker about the last deal. Trevor said, 'You see Stacker is not very professional in what he does.' I tended to agree with him on that. Trevor finished the conversation with, 'You can trust me, Lenny. No-one's gunna rip you off. It'll be sweet, mate.'

I said, 'Sweet, I trust your word, mate.' As I hung up the phone, I thought, 'Now I'm mates with and trusting a cop killer more than a junkie self-confessed body-stacking murderer.'

Late that night Stacker and Eddie arrived at Fran's home. After several bongs with Sally and Fran, they stayed the night. The next morning, Wednesday, September 1, 1993, at 9.45am Stacker convinced Fran to drive him back to Trevor's. Sally jumped in for the ride. Eddie left Fran's home in his van. Stacker had Fran park outside the twenty-storey housing commission block. He said he needed to score some heroin. He went to a phone box and made a call. He told the girls he'd called a gook named 'Le'. Stacker was upset that Le wasn't home and demanded to be driven to another address in Reservoir. Fran ended up driving around for about an hour before he rang Le again. Stacker told the girls he could buy heroin from heaps of people but Le had the strongest and the best quality. By the time they got back to the commission flats, Stacker was really 'hanging out'.

Fran told Stacker he was not going to leave them in the car again. They walked up to the twelfth floor. Stacker left them in the stairwell and walked to Le's flat. Seconds later, he told them to follow him. In the flat they were introduced to Le, Bruce, Dook and Andy. The girls immediately recognised Andy from the aborted deal in Footscray. Fran, Sally and Stacker sat around and chatted for about fifteen minutes. Fran was happy to have finally met Stacker's dealer. As Fran drove Stacker home, she noticed how he and Sally had slowed right down. They weren't the same people. Heroin had suspended their reality just long enough for them to think they were happy. At least that made Stacker a little easier to get along with. Fran later told me what upset her most was that the Asians weren't users themselves. We spoke about how Le and Andy just fed off users.

It wasn't until about a week later that I learned more about what happened that day. When Sally made her statement, she revealed that Fran had taken her eldest daughter 'S' with them. Sally also included other details. It turned out that Sally, Fran, Stacker and S were taken into the lounge room. There they sat with the four Asians, all aged in their early twenties. On arriving at the flat, Stacker kept pacing up and down. Le took Stacker into the kitchen and had a very serious chat. Stacker then went into the bathroom for five minutes. She then heard Stacker vomiting everywhere. Le abused Stacker and made him clean it up.

Sally said that while they were there, the front door bell kept ringing. Several unknown males purchased heroin from Le and Andy. Sally said that at one point Le referred to Dook and Bruce as his soldiers. Throughout most of the meeting Dook and Bruce kept watch outside. They would not only look out for cops, but also make sure other crooks weren't going to rob them.

I pictured Fran's teenage daughter sitting in a grotty housing commission flat surrounded by drug dealers, drug users and their criminal minders. On top of this, her mum is sitting there sucking on a bong. The next time I spoke with Fran I asked why she took her daughter into a scene like that. She said she had no choice – she would have preferred S wasn't there, but she was, and that was that. I realised I was out of order. I was judging Fran by my morals and my ethics. I'm from another world, one that would never condone that behaviour. But then again, I was then in that world. I was probably responsible for making her want to go to this drug dealer's flat in the first place.

At times I felt uncomfortable about everything. I was with the Victoria Police drug squad somehow condoning the trafficking and personal use of heroin and cannabis. Technically, I was a drug trafficker. On tape and in statements we had Fran smoking dope with Sally and other criminals. This on many occasions was done in the presence of her children. I felt uncomfortable with this.

The following day, Thursday, September 2, started with several calls to and from Fran. Our biggest problem was still Stacker. As on most mornings, I grabbed my black shoulder bag and walked off to the nearest railway station. I only had two months left to study for my sergeants' exam. I caught the train so I could study for nearly an hour travelling to work each day. That was the plan anyway. I found that my mobile would ring most of the time so actual study rarely occurred.

As I arrived at Russell Street, I ducked into a doorway, pulled my wig on and entered the huge swinging doors of the station. At the drug squad I sat down with Steve. The next deal was organised for the following day at 2pm. The deal was to go down at Trevor's flat. I told Steve I really needed to talk to Trevor again to sort out who I was buying heroin from.

I gave Trevor a quick phone call and he agreed that we needed to talk. So at 4.40pm I parked outside Trevor's flat. Trevor met me at the front door. We shook hands and I walked inside. Trevor locked the security door then the main door and all its locks and put the key in his pocket. I followed him into the kitchen. As I sat down at the kitchen table I noticed someone sitting on the couch in the lounge. It was Stacker watching television. I'd hoped to get Trevor alone. As I entered the kitchen, I said, 'So how's Lord Trevor going?' Trevor laughed. I said, 'How's your kingdom?'

Trevor said, 'My servants are a pain in the arse.'

Stacker in a low monotone said, 'Fuck you, too.'

I called out, 'Hello Mr Stacker.'

There was a pause, then Stacker replied, 'Lenny'.

Debbie appeared out of the hallway and in a very jovial voice said, 'Hello Lenny. Do ya want a drink of sumfing?'

I said, 'Hello Deb. May I have a glass of water, with some ice if you have any?'

Deb said, 'Sure you can.'

I spoke in my politest voice. I was starting to realise that Deb and Trevor were just like old Kath. They'd never met a yuppie. Trevor would assume that any undercover cop that was going to try and get him and his mates had to be a real tough bastard. They were looking out for a 'Steven Seagal' type character. So Lenny was exactly what the Pettingills were not looking for. My polite, non-threatening half-baked yuppie character was not like any cop they had ever met.

In a low quiet voice, Trevor said, 'Are you right for tomorrow?'

I whispered, 'Yeah, but I'm still not happy with Stacker. If I buy large amounts he's just going to tax more of my gear.'

Trevor said, 'You should be there when he taxes it.'

I said, 'I'll be honest. Stacker makes it very hard for me to trust him.'

'I know what you mean,' Trevor said. 'Everything will be sweet with him, Lenny.'

I said, 'Good.'

Trevor said, 'I've got this ready for you.' He put two fingers to his mouth to indicate smoking. This meant cannabis. He continued, 'It's all that.' As he said this he touched his head indicating cannabis head, which is the strongest and best part of the plant.

'Good stuff,' I replied.

He said, 'Do you want this or that first?' He touched the inside of his arm meaning heroin and then his lips meaning cannabis.

I touched my inner left arm and said, 'Is this (heroin) with you or him?' I pointed toward Stacker.

Trevor said, 'I wanted to purchase that up front for you, but Stacker is stopping me. You have to do that with him and the green with me.'

I said, 'I would be doing large ones now if I could trust Stacker.'

By 'large ones' Trevor knew I meant ounces of heroin. It was obvious that Trevor was having just as much trouble with Stacker as I was. I was resigned to the fact that it was never going to change. I leaned back in my chair and said, 'Hey Stack, come in here. I don't want you thinking that I'm talking behind your back.' Stacker walked straight into the kitchen. As he pulled out a chair, Eddie started knocking at the door. Trevor let him in. I smiled at Eddie as I shook his hand.

I found myself with Stacker on my left, Trevor on my right and Eddie sitting up on the kitchen bench right behind me. With the table in front of my I found myself surrounded. If I was ever going to be robbed, now was the time. I started to panic. I could not watch them all at once. I didn't want them to see how scared I was. As I squirmed in my chair I realised that some of my fear must be leaking out. I was petrified. As Eddie was in the best place to whack me over the head, I kept trying to keep an eye on him.

I said to Stacker and Trevor, 'The last time you chewed on my rock you took .5 of a gram, for me that's about 250 bucks worth. I just want safe regular business that I can make a dollar on.'

Trevor said, 'You should buy large ones.'

Stacker said to me, 'Trust, you don't trust me or something.'

Trevor said, 'Everything is hostile, right. It has to stop.'

Stacker said, 'I'm not going to rob ya. Get it in your head, I won't fucking rob ya.' That convinced me I was about to be robbed.

Trevor held out both his hands and said, 'Just calm down, we're mates here. It's all hostile.' I was sick and tired of negotiating with the unnegotiable. I didn't need this. Eddie moved behind me and I spun around. Eddie smiled as though he knew how scared I was. I was trying to stop being scared. Then I realised that it was okay because if I was a real crook I'd be scared as well, but maybe not as much as me. After the initial assault, they would rob me of my money, gun and recording device. They would initially think I was a dog, a police informer trying to set them up. I would probably not survive the immediate intensive attack that would then take place. Questions jumped into my head. Would I try and explain that I was in fact a cop, and would that help me? I don't think so. Next question. Why the fuck am I carrying a gun when there is no chance in hell of them ever giving me enough time to use it?

All this was running through my head as I continued on with the meeting. Eddie slid off the bench behind me and sat at the table with the rest of us. Thank God for that. I said, 'Stacker. It's more than you robbing me. It's you never being on time, you taxing my gear and you threatening me every five fucking minutes. I'd prefer to pay you cash for setting up the deal rather than you taxing my gear.' I was pleading with him. I went on, 'You must know by now that I'm a lover not a fighter, right. If you want to rob me, go for it. Rob me, take my money and we'll never do business again. I'm wanting to do big regular deals. We started off on the wrong foot. We need trust now.'

Trevor looked uncomfortable. He said, 'Hostility, there's too much hostility.'

I said to Stacker, 'Tomorrow I'll buy you a big breakfast so you won't go chewing on my rock again.' We all laughed and Trevor said, 'Me old mate Stacker here is a shithouse drug dealer.'

Stacker smiled and said, 'My good deals make up for my bad deals.'

I said, 'You must do a hell of a lot of good deals then.'

Only the tension on the surface had gone. I could still feel seriously bad vibes from Stacker. Stacker laughed as he said, 'I nearly broke one of me front teeth when I bit the rock last time.'

I stood up. As I walked to the front door, we agreed to see each other here again at 2pm tomorrow. I stood there for several seconds as Trevor unlocked all the locks. I said, 'This is just like Maxwell Smart's front door.'

Trevor said, 'Security is very important. I feel safe in here.'

I thought, 'Not for long.'

As I drove back to my office I rang Steve. At the end of the update I lied. I told him I felt fine. I was mentally and physically drained. Sensory overload. Nothing a few litres of wine wouldn't fix.

I SPENT the morning of September 3, 1993, organising the girls to come into the city early. We had statements to take. Fran drove in with Sally and the children. Our crew tossed coins to see who was typing statements and who was entertaining the kids. We met at a motel and took statements until about 1pm.

I sat with the girls in a room and went over what was happening that day. We sat there on the bed counting the money. For the first time it had arrived early. I handed Fran $6500 for the half ounce of heroin. Fran was wearing a long light summer dress. She stood, lifted her dress and revealed a thin red G-string. 'You are kidding, aren't you?' I said. She then began to tuck three large wads of cash under the G-string. 'You need cottontail bloomers, not bloody that tooth flossy thing.'

She laughed and said, 'Relax Lenny, I've had more than six and a half gorillas down me knickers before.' I think she was talking about money.

Sally was immediately jealous at all the attention Fran was getting and stood, lifted her dress and said, 'You could stick a few gorillas in here too, Lenny'. Sally had a bright pink tiny G-string on.

I said, 'For Christ's sake. You don't do that to Stacker, do you? No wonder your drug deals take so bloody long.' As we left the motel room, Baldrick and Laurie were leaving the room next door. Sally saw them and immediately lifted her dress and said, 'Come on boys, I need some gorillas'. Baldrick and Laurie laughed as I grabbed her by the arm and pulled her dress down at the front. She spun around and lifted the back of her dress and stuck her bum out at them. I realised I was fighting a losing battle. Not to be outdone, Fran lifted the front of her dress and said, 'Look what I've got'. By now there were several interested motel patrons and staff looking at all the commotion. I stepped into my car and started to reverse out. The girls jumped in. I said, 'Receptionists my arse.'

Fran said, 'Show us your G-string Lenny.'

In a serious voice I said, 'Fran, how can the money stay there?'

Fran said, 'If it falls out I'll feel it. Trrrrust me.'

As I drove, I thought, 'I only have to last another thirteen days.' To the girls this was all a great adventure and they were making the most of it.

We had fifteen minutes to travel about five kilometres. Each major road I tried to go down was at a standstill. I started to panic. I said, 'Always late for a drug deal. I reckon Trevor Pettingill is the only drug dealer in Melbourne who wears a fucking watch.' As I drove into Dight Street, I put on the brakes. There were three marked police vehicles right outside Trevor's. Trevor, Stacker and Eddie were standing on the balcony looking down on them. I pulled over and parked about 50 metres short of Trevor's. The girls kept telling me to drive off. I calmed them down. I had a good look at the cops and made sure I didn't know any of them. I said, 'Come on, let's do it.' We got out of the car. I said, 'Just ignore the cops and they'll ignore you.' Stacker appeared out on the footpath. I nodded my head at him to say hello. He nodded back and walked off in the direction of the heroin. The girls followed. I said, 'Go girls.'

I walked past the cops and up the stairs leading to Trevor's flat. Trevor and Eddie were standing in the doorway holding the door open. As I approached, I smiled and said, 'What sort of a neighbourhood is this? Are there some criminals around here?'

Trevor said, 'Yeah, they drive them white cars with them blue lights on them.'

I said, 'They can't be good for business. Scaring the customers.' I walked inside and Trevor went through the ritual of locking the security door, then the main door. He locked two large dead bolts, took the key out and put in his pocket. I'd seen him do this several times but it was hard to get used to. Again I thought if I get into trouble I can smash the front window and jump off the balcony. I thought, 'Shit'. I'd forgotten to take a look to see where the cars were parked out the front. Last night

I thought if I have to jump off the balcony I should try and land on top of a parked car. A cop car would be good, I thought.

Trevor took me into the kitchen. Debbie was very friendly again and got me a glass of iced water. Deb seemed to fancy me. Then again, she's a Pettingill and I had money. Eddie and Trevor spoke about how the cops were chasing some bloke. I said, 'I drove into the street and saw cops everywhere. Then I saw Lord Trevor standing up on the balcony and I realised you guys were all right.'

'Most cops don't know what to look for,' Trevor advised.

I asked him, 'Do you think those cops know you live here?'

Eddie said, 'Every cop in Victoria knows Trevor lives here.'

Trevor added, 'That's why I feel safer in here than walking around outside.'

I could hear cars out the front slam doors and drive off. We all got up and walked over to the balcony. Trevor opened the door and we stood there looking down on the empty street. It was like the sharks had just left a reef. Within seconds the dead street came to life. People started leaving their homes and several cars drove up and parked outside their addresses.

As I botted a smoke from Eddie two young women walked down the footpath toward us. Trevor closed the balcony door behind us and said, 'Watch this'. Trevor held out both his hands. As he waved his hands in an upward motion he said, 'Hey girls, show us your tits'. The girls stopped and lifted their tops to reveal their breasts. Then they walked off on their merry way.

I said, 'You are the man.'

Eddie said, 'Lenny, that's cool, hey.'

'I'm going to get myself a balcony,' I said.

Trevor then said, 'Lenny, follow me. You got the money here?'

'Yeah,' I said. I followed Trevor to the front door. He undid all the locks and I followed him down the stairs and around through a walkway that led to the rear of the poofters' flat. He opened the back door of their flat and took us into the kitchen. He stood on a chair and reached into a small cupboard above a fridge. He pulled out a sausage-shaped parcel and handed it down to me. It was just like the others. He got down and started to dig a small hole in one end while I was holding it. Trevor said, 'I want you to smell it. It's the best head you'll ever get.' There was a line there but it was no time for jokes. Trevor's face was hard and cold. His words were short and to the point. This was 'game on' for Trevor and he didn't fuck around. This was the only thing he was good at, or thought he was.

I handed Trevor $4800 cash. He didn't count it, just shoved it straight down his pants. A voice said inside me, 'You're in Lenny. He trusts you.' As we walked out the rear door of the flat, Trevor stopped to lock it. I whispered, 'I'm after some gowie (speed) and Trevor replied, 'I was speaking to a bloke yesterday who has some grouse gowie.'

I said, 'See if you can get me an oz sample and I'll take one of these.'

I pointed to my elbow, indicating I wanted a pound. Trevor's eyes lit up and he jumped on the idea straight away. 'Sweet,' he said. 'I'll call you Monday or Tuesday.' We shook hands.

We walked off toward Trevor's flat. I could hear that the girls were back. So could half the street. As I approached, I said, 'What's going on here?' This was the first time I felt like a drug trafficking pimp who couldn't control his girls.

Fran said, 'That thing doesn't want us in her flat.' They were referring to Debbie.

In a low voice I said, 'Fran, take this and get into our car, would you. You got the gear?'

Fran said, 'Yeah, but this shit …' I stopped her mid-sentence and said, 'You're doing a brilliant job, both of you, but just get in the car. Now. Keep your voices down.'

I looked over at Trevor. He waved me to come over and speak to him. He looked really pissed off. The girls reluctantly walked off and I threw Fran the keys. Things got worse as I saw Trevor walk back into his flat. I followed him into his territory. Not good. Debbie was off to my left in the kitchen, mumbling away about sluts and bitches. Trevor appeared to compose himself before starting one of his 'world according to Trevor' speeches.

In a low voice he arrogantly closed his eyes and said, 'Sometimes you just have to smack 'em. Watch this.' Trevor turned toward the kitchen and called out, 'Hey Deb, can you get me a glass of water, please?' Deb called out, 'Sure.' He paused for a few seconds as Deb stopped what she was doing, poured a glass of water and did the eight-month pregnant waddle over to us. As she approached, he said, 'Thanks, Deb, you can take it back now.' Deb turned around, shaking her head and walked back into the kitchen, mumbling. Trevor's voice and face changed as he said, 'Now, see that. I was polite and I was fair. She got me the water. If she didn't …' Instead of finishing the sentence in words Trevor smashed the back of his right hand into the palm of his left hand. He did this right in front of my face.

I held both my hands out and said, 'Yeah, okay, but I'll handle the girls.'

Trevor said, 'If you don't want to, I'll smack 'em for ya.' Trevor let that sink in and added, 'I was going to smack 'em outside there but out of respect for you I didn't.'

I said, 'Thanks Trevor. I'm listening. I'll see what I can do.' I walked over to Debbie and said, 'Debbie, I'm sorry about that.'

Debbie said, 'You're welcome here in my home, Lenny, any time but not those sluts.'

Happy families … check out Kath's fridge door. Cute little magnets and the picture of her son Dennis Allen pointing a gun at her head.

One of these bottom dwellers has a head full of crap. Me with a giant crayfish.

I like to catch things including fish and drug dealers. But they weren't the same. I sometimes threw fish back. And fish smell better.

A dismantled pen pistol … no wonder I wore gloves.

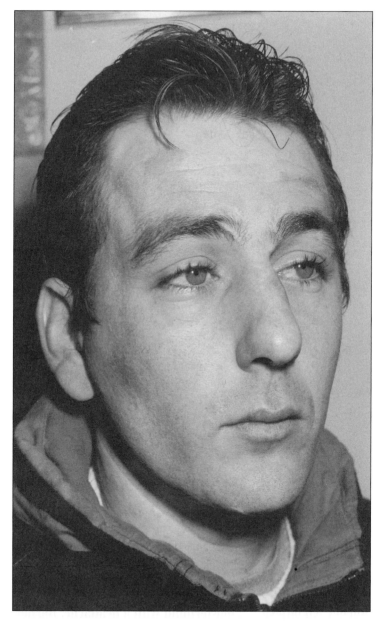

Trevor Pettingill … thought Mensa was an unraced two-year-old.

They say drug dealing is a victimless crime.
Then why do dealers need guns like these?

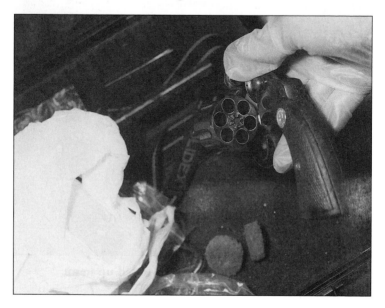

They call them love drugs but they were ready for war.

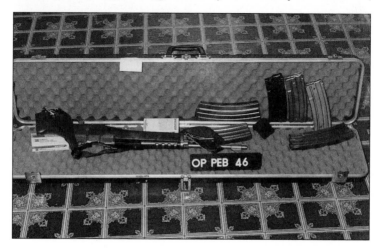

The heroin dealer
had stashed his
money. The police
dog could smell the
heroin on the notes …

... **bingo.**

Kath Pettingill … just a granny in her curlers. Who would have thought she was the mother of Australia's worst crime family?

I said, 'I really must go. Thanks again for everything.'

We shook hands. Trevor undid all the locks and let me out.

As Trevor closed the door behind me I thought, 'You'll get your right whack.' I whispered to myself, 'Your smack is coming.'

Halfway down the stairs I suddenly I got a cold chill down my spine. I grabbed my automatic 9mm pistol from the front of my pants. I hadn't seen Stacker. I held it under the front of my shirt with my finger on the trigger. I walked sideways down the stairs trying to look behind me and in front of me at the same time. As I got to the bottom of the stairs, I quickly drew my gun out and pointed it under the stairs. Nothing. I whipped the gun back into the front of my pants in case someone saw me from the street. I carefully walked out onto the street. As I walked over to my car I mumbled again, 'It's okay to be scared. If I stop being scared, that's when I should worry.'

As the girls gave me a full rundown of what happened with Stacker, Fran handed me the half-ounce of heroin we'd bought. I looked down at the pound of green on the floor at Fran's feet and said, 'See that pound, that's the first lot of drugs we've bought that hasn't been taxed.'

In unison they said, 'We can fix that Lenny.'

I screamed, 'No, leave it!' As I drove, I wrestled the package from Fran. She whinged, 'We have to have some smoke to look good – what if Eddie and Stacker come over for a visit?'

I said, 'Tell them the truth, that I'm a son of a bitch and wouldn't even give you a leaf.'

I added, 'Things are changing around here. I'm going to do what Trevor says.'

Sally asked, 'What's that?'

I said, 'I'm going to start smacking you around. Trevor reckons you both need a smack.'

I let a smile creep over my face. Fran smiled and said, 'Well come on, you smack first.'

Sally said, 'Can you handcuff me first, Lenny?'

As we were all laughing I got serious. I said, 'From now on you're going to have to be careful. Trevor means it. He or Stacker would drop you two on your arses without even thinking about it.' The girls went on to talk about how they hated Debbie. I said, 'Let's just be careful from now on. There's not long to go. I'm not going to let anything happen to you.'

Sally said, 'What if they just pull out a gun and shoot us and take our money?'

I said, 'Well, I can't stop that.' The girls went on with stories about blokes who had hit them. I interrupted them with one of my own. 'Once I was having this big argument with this girl I was living with and right in the middle of it she punched me in the middle of my chest. I couldn't believe it. I went straight outside. I went for a drive and thought "Hang on, it's my house." So I went back and she refused to apologise. How bad is that?'

Fran retorted, 'That's not bad; that's funny. I went out with a bloke once and he was being an arsehole so I whacked him. He left and I never saw him again.'

Sally continued, 'Well I was going out with this speed head, he was a mad armed robber.'

Sarcastically, I interrupted, 'As you would.'

Fran added, 'I would. I'm married to one.'

I said, 'Sorry, I forgot what planet I was on. I'm the odd one out here. Go on, Sally.' Sally continued as though she had been rudely interrupted, 'And one night he punched me right in the face. I had to wear dark sunglasses for a week, right. So the next morning he woke up and I was holding his dick in the middle of a big pair of scissors.' We all laughed. 'What happened?' I asked. 'We were in a motel in New Zealand. I led him by the dick, out of bed and straight out the front door and locked it.' I said, 'That would have got his attention.'

Sally went on, 'I peeped out the window and there he was checking out his old fella to see if it was okay.'

I said, 'Did he come back and get you for doing that?'

Sally said, 'I let him back inside eventually and we did a few more armed robberies. But he never did hit me again after that.'

SATURDAY, September 4, 1993, was my day off. But no, Fran managed to find new and creative ways to jeopardise our covert operation and send me round the twist. Not to mention putting us all in even more danger. At 9.38am, my mobile phone rang:

Lenny: What? (Remember, I got that off Stacker.)

Male: Who's this?

Lenny: Who's this?

Male: This is Prison Officer Richard Dillon at Barwon Prison. I have Fran (surname) here. Who am I speaking to?

Lenny: Can I speak to Fran for a second, just one second?

There was a pause, then he handed the phone to her.

Fran: You can talk to this bloke. I'm at the fucking prison and they've arrested me.

She sounded really bad.

Dillon: Who is this?

I thought, 'Shit. Who am I today?' Then I asked him why they'd arrested Fran.

Dillon: We are holding her because she tried to smuggle some sort of recording device into the prison.

Lenny: You are kidding. That device is mine. I am Detective Senior Constable Lachlan McCulloch.

Dillon: Why are you sending her in here with a tape recorder?

Lenny: No, no, no. Please understand. This has nothing to do with you guys. Nothing to do with the Barwon Prison. She's just a fucking idiot, right. I'm with the drug squad and her life has been at risk and she has to carry the recording device because she's being threatened. Her husband can't find out about this ever or he would be killed. Please don't tell any other prison officers or the word might get around that she's carrying a tape recorder.

Dillon: Every time she comes into this prison she causes trouble and now she's trying to tape us or something.

Lenny: No, she's just a fucking stupid idiot. That device is worth over $12,000. Please don't touch it at all. What I'll do is get my officer in charge to call you immediately. This is life-threatening to several people. Please don't tell anyone about this. Can I speak with her?

Fran: Hello. Can you help me?

Lenny: You ... I ... You try and take that into the prison?

Fran: I didn't want to leave it in the car in case it got stolen.

Lenny: You risk everything. Everything we've done.

Fran: I'm sorry. Do you still love me?

Lenny: You're making it hard. If word gets from the prison guards back to Butch and every other bastard in there that you're carrying a hidden drug squad tape recorder it's all for nothing, the job's dead, we're dead and he's dead. Do you understand what happens if Victor Peirce finds out? Put Dillon back on.

Dillon: Hello.

Lenny: Within five minutes I'll have my bosses call the prison governor to sort this out. Please keep this in-house. This is not about you guys.

I spent the next two hours negotiating Fran's release. Her visiting rights were revoked for a month. As it turned out, for some time Fran had been suspected of bringing drugs into the prison. She had been getting hassled and thoroughly strip-searched each time she went there. She maintained she only took the recorder into the prison so it wouldn't get stolen from her car. Knowing Fran as I did, I had no doubt she wanted to tape the guards saying something they shouldn't have. I could imagine how fast a juicy bit of gossip like: 'Butch's wife Fran brought in a tape recorder hidden in her handbag and tried to tape the screws' would travel. Fran had a natural talent for pushing boundaries. I decided if the operation was successful I would henceforth believe in miracles.

Next time I met Fran I removed the recorder from its hidden compartment. The lining was all ripped and the casing had been forced open. The tape was missing. Luckily, the tape was a new one and had nothing on it. A fiddle with a screwdriver and some gaffer tape got the thing running again. I sat down with Steve and our crew and discussed whether to continue with the device in her handbag. Was it too risky? The consensus was that one more risk in this job was like another grain of sand on a beach. Who's going to notice? I agreed. While we were still just afloat, I went back to steering my papier-mâché ship named *Operation Earthquake-Tremor* straight into the wind.

OVER the next few days I spoke to Trevor several times. He got a sample ounce of speed and arranged for me to come over and pick it up. At 1.51pm on September 7, I parked right outside Trevor's flat. He was on the balcony as usual. He seemed happy to see me and said, 'Come straight up'.

I met him at his front door. We shook hands and Trevor locked the doors. I followed him into the kitchen. I suddenly stopped. There, on the kitchen table, was pile after pile of audio tapes.

It looked just like my desk. I recognised the tapes straight away as coming from the Victoria Police special projects unit. There were over a hundred telephone intercept tapes.

Trevor said, 'Take a seat.'

I said, 'What's all this?'

Trevor said, 'Telephone taps. The jacks tapped me phone and I'm just going through a few of them.'

It sort of caught me off guard and it was weird. I said, 'Am I on them?'

Trevor said, 'No. No these are from a while ago. That's why I don't talk on the phone.' Trevor casually added, 'My whole life, me phone and me house has been bugged by the jacks.'

I thought, 'That's because you're a drug trafficker.' I said, 'So the feds tap your phone?'

Trevor said, 'No, the state jacks, Victoria Police drug operations.'

I said, 'No, the phones fall under the federal jurisdiction. Only the feds can do it legally.'

Trevor sighed, 'Lenny, the Victoria Police jacks have to find some evidence and then take that to a judge and the judge gives them a warrant to tape my phone.'

I said, 'I thought it was the feds, you know federal laws and that.'

Debbie and Trevor laughed. Trevor said, 'You're watching the movies and that.'

I said, 'I don't get it. They tape your phone and give you the tapes.'

Trevor said, 'Don't worry about it, Lenny. These tapes have caused us a lot of grief. You see, my mate Donato got a copy of all my phone tapes and I got a copy of all his tapes.'

Debbie interrupted, 'And there's shit in them that Donato shouldn't ever hear.'

I said, 'Too complicated, eh.'

We sat down at the table and Trevor pushed all several piles of tapes to one side. Trevor said, 'Can you close the blinds in the lounge, Debbie?' She did. She then closed the kitchen blinds. It was almost completely dark. Trevor leant back and turned on the kitchen light. There in the middle of the table was a small clear plastic bag full of a beige-coloured powder. I put my wallet on the table in front of Trevor. I opened the bag and smelt the powder. Trevor said, 'You could add a quarter ounce of sugar to it but it's probably best to leave it and sell it the way it is.'

I said, 'Sweet. How much do you want?'

'You can have that for nine hundred.'

I said, 'Grab it, it's in the wallet.' I stood up and rolled the bag up as small as possible. I lifted the jeans above my left boot and placed the bag inside the top of my sock.

As I did this, I saw Trevor open my wallet. He stopped to look at my driver's licence and a photograph. He asked, 'What sort of fish is that?'

I said, 'A Great Trevally. That's my dad.' There was a large wad of cash in my wallet. Trevor counted out some money and took it.

He smiled and said, 'I should have charged you …' Then he held his hands open and held up ten fingers indicating $1000. He added, 'But that's fine. My bloke has promised me a … ' He touched his elbow. I said, 'Sweet. I'll see how I go with this.'

I think the phone tapes had made him paranoid. He leaned over right up to my face and whispered, 'Thanks for not talking openly about drugs. I just can't trust many people. I feel like everyone is trying to set me up. But this is me life, it's what I am.'

I said, 'Thanks for helping me, mate.'

Trevor said, 'It's sweet.'

I said, 'Get the price on a large and when you call me say it's a car.'

Trevor whispered, 'Come outside.' I said goodbye to Debbie. He unlocked the door and I followed him to a small laundry at the rear of his flat. Trevor whispered, 'I'll say I've been to a car auction house and that I've seen a VL Commodore. The price of the car will be the price of the pound.'

'Sweet,' I said.

We shook hands and I left. I couldn't help peeping under the staircase looking for Stacker. With Stacker, it wasn't a matter of if he was going to rob me, it was when. After sneaking around doing anti-surveillance I returned to the drug squad. I tested the sample ounce of speed and found it to be average street quality. Nothing flash, but it was speed and enough to put Trevor in jail for a while.

We all entered the conference room and closed the doors. I placed a large tape recorder on the table and pushed play. Playing the recording of the meeting gave my crew another taste of what it was like to do what I did. I feel strange when I hear the tape of a meeting. Listening to the voices and background noises always takes me straight back there. Even though I was in a safe place listening, it made me feel unsafe. I'd get a different perspective. Listening, sometimes I would think I shouldn't have gone there. I shouldn't have gone into Trevor's home. It was his turf. It belonged to him and was no place for the likes of me. It was only at those times, listening to the tapes, that I realised it really wasn't safe. But I did it anyway and I knew I would do it again.

Did he forfeit all rights when he trafficked drugs? To me he did. He lived outside the law. So the law had to go inside and the law was me. I looked at the faces of my colleagues as they listened. They listened to the metallic rustling sounds. One of them asked, 'What's that?'

'That's Trevor locking the deadlocks. He locks us inside his flat. He always does that.'

I paused and said, 'I hate that.'

They listened intently.

In the middle of the deal, we all jumped out of our skins as Debbie dropped a large glass ashtray onto the laminex table. While the tape was playing, I left and made a coffee. I didn't need to taste that shit again. When the tape finished, we started a meeting about the operation as a whole. The telephone intercepts revealed that Donato Corsi had supplied Trevor the ounce sample of speed that I had just purchased. The intercepts also revealed that there was some serious unrest among the players. As Donato had been charged with Trevor over the same large cannabis crop, they had both been given the same tapes. Donato got copies of Trevor's phone tapes and Trevor got a copy of all of Donato's. The problem was that Trevor's phone conversations revealed what the Pettingill clan were best at: dastardly criminal behaviour, treachery, deceit and plots and plans. The following conversations were included in the brief of evidence:

Debbie: Trevor's gone out for a minute. Where are you, at home?

Donato: I'm at home, yeah. I didn't get to bed till about six o'clock this morning. I've been listening to me tapes.

Debbie: Did you listen to them all?

Donato: Yeah, I got all your phone tapes, phone conversations.

Debbie: Oh, yeah?

Donato: Some coming from Victor's joint (jail). *Yeah, there's a few things in there that I don't like at all. Not at all.*

Debbie: My voice isn't on them?

Donato: No, no, no.

Debbie: Nup.

Donato: Peter Allen's voice is.

Peter Allen is the brother or half-brother of Trevor Pettingill and Victor Peirce. Peter was calling from prison. He was serving his umpteenth sentence for heroin trafficking.

Donato: Kath's voice is. Peter rang Trevor from jail. Fat Albert and Victor are on the phone too. They all do a lot of talking. Victor talks about ripping off the gear, ripping me off, talk about bogging me off.

Debbie: Really. No, you wouldn't be hearing that.

Donato Corsi is talking slowly and with venom. He explains to Debbie why he is not happy. Debbie sounds like she's in shock.

Debbie: You have that on tape?

Donato: Yeah, really. Fuckin' Fat Albert is there with Trevor and he talks to Victor and Fat Albert says he's gunna get me up there, and fuckin' take me for a walk.

Debbie: Really, is all that on tape?

Donato: It's on tape, mate. I rang Trevor to say, have a listen. Listen to the tapes.

Debbie: I'm nearly eight months pregnant and I'm just trying to have this cup of coffee and a biscuit. 'Cause I feel a bit hungry.

Donato: Okay, mate. Bye.

Two hours later, Trevor telephones Donato's home.

Donato: Hello?

Trevor: Yes sir, what's happening?

Donato: The tapes are happening.

Trevor: What's on them?

Donato: This is what's on them. Remember the time you were gunna rip me off is what's on them. Taking me off for a walk is on them, mate.

Trevor: You must have different tapes, mate.

Donato: Don't you worry; I've got the tapes, mate. I can bring them over to you and you can listen to yourself, to Victor and Fatso.

As an undercover operative, I was always wanting to know everything that was going on, without knowing too much. Sometimes I didn't want to know everything so I couldn't slip up, say the wrong thing. I didn't have to worry, really. In the scheme of things, as it turned out I don't think I ever learnt half of what was really going on.

That night I spoke with Fran. Fran wanted to know what was going on. I told her everything. We were all stressed out about the fact that there were only a few days to go. Fran kept on asking me about the witness protection program. Witsec, as we called it, operated totally independently from us at the drug squad. I just kept telling her to speak with them.

I knew I was going to miss my daily chats with Fran. I felt a closeness with Fran that was hard to describe. She was so different to me. She had an inner strength of character that made you trust her, an intangible integrity at odds with her outward looks and her background. During all these months she had never done anything to intentionally jeopardise the operation, at least that I knew of. She may have acted like a lunatic but she was a good-natured one.

At 7.15pm on September 8, 1993, I was on the phone to Fran when Stacker arrived at her front door. Stacker was there to see Fran and to arrange another heroin deal. The deal had been organised to happen at Footscray with Andy. I'd decided to start dictating the rules. It was my money, so I was the boss – sort of. I had told Fran to tell Stacker that she was going to hand the money directly to Andy. Fran understood that we only had days to go and needed to cut Stacker out of the picture as soon as possible. I apologised to Fran for putting her in the middle of all this shit. Fran knew this was going to cause Stacker huge grief.

Lenny: We've come all this way. We finish next week. Push him as far as you can but don't let him kill you.

Fran: Thanks very much, Lenny my darling.

I could hear Stacker talking to Sally in the background.

Lenny: Go for it. If you need me I'll come straight over. Set the deal for 1pm Friday the 10th of this month. In two days time.

Fran: You're a prick. Love you. Stacker's here. Bye.

At 11.48 that night Fran rang me on my mobile. Just what I needed. She was paranoid from the copious bongs she'd had with Stacker and Sally. Fran felt sure Stacker had hidden a tape recorder in her home to spy on them. I assured her that if Stacker ever had a tape recorder he would sell it for heroin in an instant. Fran said Stacker had refused to allow her to hand Andy the money. We arranged to talk tomorrow.

At 12.45pm on September 9, 1993, I was in my 5.4-metre Flightcraft sports profile boat cruising at 38 kilometres an hour when my mobile rang. It was Fran. She was most upset.

Fran: Where are you, I've been trying to ring you all morning?

Lenny: In my bloody boat. I am looking at a nine pound, seven ounce crayfish. It is huge, and three other smaller ones.

Fran: You're meant to be here at Trevor's. Fuck.

I then heard Fran talking to someone in the background. Fran said something about the fact that I was out diving and fishing.

Lenny: The deal is on for tomorrow at 1pm at Trevor's.

Fran: No, it's today.

In the background I could hear Stacker was very upset. I cut the motor and we glided to a stop. I was about a kilometre south of West Head in the entrance of Westernport Bay. My brother-in-law John looked at me, bewildered. I covered over my phone and whispered to him to be quiet, then waited while Fran argued with Stacker in the background.

Lenny: Fran, speak to me, speak to me. Are you all right?

Fran: Yeah, but I'm not happy. Stacker is going off his nut.

Lenny: See, this is what happens when you smoke too much. Tell Stacker I'm out in my boat with a huge fucking crayfish and the deal is on for tomorrow.

Fran: You must bring the money now.

Fran was on the verge of tears. Stacker was screaming about how the deal had to happen now!

Lenny: Put Stacker on the phone, now.

Stacker's voice was breaking with anger: *You fucking well get down here, right; give me a time that you'll be here.*

Lenny: G'day Stacker. I'm out in the middle of nowhere. Right in the fucking middle. The deal is on for tomorrow.

Stacker: You don't understand. It was for today. Just give me a time that you'll be here.

Lenny: My money will be there at 1pm tomorrow as planned.

Stacker raved on and on. Fran eventually grabbed the phone off him and I made sure both she and Sally were fine. I then threw my phone up into the cabin and said, 'Seven more sleeps and it's all over'.

My phone started ringing again. I tried to ignore it. I couldn't. I picked it up. This is the transcript of the conversation:

Lenny: What?

Trevor: Lenny, it's me, Trevor.

Lenny: Sorry, mate. I'm a bit stressed out by your mate. Christ, I wish I was dealing with you.

Trevor: So do I, mate. Listen – I went into the auctions right, and I had a look at a few cars. I had a look at a … a fucking VN Commodore, right.

Lenny: Yeah.

Trevor: Like 1990 models they're going normally for about fourteen, fourteen grand, right?

Lenny: Fuck, but fuck that's a lot.

I thought, 'I can't pay that. I know we are talking about a

pound of speed from Trevor Pettingill and the money's not mine, but Christ I'm not an idiot. The sample was shitty low-quality speed. You could almost put it on your cornflakes.'

Trevor: Yeah, well that's normal, right, but I can pick one up for eight and a half.

Lenny: You're kidding?

Trevor: That's it.

Lenny: Yeah, well that's fine. Sounds great. Excellent.

Trevor: Well usually you pick them up for about seven or eight fucking smashed. This is eight and a half with rego.

Lenny: Shit, that's excellent. I'll see you at 2pm?

Trevor: 2pm is great. See you then.

I started up the motor and roared off. Flat out. Over the sound of the screaming engine I yelled the answer to the obvious question. 'Well. It's nearly over. Then I've just got a couple of years of court cases and death threats and **then** it's all over.' I smiled at my mate John, the biological scientist.

He said, 'Why do you bother? You could just direct traffic or something.'

'Someone's got to do it,' I replied.

John said, 'No, they don't.'

I glanced at him and thought about that for a second and said, 'I suppose you're right. Ah well. It's too late now'.

I thought how my job had neverending dramas and problems to solve. Through it all, at the end of the day, I wouldn't be dead for quids. A smile crept over my face as I squinted into salt spray. I screamed out, 'I love it.'

'You love what?'

'I love it all, mate. The job, the crooks and the great big crayfish.'

We laughed as I powered through the next wave.

Diving for crays is hard work. They love to hide in narrow

deep crevices. At times I have to take my tank off my back in order to fit into their hiding spots. On this dive I had found this huge cray and removed my tank so I could go in and get it. Well when I eventually got a grip on this cray I found I had to hold it with both hands, which meant I couldn't get back out. So I crossed my fins. Then I hoped that they were sticking out of the ledge. John saw them crossed over. This was our 'Pull me out I'm stuck' signal. When he pulled me out he saw that I had the cray and the cray had me. It was the biggest cray I've ever caught. It was too big for our catch bag, so I had to swim back and put it in the boat. John took home the three smaller crays and I took the great big one. Later that evening I took it over to my parents. We invited a couple more friends over because it was just too big. In the end six of us could only eat the tail and some of the knuckle joints. All the legs remained untouched. One of its front legs weighed just over nine ounces.

Believe me when I tell you that you can eat too much crayfish. I do it quite often. It is one of the longest digesting foods you can eat. Therefore it tends to sit in your stomach for days. Most people buy a small cray or order one at a restaurant. At the end of the meal you would be quite happy to eat more. I regularly dive for crays with John and some other mates and we catch our legal limit most dives. Cray is beautiful but there is a limit. We often camp along the west coast of Victoria in my 4WD camper trailer, usually right next to the beach. Most of the time there are three of us divers catching our limit of two crays per day. That, with abalone and heaps of fish, makes for some great meals. After about a week when we've had crayfish freshly boiled, stir-fried, mornayed, in a Thai chilli sauce, eaten cold in sandwiches, omelettes and even crayfish cakes they get a bit hard to look at. Anyway, back to the crooks. They are quite similar really. Both are bottom dwellers, a bit rich and have shit for brains.

FRIDAY, September 10, 1993. At 7.24am I was sitting on a crowded train on the way to work. I was dressed as Lenny does and reading study notes for the Victoria Police sergeants' exam. Therefore I was trying to be as inconspicuous as possible. My mobile phone rang. It was Darren. The real Darren, my police mate from St Kilda days. I hadn't heard from him for a while. Darren was the only person not on my crew who I could talk to about *Earthquake*. After the normal pleasantries, I could tell there was a serious tone in his voice.

Darren: I was just wondering if you had any meetings at all today?

Lenny : Yeah, I have. Why?

Darren: What, like serious sort of meetings.

Lenny: What, what's the matter? Talk to me.

Darren: Well, look. I felt like I had to ring you. I had this dream right. You were buying drugs in this house and the crooks shot you.

Lenny: You are fucking kidding me. Are you serious?

Darren: Yeah, I'm serious. I've never done this before, right. But last night I had this dream that you were in this house and they searched you. They found your 'wire' and shot you in the head.

Lenny: This job is fucking hard enough, right, without you telling me this shit. Besides it's in a flat, not a house.

Darren: Who with?

Lenny: Trevor. A pound of sugar in his flat.

Darren: There you go, that's it.

Lenny: You are an arse. So now you'll be able to live with yourself if something happens to me, because you warned me.

Darren: I just had to tell you.

Lenny: Well if you have any more dreams can you keep them to yourself?

As if this job wasn't hard enough. Darren had introduced Fran to me in the first place so he felt like he could be partly responsible should something happen to me. My meeting with Trevor wasn't until 2pm so I had all day to think about it. Great. At 8.48am while walking up Russell Street, I rang Stacker. Stacker sounded like I had just woken him up. We didn't mention yesterday's dramas. It was a new day. Stacker wanted to do the deal earlier. We changed it to 11.15am at the corner of Johnston and Hoddle streets, Collingwood.

I met the girls at 10.40am at a service station in Toorak Road, South Yarra. I handed Fran $3500 in cash. I had counted and separated it into $500 bundles. Fran put it straight down the front of her pants.

Lenny: Fran, Sally, are you happy? You right to do this?

Fran: Happy would be exaggeratin' a bit. Stacker won't lash me.

Sally: Or me.

Lenny: Fran, safety first. Any danger, just give the money away, drop it. Whatever. But don't lose the money. Your safety comes first of course but even if your life depends on it, don't let anyone take the money.

Fran: So our two lives are worth about 3500 bucks?

Lenny: If not more. Take this mobile for protection. You can ring me if you're in trouble.

Fran: You can talk them to death.

Lenny: Remember, one or two dead informers and a missing $3500 would look shithouse on my resume.

Sally: We'll remember that as we're getting raped and murdered.

Lenny: If that happens, don't forget to tape it.

Fran started to drive away. I called out mockingly, 'Bye bye, I love you, safe drug-dealing.'

An erect rude finger appeared from either side of her vehicle as it coughed and spluttered off up the road. As I got back into my car, I mumbled to myself, 'How rude was that? I'm dobbing'. As I drove off, I called Steve and said, 'Steve, as the girls drove off up the road they stuck their rude fingers up at me. Can you ask them to show me a bit more respect?' Steve laughed and said, 'I'll certainly try big buddy. What's going on?'

I gave him the full rundown. I told him that Fran had the money and that they were on their way to do the deal. Steve contacted the surveillance crew and all was set. There was nothing I could do but wait. Moments later, Steve rang me to say the girls had entered the twenty-storey housing commission block of flats at 229 Hoddle Street. My biggest worry was that they were in possession of $3500 in cash and an operating tape recording device. They were in a building containing about 400 flats. If they did go missing, where would we begin to look? And they were buying heroin from unknown criminals in company with a self-confessed murdering lunatic. Why worry? I worried and waited at the KFC restaurant on the west-bound side of the West Gate freeway, near the bridge.

Fran and Sally later made statements about what happened. As Fran parked her car near the housing commission flats, she saw Stacker standing there with a male called Theo. Fran had previously met Theo at Trevor's. Stacker led the girls and Theo to the lift well. They all got out at the eighth floor. Stacker told them all to wait there.

Fran: I'm coming, remember?

Stacker: Sweet, stay behind me.

Stacker knocked on the security door. Le answered it. Without a word being spoken, Fran handed Stacker the $3500 and he immediately handed it to Le. Le took the money with his left hand and handed Stacker a small white package with his right.

Le nodded his head and closed his door. Stacker handed the package straight to Fran. As they walked back to the stairwell, Fran broke a tiny piece off the heroin rock. She handed it to Stacker. Once they got back to the ground floor Stacker and Theo left. At 12.20pm, Fran and Sally parked next to me at the KFC. Fran raved on about how easy the whole thing had been. I took Fran's tape and the heroin back to my office.

At the office I weighed the small package: it was 13.65 grams. Spot tests indicated it was heroin. This was all too good to be true. A drug deal with Stacker that went smoothly? Of course it was too good to be true. During the drug deal, something had gone seriously wrong. None of us knew what it was just yet.

I started to get ready to buy a pound of speed from Trevor Pettingill. I felt myself starting to change again. I could feel my heart start to beat a fraction quicker. I knew this time was worse. Bloody Darren had added another dimension. He called it his dream. It wasn't. It was my nightmare. I'm not really superstitious – I like the number four, I sometimes glance at my horoscope predictions, and at night when I drink from a glass of water I do so in groups of twelve mouthfuls. That's it. Today, is my time up? I decided, why risk it? Darren had said that in his dream the crooks searched me, found a wire and shot me. Get rid of the wire. Simple. I asked Steve if I could have a chat with him in the 'cone of silence'. He followed me into our usual interview room and closed the door.

I began, 'Today, I really don't want to wear a wire. No recorder, nothing. Is that okay?'

Steve replied: 'Sure. You've got heaps of statements to make. Just sit at your desk and do them.'

'Don't, don't do that to me,' I said. 'I still want to do the meeting, but not with a wire.'

Steve said, 'We need evidence. As much as we can get. There's no point to the meeting if there's no evidence.'

With respect to your rank and everything Steve, you are a bastard.

As I left the interview room, I mumbled obscenities out aloud. As I walked off I thought to myself: 'Do I believe in dreams? No. Do I think I can do this? No. Do I believe I can do this? No. Or do I know I can do this? Yes. I know I can do it. I've done it before so I can do it again. Well, then do it.'

I sat at my desk and started to get ready to meet Trevor. Baldrick asked, 'Is everything all right? Are you taking the stubby holder with you today?'

'Shhhhhhhh. No. My mate Darren rang me this morning and said he had a dream that Trevor and that searched me, found the wire and shot me in the head.'

'What a prick,' Baldrick said.

'Tell me about it.' I counted my money and wired myself for sound. A few minutes later I was driving toward Trevor's. At 1.50pm I telephoned Trevor:

Trevor: Hello.

Lenny: Mate, Lenny. I'm just around the corner about to come into your street.

Trevor: That's good mate, I'll meet ya out the front.

As I drove into Dight Street, I saw Lord Trevor leaning against the railing of his balcony. As Trevor saw me, he turned and disappeared inside his flat. I parked and stepped out onto the roadway. Trevor appeared, walking toward me. We shook hands. Trevor asked me all about my car. This time I was driving a two-year-old Nissan Patrol 4WD. I told him I knew someone involved with a lot of car auctions. After a quick chat Trevor smiled and said, 'Come on, follow me'. He quickly turned and walked up a small laneway on the south side of his flats. Just as I entered the walkway I saw Brydon Shabbo appear in front of me. I dropped my head forward and whipped out my sunglasses. I put them on as Trevor said to Shabbo, 'Not now, mate, I'm busy'. Shabbo looked at me. He said nothing and kept walking toward me. I dropped my head forward so my long hair fell forward covering most of my face. Shabbo would have recognised it as a drug deal and ignored me. As Shabbo walked off, I thought, 'Thank Christ for that'.

As I got to the rear of the flat, I found Trevor rustling through his large set of keys.

Lenny: You look like a security guard with all those keys.

Trevor: They all look the fucking same.

We were standing at the back door of the so-called poofters' flat. He finally opened the door. I followed him inside. The flat smelt strongly of cannabis. Trevor then deadlocked the door from the inside and put his keys back in his pocket.

Lenny: You're the most security conscious bloke I've ever met.

Trevor: This ain't no game, is it?

Trevor was right. I looked around and listened. The flat seemed empty other than the smell. Trevor reached up and opened a kitchen cupboard. He grabbed a small silver-coloured cardboard box and handed it to me.. I opened it. It contained a clear plastic bag full of a yellowish beige coloured powder. I closed the box and said, 'I trust you, mate'. I unzipped my small leather bumbag and grabbed out the bundles of cash. As I put them into Trevor's hands, I said: *This one is four thousand and this one is four thousand five hundred. Eight thousand five hundred.*

Trevor: Sweet.

He shoved them down the front of his pants. Trust is a wonderful thing. As Trevor reached into his jacket pocket to his keys, he said: *Stacker is a rat, right. I've told him not to come here again.*

Lenny: What's going on?

Trevor: On the phone right, have you ever heard Stacker say 'pound of heroin'?

Lenny: No, not that.

Trevor: Can you fucking believe that? I heard him say those words on me phone, right. I've got some blokes that will sort him out. He's a fuckwit and should know better.

Lenny: Fuckwits are just that. Fuckwits. He's a junkie, too much on the gear.

Trevor: I don't want him in me house no more.

He was speaking very quietly, and very seriously. He stopped unlocking the door.

Trevor: Listen to this, right. This junkie bloke lives out the back here. He's scoring off me, right, and got no money. So he has a little boy about a six-year-old right. His kid has one of them racing car beds, like a formula one car – a red one.

Lenny: Yeah.

Trevor: This bloke wants to sell me his kid's fucking bed – right – for some hammer.

Lenny: Fucking unbelievable. Junkies would sell their mum.

I stopped for a split second because I suddenly realised that Trevor sometimes uses heroin. I thought, 'I better not knock junkies too much'. Then I thought, 'hang on, he doesn't know that I know he uses heroin. I can knock junkies'. These are the terrible thoughts that fly through my head. This is why knowing too much stuff that I really don't need to know at times like this, can be dangerous.

Trevor started unlocking the door again. As we left the flat, Trevor looked all around. He stopped and leant right up to my face. He lowered his voice to a whisper:

Trevor: On the phone – a pound is a car right?

Lenny: Yeah, I'm going to need another pound next week if this shit is good.

I tapped the silver box. Trevor arrogantly closed his eyes. I could tell another sermon was coming. Trevor rambled on about how I could cut it and mix it and sell it. In the end he finished with, 'But I wouldn't do that, right. Just leave it the way it is'.

This is all he knows. This is all he does. I hate drug dealers.

We shook hands. Trevor walked off toward the rear of his flat. I walked back the way I'd come. The coast was clear. Getting back into my car with a pound of speed from Trevor was a great feeling. I felt ten feet tall. After the usual anti-surveillance rigmarole I walked into my office. The word had already spread. Several members gave me a little cheer as I entered the room. I placed the silver box on a table. On my mini voice recorder I made notes of handing my drug product to Detective Senior Constable Bigmore. I put a pair of rubber gloves on and opened the box. Several detectives gathered around to look. I noticed one police uniform stood out in the crowd. It was an officer – an assistant commissioner. He asked, 'Can you test it to make sure it is amphetamines?' That was what I was about to do. The officer said, 'The chief has asked me to report to him the result.'

It appeared we weren't the only ones wanting to strike back after the Walsh Street murder acquittals. Within seconds, my spot test indicated the presence of amphetamines. Now I was happy. I did buy speed, not soap powder or sugar. The officer shook my hand and said, 'Well done. The chief commissioner and I would like to congratulate you.' I thought of asking for a pay rise but thought better of it. Even though I looked like Lenny, I tried to be as professional as possible. The officer turned and quickly left.

I was so proud of myself. My crew were in the middle of telling me what a great job I'd done when another detective approached. He is a short little bloke. We knew each other well. We had gone through the highly secret undercover operatives investigations course together. In a loud serious voice he said, 'So Trevor's your mate now, is he?'

In one of my proudest moments I was stabbed in the heart. I couldn't believe it. All I could say was, 'What?'

He said, 'He's your mate. I couldn't even be in the same room as him and breathe the same air.'

Accusing me of being mates with Trevor, an acquitted cop killer, was the lowest of all acts. All I could say was, 'What?' in disbelief. In all professions, office politics can be brutal, but cops are up there with the worst. At times I preferred being with the crooks. At times they were nicer. This was one of those times.

My mobile phone rang. I quickly started walking from my desk to an interview room where my end of the phone would sound less like the drug squad. As I closed the door behind me, I answered it. It was Stacker. The phone line was really bad. The only thing I could make out was, 'Something is wrong, it's urgent'. He also said something like, 'Don't go there'. The line went dead. I rang Stacker's home but there was no answer. As I tried to ring Trevor, my phone rang.

Fran: Eddie just rang me; the gooks are going off their heads.

Lenny: What are you on about?

Fran: They gave us too much heroin. We paid for a quarter ounce and they gave us a half ounce.

Lenny: Shit, you're right. 13.65 grams is a chew or two off 14. So what's going on?

Fran: Stacker and Trevor have been copping it from the gooks. That Le bloke wants his quarter ounce back or another $3500.

Lenny: You know the flat, number 82. How about you take me there and we'll give Le the extra money or the smack back?

Fran: We can't. That was the first thing Stacker said, 'Don't you fucking go there or I'll kill you'. Stacker thinks we're going to cut him out.

Lenny: We are trying to cut him out. This is perfect. Fantastic. This is the first time a fuck-up has gone our way. Leave Stacker to me. I'll work something out.

I arranged for Fran to drive back into the city. Sally didn't need to come. I briefed Steve. Steve told me that the first person Le rang when he realised he gave us too much was Trevor. Then Trevor agreed to sort it all out. Steve said that Trevor told Le that the gear was for a bloke named Lenny. Trevor told Le, 'Lenny, he's sweet. You can trust him.' Trevor told Le that he would come over and see him soon to have a chat. I decided it was better to take the seven grams of heroin back to Le rather than pay the extra money. Extra money would require extra paperwork. I couldn't be bothered this late in the day.

Fran drove back to the city, jumped into my vehicle and headed to Collingwood. I made sure her handbag was ready to rock and roll. I rang Stacker to make sure he wasn't around. He was at Trevor's down the road and told me the gooks had calmed down because he'd promised to pay for 'the extra' at the next deal. Stacker said that his bloke Le would only deal with him. I agreed with everything he said and promised to do another deal soon. I added a little something to keep him happy:

Lenny: Next week, I'm going to be doing some big business deals, right? I'll need you to watch my back. I'll pay you five hundred bucks just to come along.

Stacker: That's sweet. I'll bring a gun.

Lenny: No, it's not that big. I'm going to do some bigger stuff soon. I'll talk to you more about it later.

Stacker: Yeah, well I can bring me mate as well. He has a machine gun and can shoot cops or whatever. He doesn't care, Lenny. But he would cost more like eight hundred or somefin'.

Lenny: No, no, no, that's all right, just you will do. I'll speak to you later about it.

Stacker: Okay, my mate. He's in jail but gets out any day now.

Lenny: That's all right, see you mate.

Stacker: See ya, mate.

I pushed the 'end' button on my mobile about twenty times to make sure I'd hung up. I was always paranoid about my phone being left on.

'What did he say?' Fran asked.

'He said he was a fucking lunatic and he needs a bullet in his head. Come on, let's go.' I was paraphrasing, of course. I started to climb out of my car. Fran followed. As we walked up to the lifts Fran kept asking me what Stacker had said.

'He was rambling on about machine guns and killing cops. Let's just concentrate on this job. I'm going to stop short of Le's front door. I'll hold the gear. You tell Le that your bloke has brought back the extra smack. I can't help it. I'm just the most honest drug dealer the world has ever seen.'

Fran commented, 'You're the most full of shittiest.'

The lift door opened. The smell of stale human urine filled our nostrils. We stepped inside. Each of us stood on our tiptoes in between the puddles. As the lift lurched upward little yellow waves splashed onto our shoes. Fran said, 'Oh … fuck. This shit never happened in *Miami Vice*.'

'Today, it's more like *Hill Street Blues* goes to *China Town*,' I said. 'Except they're Vietnamese.' I pointed to her handbag. She reached inside and turned the tape recorder on:

Fran: It's Fran here again. It's 7.15pm on Friday the 10th of September and I'm in a lift with Lenny.

Lenny: Detective Senior Constable Lachlan McCulloch speaking, today I'm using the name Lenny. We were given fourteen grams of heroin instead of seven so we're giving seven grams back to a person named Le.

Fran: And we're both standing in a puddle of piss.

Lenny: Urine.

Fran: Piss, and it stinks. We're in a lift at 229 Hoddle Street, Collingwood.

Fran: Are you going to pay me for a new pair of shoes?

Lenny: No comment.

Fran: You can't say 'no comment'.

Lenny: You're taping me. It's my right. I know my rights. Now come on. Concentrate.

*Fran: Give me a look at your badge again. I don't reckon you're a cop. Besides, in the movies drug dealers are glamorous. Lenny, this is **not** glamorous.*

Lenny: Glamorous is coming. Now stamp your feet, get all that urine off them.

Fran: This is piss, Lenny.

Fran muttered away to herself as she stamped her way up the corridor. She knocked on the security door. Le answered. I heard him say in a heavy Asian accent, 'Wait, I get key'.

Le, like Trevor Pettingill, was in a habit of locking the inside of his doors.

As the door opened, Fran said, 'You gave us too much. My bloke here and I have brought it back.'

Fran pointed toward me. Le leant forward and peered at me. He smiled and started walking over. Fran walked with him. Le was very thin, about 165cm tall with a hard, gaunt face.

I was taken aback at the intense look on his face. He had very long straight hair and a large gold medallion on a long chain around his neck. He was the drug dealer from central casting.

Le gently grabbed me by the arm and stepped into the stairwell. Le obviously wanted to hide out of the way. He gave me a huge smile and a big handshake. His smile disappeared as quickly as it had come. He clasped my hand with both hands. Then he grabbed both my arms. I thought he was going to kiss me. I wasn't looking forward to it.

He reminded me of the bloke who tied Mel Gibson upside down and tortured him in the first *Lethal Weapon* movie. Except Le was a smaller, skinnier, scarier version. This touchy, feely rat-faced little bloke scared the crap out of me.

Fran: This is my bloke Lenny. Lenny, this is Le.

Lenny: It's great to meet you. Here is your gear. You gave me too much.

Le took it from my hand. He continually looked all around. He grabbed me by the left arm and gently squeezed it. We were all speaking in whispers as our voices echoed in the concrete stairwell.

Le: You are very, very kind. You could have paid me next time but this is very good. I trust you – we have trust. Lenny, I have wanted to meet you – I know all about you.

This was a worry. I was hoping he didn't know **all** about me, or he mightn't be so friendly. Le suddenly looked concerned. In his serious voice he said:

You must be careful. Never, never tell Stacker you come here. For me, and for you. He be very angry and too much trouble.

Lenny: I agree. We no tell Stacker. We can do business now?

Le: Yes, very much. I know about you – there is trust in us.

I didn't want to ask exactly what he knew about me. An Asian male appeared around the corner. Le introduced him to us as John. Le called him his brother. It wasn't his actual brother, just a good friend. He just stood there and smiled.

Lenny: Are you good friends with Stacker?

Both Le and John in unison: No, no, he craaaaaazy.

They both motioned to the inside of their forearms. They simulated injecting syringes into their arms.

Le: He junkie, very bad, very bad. I trust you.

With that comment I pulled up both my sleeves and showed Le my inner forearms.

Lenny: I no junkie. You both no junkie?

I looked at both of them. They exploded with, 'No, no, no, no.'

They pulled up their sleeves as well. Fran must have felt out of all this as she suddenly exposed her arms.

Lenny: Very good. I do only big business with you now. I can trust you.

Can I lie or what? Le was big on the trust business so I jumped on the bandwagon. I decided I was going to trust this guy the moment I trusted Stacker.

Le: Trust is good. Trust very good.

Lenny: I think Stacker crazy. I only know him because he can buy rock, good rock. He junkie so I only buy quarter ounce of rock with him. Now you, me and Fran can do big business, okay?

Le: Yes, when you get from me the rock, I all the time give you more never less. You will see.

From his pants pocket Le produced a piece of paper with a mobile phone number on it. I had prepared a similar piece of paper for exactly this occasion.

Le: Now, I call heroin a 'Tie' sometimes. But you just want rock heroin yeah?'

Lenny: Yeah

Le: You call it one CD when you want quarter ounce, you call two CD for half ounce, three CD for three quarter ounce and four CD for an ounce.

Lenny: Only rock, pure rock. What price?

Le: $10,500 for one ounce. Price cheaper the more you buy. No discount for quarter ounce.

Lenny: Now I only buy one ounce or more.

We shook hands again. I told him I was very happy now. Le went on to say that he was very careful around the flats.

Le: Police here dress up as garbage men, mailmen and try to catch him. You want to come here, you catch lift to top of building then walk down stairs to floor eight. Confuse police.

He rambled on about security. Just when I was feeling more comfortable with him.

Le: The more you buy the better. I do small deals here. Bigger deals with you at restaurants. I have restaurant one and restaurant two. There I bring my soldiers. My soldiers protect us.

Lenny: Great, that would be good.

Le: Never phone after 6pm – I have my time then – time off for me.

After a hard day drug dealing, he needs some time off. I'll give him some time off. We left moments later. Down the stairwell we whispered to each other. I was very happy about the whole thing but the soldiers were a worry. I dropped Fran back at her car and gave her a cuddle. She had done a brilliant job. We had finally made it past Stacker. Fran and I couldn't wait to do more deals. Not long to go now. I drove home and had a chardonnay or ten.

IN the police force, our days off are called rest days. They were not really days of rest for me. I spent most of the weekend talking to Fran. I was not allowed to speak to Fran inside my house. Apparently the subject matter and my language offended delicate ears. I would wander around my back yard plotting and planning with my mobile in one hand and my mini recorder in the other.

On Monday morning September 13, I was back at work. I

researched Le. His correct name was Cong Viet Le and he had been born in Vietnam on January 1, 1968. He had recently served two years in jail after being charged with murder. Le had allegedly been involved in a large street battle in the predominantly Asian suburb of Springvale. Two rival gangs fought in the middle of a busy shopping centre. Witnesses saw Le chase and hit a man several times with a meat cleaver. Le was charged with murder. While Le was on remand, the witnesses disappeared and he was released. He was as mad as he looked. Appearances often aren't deceiving.

In the middle of a crew meeting, Stacker rang. He was mad keen to sell me more heroin. I put him off till D-Day, meaning the following Thursday. I told Stacker that I was planning a huge deal on Thursday. I told him I was going to pay him five hundred bucks to watch my back, to protect me during the deal. Stacker was very happy with that. I told him when we finished that we could do the other deal as normal. When we did that deal, we could pay for the extra heroin we were given. I'd ring him Wednesday with the details.

After the phone call, we started to formulate the final plan for D-Day. On the top of the list, first cab off the rank was Stacker. The order was Stacker, Le, Trevor and Eddie. It would be a big day out.

CHAPTER 7

Endgame

By the time the cavalry
came to our rescue,
Fran and I could be
that pork-like substance
in the chop suey.

AT 11.15am, I entered the cone of silence. Steve sat next to me. I rang Le. He was pleased to hear from me. I told him that I needed to buy some CDs on Wednesday. Le agreed. He asked me to come out to lunch with him the next day. We agreed to meet at the Van Mai Restaurant in Victoria Parade at 1pm. He asked me to bring Fran. I said that was good because I was teaching her about music. Le laughed and said he was teaching John to play music.

The next day Fran and I parked outside the restaurant. As we got out, Le and John appeared and Le explained that the restaurant was closed. He offered to drive us to what he called his restaurant number two. It was the Kym 2 restaurant about three kilometres up the road. Le took us to his car – a brand new silver Ford Ghia sedan. Fran and I got in the back. Le drove with John in the passenger seat. Le asked me what music I liked. I told him I didn't mind. He picked up a large remote control from a holder on the dashboard, pushed a few buttons and the car exploded with rap music. I couldn't believe the windows didn't break. My bones and skin shook to the beat. Le started screaming something about the seats. Then I realised that our back seats were in fact massive soft speakers. A huge ten-stack CD player was mounted into the dashboard. Le screamed, '$6000 cost me'. I hoped the loud noise would not blow up my 'wire'.

As we walked into the restaurant, the staff were pleased to see him. Le took us to 'his' table. It was in a corner with a clear view of the place. It was quite busy. This was the heart of Vietnamese town, Victoria Street, Abbotsford. Fran and I were the only Anglo-Saxons around. This was to be a long lunch. Long as in painful. John was as quiet as a mouse. If he spoke, it was so quietly I just nodded as if I heard him. Le sat next to me. I mean next to me. He sat on my right and pushed his chair right up next to mine. What upset me was he kept squeezing my right thigh. I didn't want to be rude, so I put up with it. I noticed the strongest squeezes occurred whenever he mentioned the word 'trust'. Unfortunately 'trust' was sprinkled through every sentence. The food was beautiful. Every five minutes another course arrived. But just when I was enjoying it, Le picked up a clump of pork with his chopsticks and dropped it onto my plate. His disgusting, used chopsticks. I had to pick at the sides of the dish. It was a very long lunch.

I soon found out why we were invited to this lunch. Like Trevor, Le had certain operational procedures that we needed to be aware of. He stressed these in a voice straight out of a Jackie Chan movie. Excerpts from the recording:

You must pay in $100 or $50 notes so the bundles are small. Money must be wrapped in newspaper with white plastic bag on outside. You put noodles on top of money.

If you use heroin, nobody will trust you and it's very hard to stop using heroin. That was a good tip from a drug dealer. I don't think he understood the irony.

Forget CDs. An ounce of heroin is now one video.

See my phone, cost me $1900. You must call me if you late. But if you do, I get upset. We come here at 1pm. You say okay to me, John will say he going to toilet, you get money. Back here at table you give money to John, John give you heroin and I get money.

Imagine this guy organising a root in a brothel? Like Trevor, it must be his only job so he has to stretch it out.

I no count money, I trust you.

Another squeeze. I think he wanted to truss me. Throughout this two-hour marathon Le spoke of a very close friend who had been caught by an undercover cop. He warned me several times to watch out for them, meaning undercovers. I thought, 'I do look out for them because some of them are pricks.' Le stated that Stacker had told him all about our aborted drug deal on August 12 in Yarraville. He also stated that his best friend Andy (the heroin supplier that day) had also told him about it. Le blamed Stacker – it was his fault for sure. Le then went on about his own criminal past. He said he knew all about me because he had spent two years on remand in a prison cell with Victor Peirce. He also said he was good friends with Peter Allen (Trevor and Victor's other brother). Le said Victor told him I could be trusted because I was buying 'much' from Trevor. He said he had been charged with murder. He said it was a street fight. Let's cut to the transcript:

Le: We fight, I cut him. I win fight. I go jail two years.

Lenny: The winner always gets into trouble – although losing is bad, too.

Le: We were on TV news – someone had camera.

Le: You buy pound of speed from Trevor. I know this. You should buy from me. Next time we meet I have sample for you to try.

Everyone wants to cut Trevor out. At this rate he'll lose the only job he's qualified for. This began to explain why Le was always saying, 'I know what you do'. Toward the end of lunch, he came up with another classic:

Le: We must search each other.

He sat in the chair and started patting himself down. I think this was a demonstration.

Le continued: My friend he get caught. Undercover policemen wear listening device. We search each other.

Lenny: When did you want to do that?

Le: Tomorrow.

Lenny: Good, fine.

He had me worried for a moment. I hate being searched when I am wearing a listening device. Where did all that trust go when I needed it most? He trusted me enough to not count my money but not enough not to search me. There was some sort of logic there. If I was a cop I was likely not to rip him off and I would wear a wire that he would find. While he did that, I'd search him for a meat cleaver.

The bill came and he signed a piece of paper. He had an account or something. As Le drove us back to our car in his mobile supersonic jukebox, I wanted to clarify something:

Lenny: When you say soldiers, what do you mean?

Le: I have soldiers – soldiers protect me. They will be here.

I can't wait.

That night Eddie rang me. He was his normal jovial self. While in my backyard I organised five pounds of cannabis head at $4400 a pound. In code, of course. After Eddie finished talking to me, Sally got on the phone. Eddie got on very well with Sally, so I put her in charge of organising the details. Sally loved being given a job and that was it. In a second call to Sally I told her that Eddie was going to be last. The last arrest of the day. I had no idea what time it would be, just late. She promised to keep him happy until then. I stressed that we had to make sure that each of our targets didn't know what each other was doing that day. Otherwise they could have smelt a rat in the drug pile.

It was starting to get tricky. I'd cut Stacker out of the heroin and gone straight to Le and cut Trevor out of the cannabis and gone straight to Eddie. I didn't want to cut Trevor out, but Eddie offered me the cannabis at $4400 per pound, which was $400 cheaper than Trevor. Luckily, Trevor still had the speed to sell me. The girls were all excited, nervous and sad. Our adventure was nearing the end. In two days they were to enter the witness protection program and change their lives forever.

Again, I spent most of the night talking to Fran. On top of everything else she had to worry about, there was her husband. He was still in jail. His life was about to change too. Fran wanted me to go with her to give him the news. She was petrified. I supported Fran and she supported me. These were difficult times.

WEDNESDAY, September 15. The day was cold and windy. At home that morning I opened my cupboard to look for a jacket. I smiled when I saw my 'cloak of steel'. I got that name from the cartoon *Bat Fink*. It was my long dark blue Country Road overcoat. I bought it the day I became a detective. Cashmere wool blend with padded shoulders. $1200 worth in 1988. I didn't pay that, of course. I got a bit of a McDonald's discount. That's about twenty per cent off wholesale. Only joking.

Memories flooded back of walking slowly down Lygon Street, Carlton, when I had been a detective there. With the coat on, I could see Dick Tracy, ace detective when I looked at my reflection in the café windows. Late one evening I met Melbourne's most well-named gangster Alphonse Gangitano. He was wearing the same sort of Country Road overcoat. Except he was trying to be a tall version of Al Pacino in *The Godfather*. That was so weird. Given the current climate of police corruption and gangster killings, isn't it ironic that Dick Tracy and infamous gangsters want to look the same? Maybe there is a subliminal message: are they really trying to emulate each other? Anyway.

The drug squad office was a hive of industry. Operation orders and search warrants were being prepared. Interviewing members were being selected. There was a long list of what had to be organised: exhibit officers, log keepers, video operators, photographers, the dog squad, special operations group, surveillance unit, assets recovery section, tactical investigation unit, criminal intelligence section. Even the media liaison officer had to be informed that we weren't allowed to tell him anything. Not yet. The force is funny like that. We spend so much time hiding all our secret stuff from the media, both print and television. Yet when we really want to know something secret, we call them because they always find out first.

Everyone was vying for position on their favourite arrest team. Some wanted Trevor Pettingill, Le and his mates, others wanted Kath. There was one detective in the office who was going to miss out on all the action. The one who bagged me over getting close to Trevor. He was telling anyone who would listen what he wanted to do to Kath if he was on the arrest team. I didn't need a mental pigmy trying to do a bad impression of Clint Eastwood and ruining the case. I had a chat to Steve. He said he would handle it.

I started to get ready for my next deal. I no longer had to

become Lenny. By now I had realised I had become him. No acting required. I only had to be myself. Soon, when it was over, I would have to get back into character as Lachlan McCulloch. I grabbed my coat off the back of my chair and went to work. I picked up Fran and we drove to Victoria Street. It was lunchtime and the place was packed. I suddenly realised that I had forgotten one vital ingredient. The noodles. Fran started laughing. I cursed Le as I walked into one of the million noodle shops and asked for a bunch of noodles. The shop assistant looked at me blankly. I looked around at the thousands of packets of noodles. I told Fran I'd forgotten to ask him what type of noodles. In true police style, I realised what type I should get … the cheapest. I splashed out and bought four packets of dried rice noodles for $1.20. Bargain.

About 12.55pm, Fran and I entered the Kym 2 restaurant. The place was very quiet. We took our seats at the same table. I sat with my back to a blank wall. I had a clear view of the whole restaurant. Big windows allowed me to see out onto Victoria Street and a small side street. Fran and I ordered scotch and Cokes.

Fran: I feel like I'm in the movie Chinatown.

Lenny: Stop it, Fran. You could pick a better movie than that one. Besides there were more bullets fired in that movie than in the Second World War.

Fran: I hope it's like Bambi then.

Lenny: Bambi's mum got shot and I think Bambi copped it in the neck as well.

Le appeared, followed by six lookalikes. They were all the same height and wore the same tense serious faces. Three of his soldiers took up positions just outside the three entrances. The other three entered with Le. John appeared out of the men's toilet. Le walked up and gave us one of those forced smiles, the one kids do when you ask them to smile for the camera. Le then said he wanted us to change tables. I wasn't happy but he insisted. We sat down right in the middle of the restaurant. I couldn't decide if this was better or worse.

It looked ridiculous. Six scruffy looking young blokes, all doing oriental secret service agent impressions. Each one had at least one hand inside their jacket. Le and John sat with us at the table. I placed a white Safeway bag on the middle – $21,000 of the cold hard stuff surrounded by the long noodley stuff as requested. Le again sat on my right. He pushed right up against me and reached over to squeeze my left thigh with both hands. He looked into my eyes and said – you guessed it – 'I trust you'.

Lenny: We have trust, we have trust.

One of the soldiers decided to stand up and sit at a table right behind me. I spun around and gave him a filthy look that I had learnt from my girlfriend. He just stared back.

Lenny: Is this bloke with you?

Le: My soldier.

Lenny: Can you move him back where I can see him?

Le spoke to him abruptly in his foreign tongue. This was one very scary drug deal. Fran and I were trying to put on brave faces, but it was hard. I had soldiers too, but the problem was that Le didn't know that. Le and his soldiers could have set us up for a robbery. His soldiers were feet away from us and mine were at least 50 metres away. I was taught action beats reaction. By the time the cavalry came to our rescue, Fran and I could be that pork-like substance in the chop suey.

An Asian male entered via the same side street door. He continually stared at us as he walked over and stood about four metres to my right. He had this huge football-shaped deadpan face and a thick padded beige ski jacket. Le spoke to 'Football Face' in Vietnamese and they both walked up a set of stairs on my right. They spoke up there for a while and returned. Football Face left. Moments later they repeated their up and down the stairs routine. Finally Le nuzzled up to me again. This time, instead of squeezing my leg under the table, he pushed two golf ball-sized packages onto it. This was followed by numerous 'I trust you'. I tucked them into the top of my left boot. I nodded at the plastic bag in the middle of the table. I was feeling generous, 'You can have the noodles for free'.

Le and I spoke the next day. I told him that if I was happy I would want half a pound, or eight videos. Le told me it was $65,000 for eight ounces. I said I wanted about eight ounces every month. Le said he could do eight ounces of heroin at one o'clock at restaurant number one, the Van Mai.

During this conversation, Football Face waited for his money. Le was very nervous and was whispering very quietly, 'This today go very well. We can do much business in the future'. Le left with John. The soldiers surrounded Football Face and Le. They could not have been more conspicuous if they tried. Fran and I got the hell out the door of the opposite side of the restaurant. I had a peek at my product. It was just like the rest I'd bought. We celebrated. Happy times were here again. I phoned Steve. By now Fran and I had developed a friendship that was forged by adversity. It was all about to end. One day to go.

ON returning to the drug squad, Baldrick had some news. He had identified Football Head. His name was Meng Kok Te. I'd heard of that name. It turned out that several months ago I had gone to his house in Footscray. We had gone to serve a summons on behalf of the New South Wales drug enforcement agency. By sheer chance he wasn't home at the time. I imagined what might have happened had we recognised each other in that restaurant surrounded by soldiers. I quickly imagined something else. Did I ever say, 'Luck's got nothing to do with it'? Baldrick went on to say that Football Head was a major target of the National Crime Authority. He was importing large amounts of heroin into Australia via Sydney. Moments later, several members of the NCA arrived at our office. They wanted to be the arrest team at my 'buy bust' tomorrow. We sat around the office for hours plotting and planning our last day.

At 8.05 that night, Le rang my mobile. He wanted me to wait until Monday for the eight ounces of heroin. He called them videos. All he could supply me tomorrow was one ounce. What a tragedy. I agreed to buy the one ounce tomorrow and my original order on Monday.

Le also said he would give me the sample of speed tomorrow. Le seemed upset that he had let me down. At 9.40pm, he rang again. He said all was okay for the eight ounces tomorrow. I told him I would have the $65,000. At 10.12pm, my phone rang again. My brain was well and truly affected by chardonnay. I thought, 'I'm sure he told me he stopped doing business at 6pm.' This time he said he could only get six ounces of heroin that he could do for the bargain price of $56,000. I told him I'd take it and if there were any more changes could he ring me tomorrow. I had some serious drinking to do. One more sleep and it was over.

At last it was Thursday, September 16 – D-Day. I arrived at the office at 6.45am. The drug squad was humming – 180 members from squads and stations packed into our office. As they arrived, team leaders received a copy of the operation order. At 7.30am, the briefing commenced. The op order was read out aloud. You could hear a pin drop from the moment it began. They listened as the details of each drug deal over the past seven months were read out. I stood at the back of everyone, my head bowed, listening. To the majority, these were just words and interesting events. To me, this was grand final day. We had already won the game. All we had to do now was run onto the ground and arrest the opposition players. Up until that moment, this was the most important day of my life. It was about to get a little bit better.

At the end, there were claps and cheers. As the majority left the office, I was paraded in front of the drug squad and NCA arrest crews. I was wearing a big bright pink T-shirt, my standard black Levi 501 jeans, and my bikie Blundstone boots. I held my arms up in the air and said, 'I am going to wear this all day. So, remember, don't shoot the pink guy.'

Someone said, 'Just bash him.'

I said, 'I'll be wearing an extremely expensive listening device and you don't want to break it.' Everyone laughed. I knew that wouldn't stop them bashing me but it was worth a try. I went on, 'Seriously, today I am not armed, I will not be carrying a firearm today. So if shit happens, it's up to you.'

At the end of that, I had a closed door meeting with members of the special operations group. They were to be deployed to arrest Steven McKinnon alias Stacker and Trevor Pettingill. I will never tell anyone how these guys operate. Suffice to say if you are a suspect, a possible suspect or a criminal and you think they may be headed in your direction, arrest yourself immediately. Lie spread-eagled, face down on the floor and don't say a word. But remember, this action will in no way diminish the hailstorm of violence you are about to receive. The idea is to make the arrest as boring as possible and they may just move on. Action causes reaction. Trust me, you don't want that.

I spoke to Fran and Sally. Everything had been organised for the witness protection program to whisk them away. But first they had some work to do. I drove out to Reservoir alone. I woke Stacker up at 9.15am. I had previously asked him to protect me at this big drug deal I'd planned. I was to pay him $500 at the end of the deal. He was all excited and said he could do this every day if I wanted. As I drove him down St Georges Road, Preston, my mobile rang. I pushed the answer button and the voice said, 'Is this Detective Senior Constable Lachlan McCulloch of the drug squad?' I pushed the earpiece as hard as I could into my ear.

I glanced at Stacker to see if he had heard. It didn't look as if he had. I said, 'No,' and hung up. Unbelievable. I found out later that Sally had a court case that day and that phone call was a prosecutor looking for her. That was another debacle that I would sort out later.

Anyway, I was driving Stacker down St Georges Road. Let's cut to the transcript:

Stacker: Yeah – right – my mate's got a machine gun right and can kill anyone. He gets hired to cover big drug deals.

Lenny: Yeah – you told me on the phone – that's okay but I don't need that.

I thought that this was Stacker trying to be a tough guy. But then he went on with the story:

He's in prison and gets out in a week or so – his name is Nam. Do you know him?

I told him I didn't but I knew who Nam was all right, and he was as deadly as Stacker said. He was without a doubt the most dangerous Asian gangster in Australia – an oriental 'Chopper' Read with ears.

Stacker: He is worth getting to work with me when you do a pound or half pound of smack. He's me mate – we did time together. But you gotta see this bloke. He scares you right, that's without a gun, but he does have guns. Big ones – he's wicked, right?

I pulled into a service station. I told Stacker that I'd had a few too many drinks last night and I needed a 'slurpie'. I talked him into coming inside with me to pick some flavours.

Stacker: I don't drink fucking slurpies.

Lenny: Come on, you mix the flavours up.

After a short argument, I dragged him inside. After we got our slurpies, we began to leave. I opened the door for Stacker. He walked out first, I followed.

Suddenly a gang of black ninjas carrying machine guns appeared before us. Now I knew it was going to happen. But, no matter how much I prepared myself, it still frightened the hell out of me. They wore gas masks and bad attitudes. They screamed, 'Police, get down on the ground.' One hosed Stacker in the face with an industrial-sized fire extinguisher. The high pressure capsicum sprayer hit Stacker so hard in the face it nearly took his ears off. They did that and Stacker didn't even spill his slurpie. How tough is that? I, on the other hand, was hit by Stacker's capsicum spray splash-back and lay face down on top of mine. I wasn't taking any chances. Other secret police agencies use nasty chemical gases. It's nice to know our SOG uses an organically-based, environmentally-friendly pepper product, which dissipates without leaving any toxic residue.

A little while later when I could see and breathe again, I looked over to the arrest scene. There were still ninjas everywhere. A police inspector was trying to take a petrol bowser nozzle from the hand of a woman. She had been filling up her car when the ninjas struck. She was so scared she went into a trance that caused her to wander around with the nozzle still in her hand. Someone came and moved her car because she was unable to drive. I don't blame her.

I gathered myself together, obtained another slurpie and drove back to the drug squad. About a kilometre up the road there was a traffic jam. There was a car in the middle of the road with all its doors open and five men rolling around on the road. I recognised one of the men's jackets. It was Stacker. Then I noticed Baldrick. I rang his mobile. He told me that the capsicum spray that was all over Stacker nearly caused them to crash. They bailed out so they could breathe. A divisional van had to be called to take him back to the office.

Back at the office I started to get ready for the next episode. I counted the $56,000 in cash. As I did that Stacker was in the cone of silence with Baldrick. They had to give him a change of clothes before he could be let in the same room with other people. Baldrick walked out of the room and said, 'Where's Lenny? Stacker wants to know where his mate Lenny went. He just sits there saying, "You guys hose me down with poisonous gas. Why? What's the charge? Drinking a slurpie? Come on, what have you done with my mate Lenny?".' No-one was talking to Stacker and it was driving him nuts. He'd been put on ice. That is, no phone calls, no access to a solicitor, nothing. The law allowed us to infringe upon his civil rights as the safety of witnesses and undercover operatives was still an issue. The girls and I still had a few adventures left. Even Stacker's official police interview had been postponed.

At 11.03am, Trevor rang me. I retreated into the boss's office and closed the door. He said he was ringing from the Melbourne Magistrates' Court building. He was there to adjourn his court case. I asked him if it was still all right for me to buy the two Commodore sedans (two pounds of speed) at 2pm. He said it was sweet. Almost two years later, a judge in the County Court commented on the fact that Trevor Pettingill had organised a drug deal from a court building.

I picked Fran up and headed off to the Van Mai restaurant. As we arrived, Fran played 'let's find the surveillance teams'. She had no idea. As we walked into the restaurant, we were greeted by the owner. I told him we were with Le. He walked us around a table packed with partygoers. We sat down at a corner table with Le. I placed my white plastic bag containing $56,000 on the middle of the table. Le looked very upset.

Lenny: I'm sorry. I'm fresh out of noodles. You cleaned me out yesterday. You could buy a shop full of noodles with that!

Le: No, okay, okay.

He sat next to me and squeezed my leg with both hands. He said he was very, very, very sorry but his friend could not bring the six ounces. He could do it later that evening, but not now. I told Le that I needed at least one ounce as promised. I was most upset. My tongue was in my cheek at the time.

Lenny: But I trusted you. Do you understand? I trusted you.

Le: Sorry, sorry, sorry. This is so bad – I so sorry. This never happen again. I smash – bash the people that let me down.

Le started to turn himself inside out. He made many phone calls. Sometimes he screamed and abused whoever it was, but on the next call he would be respectful and polite. After a polite call, he told us the heroin was ten minutes away. That must be the heroin supplier.

While we waited, we ate course after course. I felt very safe in the restaurant as there was a distinct lack of soldiers. At one point, I had to call the waiter over and ask him to tell the party next to us to quieten down a bit. They were singing and shouting so much I could hardly hear Le's whispers.

Next second Le stood up and walked toward the front of the restaurant. There was Football Head, right on time. He had a different jacket on today but that head was the same. Le bowed down as he approached Football Head. They left the restaurant. I asked Fran if she could take all the money to the toilet and take out $10,500. She thought that was a great idea. Seconds later, Le came back to our table. He gave me the small speed sample. He said it was pure. He told me I could have a pound of this speed on Sunday. 'Sunday too far away,' I thought.

A waiter appeared with a big birthday cake covered in candles. The party next to us burst into song – a loud and enthusiastic rendition of *Happy Birthday*. Fran sat back down and handed me the money. Under the table Le handed me a golf ball-size package. It looked like white rock heroin covered in clear plastic. I handed Le the $10,500. We shook hands and squeezed each other again. We said our last 'I trust you' to each other. I stood up and put on my cloak of steel. I took Fran by the hand. As we walked past the party, I paused and in a loud clear voice I said, 'Happy birthday, Happy birthday'. I opened the front door for Fran. As the door closed behind us, Fran said, 'Where is everyone?' I stopped her and said, 'Ssshhh.'

The restaurant exploded with, 'Police, don't move'. A few seconds later the noise died down. Fran and I smiled as we walked off toward my car. Suddenly, Football Head stepped out of a small white car right in front of us. Fran squeezed my arm and shook it. There were no cops around. He walked past us. As soon as he got past me, I turned and tiptoed up behind him. I madly waved both of my arms pointing at his back. I was trying to tell all the police that must be around but I couldn't see, that this was the guy, 'Take him out'. He had no idea what had gone on inside the restaurant. He was headed straight for the front door and a very uncertain future.

Two passing cars suddenly turned onto the footpath and skidded to a halt either side of Football Head. Plainclothes policemen piled out of their vehicles screaming, 'Police, get down on the ground.' Football Head stopped, looked at the men screaming at him and sort of did a double take. He didn't understand that he really didn't need to give these cops a reason. Nor did he appreciate how incredibly frustrating it is to be a surveillance policeman (dog) watching criminals all the time and not ever catching any. This was one of those rare occasions when the dogs get to have a bit of a bite. What didn't help Football Head were the facts that he was an Asian high-level heroin trafficker, Le's habit of keeping company with his soldiers and Stacker's talk of Nam the mad gunman. His nickname didn't help him either, come to think of it.

The sight and sound of his arrest made Fran and me wince. Fran started to describe how the police had arrested him. That comment made me realise my tape recorder was still running. I turned my tape off. As we got into my car, I said, 'Fran, I shudder to think what you've taped with your handbag over the last seven months.' I had a feeling we would eventually find out. Court cases are funny like that. I sat in the car and looked at Fran. That was our last drug deal together. 'It's all over,' Fran said. 'I can't believe it.'

WE were excited, relieved, sad, and emotional. We hugged. There were tears. I told Fran, 'You are the greatest ever. What an adventure. You know now is the hard part. Nothing but statements and court cases.' Fran's part in the active investigation was over. But the court cases were to come. I drove her to a designated meeting place. We got out of the car. Members from the witness protection program were there. They took Fran away. As she left, I said, 'Remember, you're a witness. A witness.' Fran was not an informer. She did not inform. She did the business. She collected evidence. We all knew this action would haunt her forever. In 24-hour protection – indefinitely. She only did it because I convinced her she would be looked after. What have I done to her and her family? I cried. Real tough guys don't cry, so I stopped. Then I realised it was all right. I'm not a real tough guy.

It was only when I saw her drive away, in protection, that I realised the implications and enormity of our actions. Forever is a long time. We were in many ways closer than lovers. What we had was more intimate than sex. We had trust. The type of trust you can't put into words. Trust developed through action, not words. Some lovers never even find that.

At 1.45pm, I rang Trevor. I told him I was running a bit late. He said it didn't matter. He said he had problems because his bloke had let him down. He wanted me to come over for a chat. I told him I had people to see nearby. Trevor was upset by the fact he had let me down and was unable to come through with his end of the deal. His word was everything. When I thought about that, I realised he was right. He's got nothing else. I asked him to ring me when he heard something.

At 2.18pm, I telephoned Sally. She was happy and nervous. She had Eddie all organised for this evening. I asked her to ring me later. I tried to relax back at the drug squad. The telephone intercepts revealed that Trevor was contacting Donato Corsi constantly. During those conversations Trevor told Donato to ring him when 'it was all correct'. Donato told Trevor he had diluted something eight times and that it was too weak. Trevor told him to only make it a pound and a half then. Donato was upset about something and said he had to 'go to the other place'.

At 5pm, I telephoned Trevor. During this call he asked me to wait on the phone because his wife Debbie told him he had another call on the poofters' phone next door. Moments later, Trevor came back and said he still had problems. He asked me to ring back in an hour. He reckons **he** had problems. What Trevor didn't seem to appreciate was that he was not just disappointing me by failing to supply speed, he was stuffing around the 'Sons of God'. They wanted to knock off. At

5.45pm, I went to an observation post. Without giving away the SOG's methods, I will describe what happened next. At 5.50pm, I telephoned Trevor for the last time. This time Trevor spoke in code. He promised me he had spoken to his man and could now sell me the two pounds tomorrow. As I was speaking on my mobile, I was looking out a window straight at Trevor's flat. I watched as a small army of special operations group members approached.

I believe it's true that top crooks feel impending danger. A lot of career criminals have at the last moment stopped and walked away from situations that would have brought them undone. When investigators have spoken to them later they can't even tell you why. Call it intuition from years of hands-on experience. Once, at the drug squad, we were working on a crook by the name of Len Reading. His brother Geoff Reading was present when Mick Gatto shot 'Benji' Veniamin in a Carlton restaurant. Len was a good old crook who was heavily involved in the manufacture of amphetamines. I investigated him on and off for the seven years I was in the drug squad.

The closest we got to catching him was when one of his close associates became an informer. Len and the informer set up a clandestine laboratory inside a building. Just as we were about to bust them, Len got one of those subtle feelings. At least, that's what I thought then.

Now that all the corruption is coming to light from my old drug squad, maybe he had received one of those not so subtle 'fuck off now' phone calls. Whatever it was, it worked. Len beat all the charges.

As I spoke to Trevor and the last seconds ticked by, I realised he was not going to pick up any signals. As we again spoke of the two pound deal next day I watched six heavily armed ninjas flow into his flat. To my amazement, Trevor was still talking to me. I looked at Steve in disbelief. While Trevor was mid-sentence he screamed into the phone. I hung up. It was over. Steve and I shook hands. Steve received a call from the head of the SOG. Trevor was in custody. We returned to the drug squad. On the way I rang Sally. I told her Trevor had been arrested and she had to make sure Eddie didn't find out. 'It's nearly all over Sally. How do you feel?'

She said, 'I'm scared. Now I just want it to finish – this one more deal, Lenny. Can you hurry up? I'm having problems with Eddie.'

'I'll be as quick as I can,' I replied. 'Hang in there.'

She was doing a great job. Over the months I had grown to understand Sally. My relationship with her was very different to the one I had with Fran. Inside, Fran was a solid tower of strength. Inside, Sally was an insecure petrified little girl. Fran was out to change the world. Sally was flat out just trying to live in it. Even on this last day I didn't really understand why Sally had joined us but I was grateful that she had. There was no doubt that one of the main reasons we were successful was that Sally was accepted by the crooks as one of them. She stood up for me. That was the only reason I was accepted. Apart from the fact that I'm an extremely good undercover operative, of course.

The best way to describe the next event of the day is to read the statement made by the sergeant in charge – a man who was later to have his own legal problems:

Bassett, Russell Geoffrey states:

I am a Detective Sergeant attached to the Crime Department Drug Squad.

At approximately 5.35pm, Thursday, 16 September, 1993, I attended (an address) Venus Bay.

On this day I was in possession of a search warrant issued under the provisions of the Drugs Poisons and Controlled Substances Act 1981.

On attendance at the address I knocked on the front door and made a demand for it to be opened. There was no reply so the door was forced. I entered the premises and immediately moved to an upstairs lounge area. I was in company with Detective Senior Constable Mutsides.

On entering the area I saw an elderly female whom is known to me as the defendant Kathleen Pettingill. Pettingill was seated in a chair in the lounge room area.

Det. Mutsides yelled, 'Police don't move. Now stand.' Pettingill stood.

Mutsides yelled, 'On the floor.'

Pettingill then moved to a semi-lying position on the lounge floor. Mutsides yelled, 'Hands behind your back.'

Pettingill did not respond.

I then placed my left foot into the centre of Pettingill's back and applied downward pressure. This caused Pettingill to fall forward onto her stomach and move her hands from under her body.

As this occurred, the top of her tracksuit pants came down. I saw a silver coloured object protrude from between the cheeks of Pettingill's buttocks.

At this time I yelled, 'Weapon'. I then handcuffed Pettingill and retrieved the object from between her buttocks.

I identified this object to be a 'pen pistol'. I placed the item onto a coffee table. I yelled, 'Do you have any other weapons?'

She said, 'It's a load up.'

I said, 'I must inform you that you are not obliged to say anything unless you wish to, but anything you say may be recorded. Do you understand?'

She said, 'This is a load up.'

I said, 'It is our intention to search these premises under the provisions of the Search Warrant (Warrant shown)

She said, 'You will only find what you have brought with you.'

R.G.Bassett

Detective Sergeant 21761

They also located the rug with the letters YNIT written on it. Fran and I had given it to her to introduce us to Stacker. We really should have kept the rug. Anyway.

Russell Bassett telephoned the result through to the control room at the drug squad. There were no drugs found. I found it interesting that it was not the same pen pistol that Kath had produced to us during a drug deal. There was no gold-coloured trim. I thought that was a bit strange. I was determined to get to the bottom of the question, 'Who put the pistol in the crack of Kath's bum?' On the one hand you had Kath screaming, 'Load up', which she had done for the past 50 years every time she'd been arrested. On the other hand she may well have been 'loaded up' over the past 50 years every time she'd been arrested. So when she screamed 'load up', who would know what was going on?

On the subject of the pen pistol, I will show you a statement that formed part of the brief of evidence against Kath.

Henry James Glaser states:

I am a Senior Constable of Police attached to the Victoria Police State Forensic Science Laboratory. I am a Firearm and Toolmark Examiner.

On October 12, 1993, I received Case no. 6145/923. This item contained a pen pistol and one cartridge.

The pen pistol (Item 41) was a .22 Long Rifle calibre homemade single shot pistol the appearance of which resembled a writing pen.

There was deposits of partly burnt grains of powder in the bore. The overall length of this weapon was four and a half inches. (114 mm) The barrel length was two inches. (51 mm)

I was able to discharge this weapon after it was loaded by drawing back the plunger knob then allowing it to slip forward under its own spring tension as it was designed to do.

The cartridge (also Item 41) was a .22 Long Rifle calibre Winchester Brand Subsonic loaded with a Hollow Point bullet.

Subsonic cartridges are cartridges that are loaded with a reduced quantity of power or propellant powder so that the discharge bullet travels just below the speed of sound, which has the effect of reduced sound and reduced recoil.

Subsonic cartridges would therefore be more comfortable to fire in a pen pistol than high velocity cartridges.

H.J.Glaser

S/C 16442.

What a classic. Kath Pettingill, just like 'Madge' in the dishwashing liquid commercial, had found that when she shot subsonic bullets from her pen pistol they were 'softer on the hands' than other more commonly used bullets. Only a regular subsonic bullet user could reap the benefits. The burnt powder residue inside the barrel seemed to indicate she'd done a bit of pistol practice.

Who or what had she been practising on? Kath could quietly slip one into a troublesome rival at bingo, in between calls of legs eleven and two fat ladies, 88.

All this indicated to me that it probably was Kath's pen pistol after all. If it had been 'planted' I'm sure no detective, in particular Russell Bassett, would have considered nor cared about the ergonomic comforts of subsonic bullets. In fact I'm positive. Another interesting fact is that pen pistols are not the preferred weapon of bank robbers. If a robber was to run into a bank and point a silver-coloured pen at a teller, the robber would not be likely to receive the urgent respect that armed robbery requires. The robber would spend far too much time explaining to the teller that it really was a gun. I know this because I often watch *Get Smart*. He had a pen gun. When he pointed it at the bad guys, they never believed it was a gun. So Max would fire it into the air. Then Max would be in big trouble because he was out of bullets.

The point I'm getting at is that there is no 'fear factor' in a pen pistol. They're only useful if you want to bypass the scaring and get straight to the shooting. The bottom line is, they really only give the carrier a false sense of comfort. Good crooks don't bring pen pistols to a gunfight, if you know what I mean.

AT 5.55pm, my mobile rang. It was Sally. I was amazed that Eddie still hadn't found out that Trevor had been arrested. The drug deal was still on. As I retreated into the cone of silence, Sally put Eddie on the phone. I apologised for being so late. I arranged to meet him in five minutes at Noturno's Café in Lygon Street, Carlton. I counted out $22,000. I'd ordered five pounds of cannabis head at $4400 per pound. This deal had worked out well. Eddie had decided to cut Trevor out of the cannabis. So Eddie had kept away from Trevor all day.

I was very uncomfortable about meeting Eddie in Carlton, as I had spent three and a half years as a senior detective at Carlton CIB. But I decided to take the risk of being recognised. After all, this was my last drug deal in this operation. I met with the arrest crew. I told them that this deal should be quick and easy. I told them Eddie Fiorello was a funny bastard who looked like a Mexican. I told Baldrick that he should have a funny interview with Eddie. I crammed the $22,000 into my bumbag and left the office via the secret rear entrance.

At 6.10pm, I entered Noturno's Café. As Eddie and I looked

at each other, we smiled. Eddie and I really did like each other. I really liked the fact that I was about to lock him up and he really did like me – probably because I was giving him lots of money.

I sat down at the table with them. Eddie was laughing away. We shook hands like old friends. I gave Sally a little kiss on the cheek. I slipped her a look that said, 'Well done'. We spoke about how the deal was going to take place. Unlike Trevor Pettingill, Eddie had actually done some kind of work other than trafficking drugs. Not real work of course. At times, when cannabis trafficking was slow, he would sell soap powder. Not fake heroin, as I first thought – real soap powder.

At one point in our conversation I said, 'Now Eddie, I'm not buying soap powder, am I?' Eddie laughed and said, 'Big bubbles, no troubles. Bubbles are my business.' He was a funny bastard who trafficked drugs and was good friends with the likes of Stacker and Trevor. So at the end of the day it just made him a bastard. Eddie said he wanted to do the deal at the same car repair place that Trevor had taken me a while back. It was in a little lane that ran off Rathdowne Street, Carlton. He wanted me to do the deal immediately, but I put it off till 7pm. I told him I only had $18,000 and that I had to drive down the road and pick up the other $4000.

Eddie: We can just do the deal down the lane.

I smiled at him and said 'Is this a test or something? Do you really think I want to be down a laneway by myself with my hard-earned $22,000?'

Eddie: I'm not Stacker. Come on, trust me.

Lenny: Do you trust me?

Eddie: I always trust the KGB.

We all laughed. Eddie often joked about me being a cop. It was quite funny really, to everyone but me. And later, to him.

Lenny: That's good. I just don't trust anyone that says 'trust me'.

Eddie: There's somethin' wrong with you – you won't even trust Stacker.

Now that was funny. Drug deals were not meant to be this funny. Eddie cracked himself up so much he fell off his chair laughing.

Lenny: I've got to go. I'll be parked in Nicholson Street at the beginning of the lane at seven o'clock.

Eddie: Do you know we could get arrested doing this shit?

Lenny: I don't plan on getting arrested.

Eddie: It just happens sometimes, mate. You ever been hit by a phone book?

Lenny: No.

Eddie: The worst year was the 1988 Yellow Pages A to K model. That was a bastard of a book. The cops knew it, too. I think the paper was heavier or somethin'. Even in 1991 I was still getting hit with the 1988 Yellow pages.

Lenny: Mr KGB has to go now. Seven o'clock, front of the laneway.

Eddie and Sally were cackling away. I paused and gave Sally a little nod. She looked at me with an all-knowing smile. As I walked off I mumbled, 'One more, just one more deal'. I phoned Steve and told him the location and time of the deal. In a back street I met up with the bust crew. They had recent photos of Eddie. Thunderbirds are go.

At 6.58pm I parked my car facing south in Nicholson Street. I was about a metre short of the lane. The night was pitch black. It had just started to rain. Nicholson Street was packed with traffic. The air was filled with the sound of cars driving over the wet road. Moments later Sally appeared. She climbed into the back seat.

Sally: Eddie is at the car place. It's freezing out there, Lenny.
Eddie should be here any second.
Lenny: You've done a great job, mate.
Sally: How's Fran? Is she right?
Lenny: She's great. We've been flat out, Stacker, Trevor, Le:
everyone's locked up. Eddie's the last of 'em.
Sally: My God. So this is it, then.

I had turned around and faced her. She had tears welling in her eyes. I reached over the seat and held her hand. I gave it a little squeeze and said, 'You're a champion. When we do the deal, Eddie's taken out. Just put your hands on the roof. Witness protection take you from here.' Sally's worn face looked petrified.

Sally: Lenny, Eddie thinks there's something wrong.
Lenny: What, what does he think?
Sally: I don't know, but he's acting funny.
Lenny: Everything will be fine.

With that Eddie strode out of the darkness and opened the front passenger door. He put a large backpack on his lap.

Eddie: Go, go, go. Let's get out of here.
Lenny: Relax, everything is fine.
Sally: You're paranoid, Eddie.
Eddie: Get out of here.
Lenny: What's wrong? Show me the gear and I'll give you the money.

Eddie reluctantly opened the top of his backpack. He grabbed one of several football-shaped objects and started ripping a little hole in the side of it. They were the same clear plastic-wrapped parcels of cannabis head I had been buying from Trevor. I reached into the hole and grabbed a piece of 'the green'. The stench of cannabis filled the car.

Lenny: Good stinky stuff.

I counted five parcels and said, 'I need a new backpack'. I started to get out of the car.

Eddie: What are you doing?

Lenny: The money is in the boot. I'll grab it.

Eddie: No, come on. Drive, I want to get out of here now!

Eddie was seriously worried. His eyes were wide open and his words were short and sharp. I'd seen this look on my own face in recent times.

Lenny: Hang on, relax.

Eddie: For fuck's sake drive. The cops could just drive up now and bust us. Go now!

This was one of those times I've spoken about. Some crooks can feel impending peril. Stacker, Trevor and Le had all missed it. But Eddie felt it big time.

Alarm bells were screaming all over his face. This was not paranoia. He could feel the freight train coming but couldn't get off the tracks. I pulled my car keys out of the ignition as I stepped out of the car.

Eddie looked around frantically. He screamed, 'Come on, come on.' I opened the boot of my car and reached inside. The air was cold and it was pitch black.

As I closed the boot, I paused. The sound of car wheels screeching to a halt was all the confirmation Eddie needed. I put my hands in the air when the sound of cops screaming, 'Police, get on the ground' hit us. Eddie must have already had his side door open. He burst out of my vehicle and started to run straight into the lane. Then he suddenly stopped, turned and ran back in front of my vehicle.

The first cop car had braked way too hard and had skidded right past us. One cop jumped out of the back seat and was beginning to stand as Eddie dropped his left shoulder and shunted him straight back inside. A second cop stepped around the back of his car just in time for Eddie to shirt front him flat onto his back.

Eddie ran headlong into traffic. Cars skidded left and right just avoiding him. How he made it to the other side I'll never know, with half a dozen cops in hot pursuit. Eddie had a good lead as the cops were slightly more cautious running through the traffic. One cop had hit the lead. It was Boonie. Boonie had organised a couple of undercover buy busts that day himself. Obviously that wasn't enough action for one day so he joined the arrest teams to catch 'Fast' Eddie. Eddie ran straight up the first laneway.

I turned to see Sally stepping out of my car. I walked over and gave her a big cuddle. Sally was shaking as she cried. She sobbed, 'He's got away.'

I said, 'Sally, they'll get him. It's all over.'

Sally just cried.

Two plain-clothed officers from the witness protection unit walked up to us. They greeted us with big smiles. I gave Sally a little kiss on the cheek. I was crying. My voice broke as I said, 'This life is over. Your new life starts today.'

Sally said, 'Good people, I'll be with good people.'

Within seconds, Sally's tears had dried up and she was laughing again. As she walked off with the two officers, she started telling them of her adventures.

I looked back over the road in time to see Boonie pushing Eddie in front of him. Eddie was three times his size but was no match for the little guy.

Eddie bore the scars of being rugby-tackled face first onto a bluestone laneway.

As Eddie was pushed into the back of a divisional van, I turned and walked across the footpath to a small fence. I sat down and put my head in my hands. I closed my eyes. It was over. I heard, 'Well done, buddy.' I looked up to see Steve, towering above me, smiling big time.

I said, 'I want to be a traffic cop. Can you pull a few strings and get me a nice cushy job directing traffic?'

Steve said, 'Anything you want, big buddy.'

I stood up and noticed that Steve was holding onto his back.

I said, 'What's the matter, buddy?'

Steve winced as he said, 'I've got a sore back from sitting in my car all day.'

I put my arm around him and started leading him back to his car and said, 'You've got a very dangerous job, mate. Sitting around all day, going to the gym all the time, getting cups of coffee, then you've got to get lunch. Then you have to charge your mobile phone.'

Steve said, 'No need to be mean about it, buddy.'

I said, 'No, seriously, you should get danger money taking all those risks.'

A short time later, I parked my vehicle in a back street. This was for the last time. As I gathered my stuff, my mobile rang. I said, 'What?'

Male: Is this Lenny?

Lenny: Maybe. Who's this?

Male: You're a dead man.

Lenny: I love you too.

I hung up the phone. It was dark. I looked all around and quickly grabbed my bag and locked the car. My mobile rang again.

Lenny: What?

Different male: You're fucking dead.

Lenny: Missing a few mates, are we?

Male: Yeah I am, and you're responsible.

Lenny: Correct. For getting that question right you've won a brand new pair of handcuffs. We're just tracing this call right now. We'll be over in a minute to give you your prize.

The phone went dead. The death threats kept coming. After my third threat I worked out a way to stop them. I disconnected the battery.

As I started to sneak in the rear entrance for the last time, I stopped. I walked around to the front of the station. I didn't have to hide any more. My job was over and I had no intention of working as an undercover for a long time. As I strode into the foyer I said, 'drug squad'. But the internal door did not open. A young uniformed officer stood there with his hand poised over the door opening button. He said, 'Your ID, where's your ID?'

'Shit,' I said,

I gave myself a pat down. What's the use? I didn't have my police ID with me. I said, 'Now I want to be a cop, I can't. Don't worry about it.'

I turned and walked back outside. I mumbled away to myself as I returned to sneaking in the rear entrance. It was just after 8.30pm and the squad was still buzzing. I got heaps of pats on the back as I stood at my desk taking Lenny off. I slumped into my chair. One member walked up to me and put a can of scotch and Coke into my hand. About the time twenty pizzas arrived I said, 'I'm off duty and as of now, I'm Lachlan McCulloch again.'

Baldrick said, 'What bloody planet are you on? You said Eddie was a funny bastard. He is a real fucking prick.'

I said, 'Fair dinkum? You must have upset him or something.'

Baldrick said, 'You've upset him.'

As we all sat at our desks eating pizza, they all gave me updates on how the interviews were going. Le stuck to the story that he had never met anyone named Lenny or Fran in his whole life. Eddie just sat there growling and trying to break his handcuffs and Stacker still wanted to know what happened to his mate Lenny. Baldrick said, 'Throughout the interview Stacker was saying, "No comment". Then right at the end I had to explain to him how much evidence is against him, right? So I said, "I now must inform you that Lenny Rogers is, in fact, an undercover policeman." Stacker thought about that for a moment and said, "Well, he's fucked then isn't he?" I said, "Well no, what do you mean?" Stacker said, "Well, he's a cop and a drug trafficker. He's fucked." Stacker thinks Lenny is a corrupt drug-trafficking cop.'

We all laughed. How good was that? Stacker had totally lost perspective. To Stacker I was a drug trafficker first and foremost. I found this fascinating. This went back to how important first impressions were. Before he met me, he had 'burnt' (identified) our surveillance team. When we met, he was happy to take me off to the failed drug deal at the Yarraville Railway Station car park. He didn't want to believe he could be fooled by an undercover cop. In those early days he had several reasons to declare me a cop. I had said to him on the phone, 'How the hell could I be a cop when you spent nearly three hours with me in my car? I know you could pick an undercover cop a mile away.' He agreed. I appealed to his ego to convince him I was okay. We kept doing business. He never even searched me.

What happens with first impressions is that you never want to prove yourself wrong. Everyone wants to believe that they're good at judging people. If your first impression is that a person is an idiot, what you do is constantly look for reasons to prove that theory. If your first impression is that they are wonderful or truthful, you tend to only see the good things. It's in our nature to not want to be wrong. The only thing that lasts longer and is harder to reverse than a bad first impression is a lack of loyalty.

I find these subjects fascinating. Not to mention vital in this murky covert world.

When the pizzas had all gone, members returned to their paperwork. I wandered around talking to the many interviewing members. For some reason a lot of cops love getting a crook to make admissions. This was very unusual in the drug squad. We always had large cameras and audio recorders. When we interviewed criminals, they were much more likely to get into trouble with us if they did want to make admissions than not. We wouldn't arrest them unless we had all the evidence we needed. The quickest interview is a 'No comment' one.

That day fifteen main targets were arrested and charged. Twelve of them were remanded into custody. There they remained. Late that night I went home. In the dark I lay there looking at the ceiling. The girls were gone, the crooks were gone. I could get my life back. For the first time in months I let myself think of fly-fishing for trout in the highlands of Tasmania. This was what life was all about. I drifted off to sleep as my fly delicately landed in front of a five-pound wild brown trout.

The art of catching crooks is like fly-fishing. It's not the ones you catch that bring you back.

CHAPTER 8

Court at last

She had done all this
because she was trying
to make up for all the
bad things she'd done.

THE following morning I rang Steve. I told him I was going to
be late as I had a few things to do. Steve told me the boss
wanted to see me later that day.

I drove to a nearby hairdresser. My hair was well over my
shoulders. I asked the girl to give me a 'number three' cut and
to dye whatever hair was left white blond. The hairdresser said,
'That will be a big change.' I said, 'Exactly, it's to confuse the
hit men.' She laughed. I didn't, I was serious.

At 11am, as I walked in through the front door of Russell
Street I noticed how good it felt to be back to normal. As
normal as Lachlan McCulloch the investigator could be
anyway. I was all 'undercovered' out. The best part of being an
undercover cop is being in a safe place afterwards. 'Afterwards'
felt great. I always kept my foot in the door. It was hard to
imagine I would never work as an undercover operative again.

Everyone in the squad laughed at my new look. The boss sat me down in his office and closed the door. He told me I'd done a great job. He didn't say much, but what he said was right. He said he'd seen me change over the past few months. He certainly seemed to understand how difficult the job had been for me. I sat quietly trying to play the strong silent type but the truth was if I had tried to speak I think I would have broken down and wept like a baby.

The boss directed me to take a week off with full pay. He wanted me to take my wife for a holiday into the country or somewhere. He finished it off with, 'Keep the receipts and give them to me. I'll make sure the Victoria Police pick up the tab. We need to look after members like you'. He told me I had been recommended for a High Level Commendation for my covert skills and dedication. In a crackly voice I thanked him.

My crew was working flat out. Baldrick informed me, 'If you start making your statements now, you should be finished by Christmas.' On my desk was huge box of covert tapes. I gathered everything that looked important and locked it in my cabinet. I informed my crew I would be back next week.

My wife and I drove for several hours and stopped at a little motel. We got to know each other again. No phone calls at all hours, no note taking, no drug deals and no Lenny. Most of all there was no Sally and Fran. My thoughts were often with Fran and what might happen to her. I felt responsible for her.

In no time I was back at the squad, sitting in one of the interview rooms, also known as the 'cone of silence'. As I listened to hour upon hour of tape recordings, I made my written statements. Each statement had to be perfect; it had to cover all the evidence. The painful part was my micro recorder notes. There were 48 tapes lasting 90 minutes each. They had been transcribed onto more than 9000 typed pages. These notes had to match my official diary entries and my statements. It was a nightmare but it had to be done.

My crew spent week after week with Sally and Fran taking statements. I had to work fast. I had organised my nine weeks' annual leave for the year and tacked it onto the nine weeks' leave I would be owed next year. This meant over four months' leave in one lump. And I was looking forward to every last day of it.

At one stage I was called to the Melbourne Magistrates' Court. Kath Pettingill was in the middle of a bail application. Kath was making the application to allow her to return to her son Victor's house in Rowville to look after her grandchildren. In particular Kath wanted to look after young five-year-old 'Katie'. She was in the middle of portraying herself as a caring loving grandmother when I entered the witness box. I gave a brief overview of the strength of evidence against her. Included in this was the occasion when Kath was arranging for me to purchase an ounce of heroin from one of her associates. I told the court how young Katie was present when Kath strip-searched me. I informed the magistrate I had tape recorded this meeting. The clerk of courts played the tape to the court.

There was silence in court as they listened to Kath exploding when I had had the audacity to laugh during the drug deal. Her constant use of the word 'Fuck' undermined her claims to doting grandmother status. The magistrate frowned as the tape played little Katie's voice interrupting the drug deal. Katie said, 'Kath, my head hurts' and Kath had dismissed her by saying, 'You've got an ugly head'. The magistrate refused the bail application. I returned to making statements. Kath returned to Fairlea Women's Prison. All was right with the world.

A week later, I was told the boss wanted to speak to me. He informed me the Governor of Fairlea had just telephoned him. The governor had received information from various prison sources that Kath had put two contracts out on me. She was offering $20,000 for each of my testicles. As the boss told me, it was hard not to laugh, so I did. 'What a bargain,' I said. 'They're worth heaps more than that.' The boss wasn't laughing. I added, 'I put my balls into that job, boss but I still want to keep them.'

'We treat threats against our members very seriously,' he said.

'As long as they remain threats I'm happy,' I answered. I treated death threats with total contempt. Except in bed during the early hours, when they worried hell out of me.

After two months of making statements I left for the highlands of Tasmania. My wife and I leased a house on the banks of the Great Lake for nearly four months. In between fly-fishing forays we entertained our friends and family. My wife and I had quality time together. It was sensational.

One of the hardest jobs during this holiday was doing the dishes. The lake was only a few metres from our kitchen window. Would you believe it, every time I filled the sink and put the bloody gloves on a trout would rise and eat an insect. As I grabbed my fly rod, I would explain to my wife that it wasn't my fault, 'I didn't put the bloody lake outside the kitchen window'. No self-respecting fly fisherman could ignore a rising trout. It had nothing to do with doing the dishes.

While in Tasmania I left Baldrick the phone number of the local hotel. This was the only way I could be contacted. It also gave me the most perfect excuse to attend this establishment regularly. Purely business I would tell my wife. And they didn't make you wash up after ten pots either. Baldrick contacted me several times while I was away. Most contacts involved death threats. Le, my tactile friend 'Mr Trust Me', was in prison telling other crooks he was going to have me killed and when the prison governor heard the talk he contacted the drug squad.

In my experience crooks usually accept getting caught by the coppers – they see it as an occupational hazard. But when an undercover cop dupes them they can go crazy. It is highly embarrassing for crooks, especially when you think they are street-smart tough guys. I have found that many Asian male drug dealers tend to take the whole thing very personally and believe they have lost face. Trust Me actually believed I was his real friend and I had betrayed him. What really hurt Trust Me was that he had trusted me. The only way he could save face and get his trust back from me involved me being dead. Reality was not Trust Me's strong point. Look at us: one saying, 'Trust me, I'm a drug dealer' and the other, 'Trust me, I'm an undercover cop'. This relationship was doomed to fail.

There was a big difference between Kath's death threat (I'd like to think they would put me out of my misery before cutting my balls off) and Trust Me's. I don't think Kath really wanted my balls. Where was she going to get the money? If some punter did go out and cut my balls off on credit, was Kath going to pay up? I don't think so. All the punters knew that. Kath's death threat was more a case of her following her own job description. She'd read a few of those true crime *Underbelly* books and said things that helped preserve her image. You can't be all tea and scones if you're Granny Evil.

Trust Me had more to worry about – like not dropping the soap – than trying to kill me. I'm not saying Trust Me didn't want to kill me. What I am saying is, his motive for doing so was fundamentally flawed. But logic is often not a strong suit for drug dealers. I was determined not to get caught up in the dramas and get back to fishing and not doing the dishes.

While most of Baldrick's calls were about death threats, there was one notable exception. It involved one of Fran's 'earns'. I was told Fran and Sally had rented a lot of household white goods – a big television, video player, stereo system. A person by the name of Lenny Rogers had been made guarantor. The goods were rented just before the girls were given new names and a new secret address, which was an amazing coincidence. They, of course, were never going to make any repayments. I was hardly surprised. It reminded me of the story of the frog and the scorpion. As the frog gave the scorpion a ride on its back across the river, the scorpion stung the frog. As the frog was dying it said, 'Why did you sting me – now we will both die?' The scorpion said, 'It's in my nature.' The girls hoped the witness protection program would also be the debt repayment protection program. Nice try but no cigar or even a rented cigar lighter.

In Tasmania, my biggest problem was working out where to fish each day. Most fish were released back into the water to fight another day. Every now and then I released one into my outback fish smoker. Smoked wild Tassie trout eaten cold on crackers is hard to beat. Four months and 242 wild brown trout later, we reluctantly returned to Victoria.

THE drug squad hadn't changed. Brief preparation was still in full swing. Five copies of each brief had to be made – one each for the defendant, the magistrate, the prosecutor, the police informant and an original to be kept by the court. That is five copies of all fifteen, which meant 75 briefs. Each of the 75 briefs was made up of six manila folders containing telephone intercept transcripts, listening device transcripts, drug analysis certificates and hundreds of statements. All up, 450 folders. And they wonder why there are no trees left in Brazil.

On top of all this, everyone had to get their own copies of every tape, including all telephone, listening device and covert tapes made by the girls and me. Everyone also had to get twelve folders of photographs. Brief preparation is a nightmare. More than twelve months later, the committal hearing was set to start. Fran and Sally were delivered under high security. The witness protection program had delivered them to a highly secure area within Russell Street police station. The first committal hearing was booked in for three months. It was to be a combined hearing. After days of legal argument, the case began. The crooks – sorry, I mean defendants – were Kath Pettingill, Trevor Pettingill, Steven (Stacker) McKinnon, Donato Corsi, Eddie Fiorello, Meng Koc Te and Coung Viet Le. What a lovely bunch of coconuts.

The magistrate Mr Golden sat high in the 'I'm in charge' position. Directly in front of him, but much lower down, was his clerk. Lower again was a long row of tables. The Crown prosecutor was in the first seat, then seven barristers after that – one for each defendant. Kath and her barrister sat next to the prosecutor. It was as though she had been given the prime position. In keeping with her criminal status. The witness box is just that: a wooden box to the left of the prosecutor. The witness box is elevated to the height of the magistrate.

I met the girls in a small room about an hour before Fran was due to give evidence. I felt like Kevin Sheedy the football coach, six goals down in the grand final at the last quarter break. I needed to motivate them to tell the truth, the whole truth and nothing but the bloody truth. A scary prospect indeed. As an experienced detective I was fully aware what I was about to say to the girls would be the subject of massive cross-examination. The defence try to win points by questioning each witness about the police.

I entered the room and gave Fran and Sally a big hug. The girls looked great, so I told them. Fran had lost quite a lot of weight. I said, 'Fran, you look great' and she said 'Do you want to boof me?' Some things never change. Then I said, 'Sally, you look like a bloody lady.' Sally spun around catwalk style and said, 'I'm off the gear; this is what going straight does to you.' For the first time in a year I was Lenny again. The enormity of the moment was reflected in their voices and facial expressions. A member from WPP stood at the back of the room. I looked at him. The minder knew what I wasn't saying and left the room. The three of us sat at a little table in the middle of the room.

'Everything we did comes down to today. This is your time to shine. You did it all. It all comes down to this. It was all for nothing unless you can stand in front of these crooks and tell the court what happened. Warts and all. Hold nothing back.'

Sally said, 'I've been thinking, it's all on tape. They can hear it. Why don't they play all the tapes?'

'Sally, you can tell them that if you want. Say what you like, this is your time.'

The girls started to ask me what they should say and when. I kept repeating, 'Just tell the truth. The truth wins every time. Court is all about searching for the truth.'

'So play the tapes, the tapes are the truth,' Sally said.

I said, 'The tapes are so bad, so damaging for the defendants that the last thing they want is to play the tapes. What I want you to be aware of is the defence will attack you personally. They'll attack us all. Tell the truth about everything.'

They asked me about the courtroom itself. I drew a picture of the inside of the court and told them who sat where. I was surprised no-one had done this already. I stressed that the girls should at all times face the magistrate. All answers should be directed to the magistrate. Never talk directly to the defence council. I explained, 'There are two reasons for this. The first is that it is respectful and proper. The magistrate is in charge. All your answers belong to him and him alone. The second and most important reason is, it really pisses off the defence barrister. He or she will do everything to get you to look at him. Just don't.'

I had worried over the past twelve months but now in the room with the girls I felt comfortable. There was so much passion. Passion for victory was in every word. I could see it in their eyes. They had lived for this day as much as I had. Success was as important to them as it was to me. Who was I kidding? All I had done was my job. I was professionally trained and paid to do it. They did it for free – Fran, in particular. Sally still had a prison sentence hanging over her head and was hoping for a substantial discount. Fran did it all for nothing. My respect for her was enormous. I thought I was good. Fran humbled me.

I thought Fran would be a good witness. Sally worried me. She was so much softer as a person. Her heroin addiction and terrible criminal record kept me awake at night. At the end of the day, the tapes said it all. But I was afraid some of these barristers would destroy her.

Of course, the three of us were the main prosecution witnesses. We were not allowed to know what each other had said in evidence. Once evidence began I could have very little to do with them. If I did speak to them, it was to offer comfort and support with witnesses present. So can you imagine how difficult it was when each of us had no idea what the other had said in answer to the same questions? This was why I'd taped everything and made sure there was nothing to hide.

I knew no promise or lie would ever stand up to seven experienced barristers asking questions during lengthy cross-examinations. If barristers believed a lie had been told, they had the benefit of a written transcript of each day's proceeding. Then they could recall any witness.

I am now able to paint a picture of what happened in court by speaking to barristers, police and media present.

The court was packed. Uniformed police from the force response unit were throughout the building. Outside the courtroom itself were several more police. A table and chair were set up for taking people's names as they entered. As they gave their names, another member scanned them for weapons. There were two very distinct types of spectators. The media looked as if they were coming to watch a basketball match. Friends and relatives of the defendants looked like Collingwood supporters on their way to the dole queue.

Fran was led into court by two security officers. They stood either side of her as she entered the witness box that would be her home for the next twelve days. She wore a long black dress with lace across the front. Her hair was long and swept back. She stood tall and straight. She looked for all the world like a private school teacher.

After Fran handed the court 32 lengthy statements, the prosecutor sat. Kath's barrister started. Two days later he sat reserving the right to continue his attack later. Trevor's barrister took over, then the next and the next. For twelve days they attacked her. They accused her of being a prostitute, a whore, thief and a drug trafficker. She agreed with the barristers on some points, and not on others. Day after day they tried to rip her apart, but she stayed strong and truthful. At one point a barrister was so frustrated with her he demanded she look at him. She instantly dismissed him, 'I am here to address Your Worship, Your Worship.'

Fran was questioned at length about the rug she had allegedly stolen. She denied stealing it. Kath must have insisted her barrister target this issue. No-one knew why. This was all about drug trafficking, but barristers get paid by the hour so they have to run down every rabbit hole.

They soon found another rabbit hole to run down. The barristers had been supplied with transcripts and copies of all my micro cassette tapes. These were the hundreds of phone and personal conversations I had with Fran and Sally. Like me, the barristers noticed Fran was always talking about sex. In particular about my penis. The barristers, like some of my drug squad colleagues, were convinced Fran had a sexual relationship with Lenny. Fran was asked, 'Why during many phone conversations would you ask Lenny if his penis was dressed to the left or the right?'

Fran replied, 'Because it annoyed him, I suppose.' Fran just told it how it was, warts and all. Bad choice of words: I never had warts. You know what I mean.

When Fran finally finished giving evidence, the defence reserved the right to recall her at any time. Just because they could. The prosecutor commented that Fran's evidence was better than many police witnesses. She came across as strong, truthful and credible. That was unusual in a court of law.

Sally took the stand. The barristers spent days covering every aspect of her heroin addiction and criminal convictions. She cried as she answered most questions. They hoped Sally would give the court reason to discredit us, and the case. The way they work is if they can find you lying about one thing it means everything is a lie.

As they did with Fran, several barristers tried to say Sally had sex with me during the police operation. The barristers pointed out to Sally they had her, Fran and Lenny himself on tape telling some of the defendants that she had had sex with Lenny. Each barrister thought they could break her story and find the truth. Eventually they did. Sally sobbed, 'You don't understand. My whole life men wanted that. Lenny didn't. He was different. Lenny wanted me. He wanted me for me.' That put an end to the sex issue.

The barristers concentrated on her criminal past. A barrister asked her if she had committed any robberies. Sally said she had – bank robberies. The barrister said but you wouldn't have had a shotgun would you? She said she did have a gun, it was a shotgun and it was loaded. Many of the questions had an easy way out. The easy way was for her to lie. Sally chose the truth – even if it was terrible.

The essence of Sally was found when she was asked about several assault and robbery convictions. Sally cried. She was asked who she had robbed. Sally said she had robbed old men. The barrister said, 'But you didn't bash them, did you?'

Sally cried, 'We bashed old men and old women.'

The barrister asked, 'Why?'

'So we could rob them – we wanted the money.' The barrister had her go into the details of these awful crimes.

After a pause Sally looked at the magistrate and said, 'That was me then. This is me now. I'm here. I done good.' She sobbed. The whole court was moved by her honesty. When I heard this, for the first time I understood why Sally had helped us; why she had turned her life upside down forever. I knew then she hadn't done it for a discounted sentence. Jail was part of her life, she didn't hate it. She had done all this because she was trying to make up for all the bad things she'd done. She had finally done something terrific instead of something terrible.

Toward the end of her evidence a tape was played to the court. Fran's handbag had recorded a drug deal. The court let the tape play on. I had asked the girls to tape as much of Stacker as they could, as he had made several admissions regarding possible murder charges. On the tape you could hear Stacker and Sally preparing for bed. The following conversation boomed throughout the court:

Stacker: Suck on this.

Sally: No.

Stacker: Come on, suck on it.

Sally: No.

Stacker: Come on, please?

Sally: No, I just brushed my teeth.

When the laughter died down the magistrate stopped the tape. Party-pooper.

After eight days Sally stepped down from the witness box. She'd surprised us all. When Sally saw me she said, 'The truth's a bitch, Lenny.' The prosecutor later made the comment, 'A lot of police could learn a few things from those girls'.

Then it was Lenny's turn. I was petrified. This was without doubt my most important case. I stood next to the witness box waiting for the magistrate to take his seat. I nodded my head to several of the barristers saying a silent, 'Hello, I hope you lose, you bastard'. We were about to do battle, so you can't be too friendly. When one of the barristers walked past it was different. I had come up against him many times over the years. We had socialised on several occasions and for a barrister he was almost a good bloke. No, he was a good bloke, for a barrister. We shook hands and smiled about the good times.

A voice sounding like Jackie Chan shouted, 'You're sacked, you no work for me.' We turned. It was Trust Me. Le had taken great offence to **his** barrister being friendly with me. Trust Me was furious. He was in the middle of yelling more abuse as the magistrate walking in. The court fell silent – all except Trust Me.

My mate the barrister informed the magistrate he had 'irreconcilable differences' with his client and could no longer represent him. The court adjourned for the day so Trust Me could get another barrister. Trust Me was on another planet. In his mind, I had betrayed his trust, this made me the most evil creature on his planet. Any friend of mine was his enemy as well. In an effort to pacify Trust Me I decided to stop blowing him little kisses.

The next day I entered the box firm in the knowledge that I was the hero and in a few moments my swashbuckling, death-defying deeds would become obvious to all. As it turned out, I needn't have worried about all the pins in all the medals putting holes in my good suit. It also became obvious that within this particular court there was a nasty and commonly held belief that I could be telling lies. In each of my ninety-odd statements I began with the words: 'I am a trained covert operative attached to the crime department, drug squad'. But apparently many in the court believed that was code for: 'I am a trained bullshit artist attached to the corrupt department, load 'em and fit 'em up squad'.

The seven barristers, their instructing solicitors and the magistrate were struggling with the whole concept of this undercover policing business. I spent the bulk of the first day explaining the word 'covert' and how it applied to my police work. I became extremely worried because if they were having trouble with the word, what were they going to think about all the secret shit I actually did? A barrister questioned me about me being covert.

After a few more questions, the barrister said, 'So what you are telling the court is that when you dealt with my client you were a covert, sneaky, underhanded, devious, sly and deceitful police officer?'

I thought he was being most unkind so I replied, 'Yes, but now I am telling the truth.'

The barrister said, 'That you are all of those things?'

I said, 'Was. Was all of those things.'

Personally, I didn't have a problem with it. I wanted to say,

'Hello, I'm the good guy using the bad guys' techniques back on them which is why they're upset and is what made me the good guy in the first place.' But no, it was like the whole police operation process using an undercover was just too unfair and prejudicial on the accused. They were drug dealers and killers and people who didn't pay taxes. And they weren't very nice. But I was supposed to catch them by using boy scout tactics. Maybe if I had dressed as a brownie and given them cookies they would have seen the error of their ways and confessed. Do me a very large favour.

What are the police meant to do – stand on the moral high ground and wait for the criminally inclined to collect all their evidence, climb the cliff of justice and plead guilty? No. I had to lower myself to their level, play their bullshit games for over six months, climb back up and stand in this witness box smelling like a rose and speak like a professional impartial witness.

The reality of undercover policing is the crooks instruct their solicitors and barristers that the whole process is unfair; the barristers and solicitors already know it is unfair, and inform the court. The court finds all the defendants guilty because of the huge amount of indelible evidence that spews from the mouths of the defendants onto various electronic devices. I wanted to scream, 'The defendants provided all the evidence, and I just collected it.' It's that simple.

GIVING evidence week after week is a very telling experience. To me, lying was like breathing. I didn't have to think about it. For these few weeks I had to tell the truth, about everything. Like flicking a light switch, I just turned the truth on.

As an undercover operative, I found the truth the only constant among the ever-shifting sands that were the lies that flowed from the mouths of crooks, which were regurgitated to the court. The truth is a beautiful thing, but only when you can prove it. Fortunately I had all the tapes and videos to prove my honest testimony.

Once upon a time, a policeman's word was believed in a court. Now everything has to be backed up. The truth is, I didn't convict them – they convicted themselves, with their greedy bullshit that was recorded for all to hear. Toward the end of my evidence this whole undercover operative business was beginning to wear a bit thin. I was beginning to establish who I was and what I was again. The truth was I liked being a policeman more than a low-life criminal playing both sides. And we had a better superannuation scheme than the crooks.

IN the witness box, we played a version of twenty questions. Except I got more than my share. It's like a game children play. I say, 'It's the truth.' The barrister says, 'No, it's not.'

'Yes it is.'

'No it's not.'

Then it goes 'is so' 'is not' 'is so' ''s not' and so on. In the end you're not really sure what you're arguing about. The difference was that they got paid a few thousand a day and I got a headache.

Committal hearings like this one are designed to test the evidence. At the end of the hearing, the magistrate decides whether or not a jury could convict the defendants on the evidence. If he believes the evidence is strong enough, he sends them to trial. The ridiculous part of all this is that even if he chooses to decide there is not enough evidence to substantiate the charges, the Office of Public Prosecutions could send them all to trial anyway. That is why they had the girls in the box for so long. It wasn't about getting to the truth. It was about beating them up so badly they wouldn't come up again at the trial. And then it was my turn.

Testing the evidence meant testing me. No-one actually spoke to me about evidence. Like all committal hearings if someone touched upon any evidence it was merely by chance. The evidence was so strong it was hard to contest. What tends to happen is the barristers spend most of the time trying to lessen their clients' criminality. They attempt to diminish what some might view as serious drug trafficking down to a spit on the footpath.

They moved on to bigger and better topics, refusing to leave my best mate alone. I was under the illusion my penis was not part of the evidence. Several barristers begged to differ. At one stage I thought they were going to stamp it with an evidence number and force me to hand it up to the magistrate. Like Fran, they wanted to know if my penis was dressed to the left or the right. The main offender was the only woman barrister. She was young and attractive and thought speaking about my penis was in some way going to help her client avoid jail. At the very least it would embarrass me. This women barrister asked me:

Why did Fran often refer to your penis as 'Lunch'?

The courtroom burst into laughter.

I responded: *I think some women just like talking about penises.*

They eventually got bored with my penis and moved on. Even I was bored with it, almost.

I spoke one word during my undercover operations that came back to haunt me during cross-examination. During a conversation with Fran I said, 'Have you spoken to "the witch" lately?' When Kath heard this she sprang to her own defence. She called out, 'Well where's me fuckin' broomstick then?'

I personally couldn't see a problem with the term myself. The issue the barrister was getting at was that I was supposed to be a totally impartial witness. I must collect the facts without fear or favour. Her barrister pointed out that me referring to Kathleen Pettingill as a witch implied I had formed an opinion about her character. I said, 'For fuck sake, spank me, yank me but don't bloody thank me. Give me a break, we're talking about Kath Bloody Pettingill.' No I didn't say that out loud. In fact, I stood there and apologised. After this irrelevant line of questioning, I said in my best voice, 'When I made the comment, I really didn't mean to hurt your client's feelings'. Sarcasm in every word. The courtroom cackled.

After the 'witch' comment, Kath's barrister would say things like, 'What did the witch, as you like to call her, do then, detective?' It didn't sound good and drove me mad. I found it amazing how the utterance of one word during hundreds of hours of conversations could cause me aggravation. I had uttered it only once, once on tape anyway.

At one stage when the court resumed after lunch, several large dog droppings were found on the floor inside court. Kath called out, 'Hey Lenny, you could have done it outside.' The magistrate stood the case down for the mess to be cleaned up. The police outside the entrance of the court stated that their scanner searched for weapons, not dog poo.

During the case Kath seemed to be the only person having fun. She was in her element. She continually dropped classic one-liners throughout my evidence. If I was asked what Kath thought was a good question, she would say, 'Come on, squirm yaself outta that one'. The court was informed one of the police witnesses was unable to attend court. He had been bitten by a white tail spider while gardening.

Kath called out, 'Call the fuckin' spider in. You'll get more fuckin' truth out of a spider.' When the court finished chuckling, Kath said, 'The poor fuckin' thing probably died from bitin' 'im.'

One barrister accused me of being a professional liar. It was sort of true of all undercovers but I strongly denied the accusation. During this cross-examination, Kath said in a loud voice, 'Has anyone seen his badge? He's probably not even a cop.'

I was asked:

Did you lie about who you were?

Yes.

Did you lie about what you were doing?

Yes.

Did you lie about why you were doing it?

Yes.

Lie about where you had been?

Yes.

Lie about where you were going?

Yes.

Is there anything you did not lie about?

Umm. No. I did want to buy drugs, but I lied about why.

A professional quite often is an expert in their field and gets paid to do it. I put it to you, you are a professional liar?

Umm ... Ahhh ...

There was a pregnant pause. That was a tricky one. I hadn't really thought of it. I wanted to say 'you're right' but couldn't – and I couldn't say 'no'. I wanted to say, 'Pass' or 'Can I phone a friend?' I did not want to 'ask the audience,' so I said very carefully:

I lie about what I do, and what I am. At the end of the day like here and now, I tell the truth. That is not a lie. I am a detective collecting evidence.

If you were to lie to us now, would we be able to tell?

I do not lie about telling the truth.

I think that made sense. The truth is extremely difficult to gauge when the court restricts answers to black and white. This is one of the reasons I feel safe now. I have left the greyness of the covert world.

So you expect us to find and identify a tiny drop of truth in your ocean of lies?

Yes, I do. It's more of a puddle really. The tapes of the drug deals contain the truth.

Do you lie on these so-called drug deal tapes?

Ah ...(you bastard you got me) *yes I do.* (I'd be lying if I said I didn't.)

Among my lies was evidence that their clients were guilty. Tapes don't lie. There was far too much damning evidence in them. In this case all seven defendants had legal aid. This meant that the community paid for those barristers to give the girls and me a hard time. I wanted to ask the barristers when they might start talking to me about some evidence.

Once, while I was deflecting, ducking and weaving questions, one barrister accused me of being a drug trafficker. Can you believe it? Before I could deny that scurrilous accusation the magistrate replied, 'I've been waiting for someone to say that. It seems to me Detective McCulloch is a drug trafficker'.

Your worship, I was acting under Section 51 of the Drugs Act. I am indemnified.'

Kath Pettingill said in a loud voice, 'Come on Lenny, come and sit next to me.' Kath was laughing. She slid her bum over to one side and started patting the seat. Kath wanted me in the dock. The whole court laughed.

The prosecutor stood up and objected. He stated that Section 51 of the Drugs Act specifically indemnified me from committing offences under the Drugs Act. The defence continued to accuse me of being a drug trafficker. Kath thought it was a fantastic concept and demanded I get out of the witness box and join her in the dock.

I just stood there and let them argue. The defence eventually moved on to the next topic. I'm convinced some barristers waffle on with the specific intent of giving witnesses a hard time thus making their client happy. The client and the barrister both know the case is a lost cause. The barrister's getting paid to do it, so why not? The community suffers the crime and then funds the amusement of the offender.

Early on during my evidence there was a break in proceedings. I found 'Fast Eddie' outside the court having a nervous smoke. Eddie was the only defendant allowed out on bail. Eddie wouldn't look at me. There was no-one much around, just a few court security officers and police. Eddie had his head down. I walked up to him, 'Can I pinch a smoke?' Eddie looked up and stared me straight in the eyes. After a pause, he said: 'You're fucking unreal.' Eddie looked around to see if anyone was watching. He reluctantly reached in to his jacket pocket and gave me a smoke. Then he laughed and said, 'You never have a light, either.' I smiled. Eddie lit my smoke. We had a laugh together. Eddie said, 'Those bloody Asians would go ape shit if they saw me give you a smoke.'

'They don't want me to die of lung cancer, do they?'

Eddie said, 'No Lenny, they talk a lot about meat cleavers.'

Eddie went on to say that when he first met me he was convinced I was an undercover cop. He said the more he met me, the more convinced he was that I wasn't. He added something I found interesting. Eddie said, 'Do you remember when you really shit yourself?'

'Yeah, I do,' I replied. I knew exactly the moment he was talking about. I knew he knew it too.

Eddie went on, 'I was sitting behind you in the kitchen. You were at the table with Stacker and Trevor. You were buying drugs. Did you know Stacker wanted to rob ya?'

'Yeah,' I replied. 'Of course. I was shitting myself that day. I got bad vibes.'

Eddie said, 'I got off the bench behind ya and went in front of you so you could see me. Trevor and I stopped Stacker robbing ya.'

'Thanks, Eddie.'

I made sure no-one was looking and held out my hand. We shook. Moments later we were back in court where justice was being found.

After giving evidence for a few days, I was outside court having a smoke. A group of about eight young uniform cops from court security were chatting away next to me. One of them said, 'Excuse me, but we have been having a chat about this case. We're all scared crossing Russell Street and walking over to do security on this case. How scared were you being undercover on all these scumbags for months? You were in their homes and that, taping them. How did you feel?'

I said, 'Well, I feel a lot worse now you've told me that.' They all laughed. The same cop said, 'Seriously, how did you feel?'

I said, 'I was petrified, for seven months. I convinced myself I could do it, and I did. It was my job.'

I put my smoke out and walked back into court. For once the courtroom felt safer. There was too much reality outside. As I waited for the court to resume, I thought to myself, 'I think those cops out there are serious. They are scared walking over to this court and doing security here. They need to get out more.'

DURING the never-ending Pettingill committal hearing, after a hard day telling the truth I had to go to a Lick, Sip and Suck

Nurses' Party in North Carlton. It was also called a Tequila party. The idea was you lick a small pile of salt off your left hand, scull a shot glass of Tequila and suck a slice of lemon. It wasn't long before I was drinking out of the bottle of truth serum, biting a chunk out of the lemon and sucking on the saltshaker. I have always believed in economies of scale.

A woman appeared in front of me and said, 'Hello, what do you do?'

I said, 'I'd normally tell you I was a plastic surgeon or a dolphin trainer but my job is to befriend people and gain their trust by telling them a truck load of bullshit. I lie about what I'm doing and why I do it, then right when they trust me the most I betray them by giving the very best evidence I can against them in court. I've been doing it for years, on and off.' She took a step back. I added, 'It's okay though, it's my job. I'm a professional informer and I only do it to criminals. Well if they're not criminals at the time, they soon will be. What do you do?' Her mouth opened but nothing came out. She turned and walked off. It was not a good pick-up line.

We were both shocked at what I'd said. It was like me hearing my own words made me see myself in a new light. I didn't care about the crooks. Betraying criminals, particularly drug traffickers, didn't bother me in the slightest. I never felt for any of them. But it was true, I was a paid informer. I felt like I did when my dog died.

It was at that moment I realised an undercover cop is just an informer with a cool name. My bosses and I used me just like we all used Fran and Sally. I was just a means to an end – a leech used to suck the poison out of a weeping wound.

I decided to give it away. Well, giving evidence for three months against the Pettingills with the Who's Who of disorganised crime in the public gallery sort of pushed retirement on me.

So I gracefully hung up my electronic devices and covert weapons and went back to being a real detective.

Once I finished giving evidence, the rest of the case flowed smoothly. After six weeks it ended. The crooks were committed on all charges. The girls had done a brilliant job. We went out to dinner and had a few drinks. There were not many celebrations as we still had the trial to go in a year or so. The girls were whisked off into never-never land again. I resumed work at the drug squad.

SEVERAL months later, Kath, Trevor, Stacker, Donato, Trust Me Le and Eddie all pleaded guilty at the County Court. During Kathleen Pettingill's sentencing, her barrister stated she had been involved in the criminal world her entire life. These offences were just an extension of that life. It was argued she had now, at the age of 58, seen the error of her ways and intended to retire from the criminal world. The judge, in sentencing, stated that Kath had shown signs of rehabilitation. He sentenced her to 30 months imprisonment with a minimum of eighteen months. As she had been in custody for the past seventeen plus months, she had two weeks to go. There I was thinking that Kath could never be rehabilitated. Shows how little I knew.

The judge had a different view of her son Trevor Pettingill. In sentencing, the judge mentioned some of the conversations Trevor had with the undercover operative McCulloch. He described how Trevor at the age of 29 had bragged about never having worked a day in his life. The judge concluded Trevor had no intention of rehabilitating. He was sentenced to seven years' imprisonment with a minimum of five.

Steven (Stacker) McKinnon pleaded for leniency based on the age-old excuse, 'It's not my fault, the devil made me do it'. When that started to fail, he tried, 'It wasn't me, it was the heroin'. He received a four-year sentence with a minimum of three. That's not a lot of porridge.

This reminds me of a story about Mark 'Chopper' Read. Chopper was being interviewed in relation to a charge of arson. The interviewing detective asked, 'Why did you burn Nick Apostolides' house down?'

Chopper said, 'Have you ever met Nick 'The Greek' Apostolides or been to his house?'

The detective replied, 'No.'

Chopper said, 'Well if you had, you wouldn't have asked such a stupid question.' Nick Apostolides was a young southern European drug trafficker. He ponced around with an inflated ego, a blow-waved mullet haircut and a black see-through fishnet singlet.

The moral of this story is, I believe, that the judge would have given Stacker a lot more jail time if he had actually met Stacker in a drug-dealing type social gathering. Anyway.

Donato Corsi received three years with a minimum of two. Eddie Fiorello considered himself very unlucky when he received four years on the top with three long years on the bottom. Eddie blamed his long sentence on the fact he was a friend of Trevor's.

Viet Cong Trust Me Le stated at his sentencing hearing that he was a chronic heroin addict and sold heroin only to supply his drug habit. If the court believed this, he would receive a hugely reduced sentence like our mate Stacker. The crown prosecutor called me to give evidence. I promise I did not smile or smirk at him, much.

I played tapes to the court in which Trust Me made it quite clear what he thought of heroin addicts. I informed the judge I had searched his arms for 'track marks' during a drug deal and found none. The judge ruled Trust Me was not a drug user and gave him nine on the top with seven long years on the bottom. Now we're talking.

Trust Me's sentence scared his boss Meng Koc 'Football Head' Te. Football Head had very little to lose (but a few years of his life) so he chose to have a full trial with the lot. That's like a hamburger with the lot but without the hamburger. Nearly three years after his arrest, his trial began. Football Head's barrister was a touch on the eccentric side of genius. We called him 'Mr Drag'. He commenced legal argument with the accusation that police in this case had breached international anti-discrimination laws by targeting a minority group within Australia, this being his Vietnamese client. He then made an application that his client be immediately released. He called for the police case to be adjourned indefinitely. This would have been quite funny except this argument went on for weeks. Baldrick had to sit there all day every day listening to this dribble. The only person more upset than Baldrick was the judge.

Every couple of days, I would go to court with Baldrick to catch up on the action. During an adjournment, I found myself having a smoke with one of the prison guards. He informed me Football Head's room mate in prison was none other than a mad, bad armed robber famous for his court room antics. He believed that if you can disrupt the court enough, they can't have the court case, so you can't be sent to jail. He must have passed on this philosophy to his new mate, Football Head.

After several weeks we observed other barristers attending our case. When I asked what they were doing, they laughed and said, 'We've heard this case is quite amusing'. Not for us, it wasn't.

Around this time, Mr Drag adjourned the case for a week so he could produce a report outlining his international anti-discrimination arguments. He stated he needed time to research case law and precedents. We all attended court a week later. Mr Drag handed everyone a copy of his report. In the report he had extensively quoted many cases of discrimination that supported his argument and made his case strong and compelling.

There was a problem. The prosecutor found it first. The fine print at the bottom of the pages revealed the source of these articles: *Time* magazine, *Readers Digest* and *Women's Weekly*. As the prosecutor laughed, the judge stood the matter down while a senior official from Legal Aid was called. Within an hour or so Legal Aid declared it was no longer going to pay for Mr Drag to defend Football Head. After almost nine weeks, we hadn't even started the trial. I was upset I never got to tell Mr Drag there was no discrimination as we never targeted Football Head in the first place. He grabbed the target and put it on his own head by rocking into our operation and delivering the heroin.

Football Head finally had a proper trial and was sentenced to eleven at the top with a nine-year minimum. What a drag.

I ATTENDED the many appeal hearings at the Supreme Court. Trevor, Stacker, and Donato had their appeals heard together. During a break in proceedings, I could hear someone calling, 'Lenny, hey Lenny'. I turned to see Trevor calling me from the dock. The three of them were sitting there with Trevor in the middle.

I thought, 'If I walk over there and one of them punches me in the face they won't get one day added to their sentence.' Then I thought, 'I'm not scared.' I stood and walked over to Trevor. I put both hands on the dock, leant right up to his face and said, 'What?' It looked tough on my part. Truth be known I was 'inside' his punch. If he tried to hit me, I would see it coming a mile off. Trevor looked at me and said, 'Is it true what I hear inside?'

I said, 'What? What do you hear inside?' Trevor fumbled for the words. He said, 'Um, is it true that you're going to work on me again when I get out?' I laughed. Trevor was scared of me. Scared of me working on him again. I said, 'No, no it's not. I've had enough of you and your family. I'm not going to work on you.'

In a serious voice I added, 'But there is not a day that goes by that some other copper doesn't ring me to ask when you are getting out. Every copper wants to be the next to put you back inside.' I walked back to Baldrick.

Their appeals were thrown out and sentences upheld. As Baldrick and I left the court, we met Kath having a smoke with her barrister. I nodded to her and said, 'G'day Kath'.

Kath said, 'G'day Lenny. I was just telling me barrister that this case was the first fair square pinch I ever had. The first one in 50 years. We never got fitted up, loaded up, no verbals, nothin'. It's unbelievable.'

I stopped and said, 'What about the pen pistol in your knickers?'

She smiled and said, 'No luv, that was mine. I have to say it's a load up.'

I said, 'It's good to see there's no corruption.'

As we walked off Kath said, 'Aw, there's corruption. You're in the drug squad, aren't ya? See ya Lenny.'

'See ya, Kath.'

Kath played the game, she knew the merry-go-round. Do crime, eventually get caught, go to court and then go directly to jail. That is the Kath everyone watched on television and played bingo with at the local hall. The 'doin' the business' Kath is a different story.

THROUGHOUT those years, my wife was a pillar of strength. She supported me through my most difficult times. After a hard day's work looking death in the face, she was always there. I asked her for a quote for this book. 'What was I like during *Operation Earthquake* – you know, that Kath Pettingill job?'

She said, 'You were a pain in the arse then and you're a pain in the arse now. Stick that in your book.'

I had spent half my life searching for the truth. It was there right in front of me and I never had to leave home to find it.

After it all I returned to the drug squad. I started to work on some crooks who made Kath and all her sons look like fairy bread. The problem was they were playing on my team. It turned out that on the steps of the Supreme Court Kath had given me some good oil. There was corruption, all right. For details, you'll have to wait for my next book, *Bent*.

A final thought. Throughout that operation I didn't cautiously test my boundaries, I ran crashing through them. I made stupid mistakes and so did those around me. Living through it all convinced me nothing was dangerous and that I was invincible. That was the lie I lived by. I had to. The truth is I will never be the person I was. *Operation Earthquake* will never be over for me. I can't help but feel some parts of me were poisoned by it. I put my heart and soul into that operation. Now, ten years on, I want them back.

Postscript: Fran went into witness protection, but later died of natural causes. Sally returned to the country of her birth and is believed to have stayed out of trouble.